There is much confusion between land and country.
Land is the place where corn, gullies, and mortgages grow.
Country is the personality of the land, the collective harmony
of its soil, life, and weather.

—ALDO LEOPOLD

PRICE COUNTY
MAIL-A-BOOK SERVICE
410 DIVISION STREET
PARK FALLS WI 54552

For Jennifer, Christine, Joseph,
and my Aussie grandchildren-to-be

Down Wisconsin Sideroads

by Clay Schoenfeld

Illustrations by Daniel P. Metz

With a foreword by Dion Henderson

Tamarack Press
P.O. Box 5650
Madison, Wisconsin 53705

Nubbins of this book have appeared previously in *American Forests, Audubon, Cabins, Conservation, and Fun* (Barnes, 1968), *Canada Goose Management* (DERS, 1969), *Environmental Education in Action* (ERIC/SMEAC, 1977), *Everybody's Ecology* (Barnes, 1971), *Field and Stream, Hunting and Fishing, Interpreting Environmental Issues* (DERS, 1973), *Journal of Environmental Education, Journal of Soil and Water Conservation, Nature Magazine, Outdoor America, Outdoor Guide, Outdoor Life, Outdoors, Outdoorsman, Outlines of Environmental Education* (DERS, 1971), *Proceedings of the North American Wildlife and Natural Resources Conference* (WMI, 1971), *Sports Afield, Wildlife in America* (CEQ, 1978), *Wildlife Management in Wilderness* (Boxwood, 1978), *Wisconsin Academy Review, Wisconsin Conservation Bulletin, Wisconsin Sideroads to Somewhere* (DERS, 1966), *Wisconsin Sportsman,* and *Wisconsin Weekend.* Some other materials appeared originally in the author's "Outofdoors" columns in the (Madison) *Wisconsin State Journal,* 1955-1967.

Text copyright © 1979 by Clarence A. Schoenfeld.
Illustrations copyright © 1979 by Tamarack Press.
All rights reserved. No part of this book may be reproduced in any form or by any means without the written consent of the publisher.

Edited by Jill Weber Dean.
Copy edited by Sue McCoy.
Designed by Patricia Dorman.
Printed in the United States of America
   by George Banta Company, Inc.

First printing 1979.

Library of Congress Cataloging in Publication Data

Schoenfeld, Clarence Albert, 1918-
   Down Wisconsin sideroads.

   1. Outdoor recreation—Wisconsin. 2. Outdoor recreation—Environmental aspects—Wisconsin.
3. Wisconsin—Description and travel—1951-
I. Metz, Dan. II. Title.
GV191.42.W6S36   301.5'7   79-17161
ISBN 0-915024-24-1

Foreword

I have known him since we were very young, although of course Clay is older than I. Much older. He was being motivated toward his distinguished career by the great work being done at Faville Grove while I was getting in trouble for trying to steal the German shorthair puppy that Aldo Leopold got from Joe Burkhart after watching Sam Kisow's dog hunt. We both began our journalism careers at the Lake Mills *Leader* while we were in high school, although of course he was there quite a while ahead of me. Both of us, I might add, were recognized as conspicuously promising, although in the case of one there was some unpleasantness involving a wedding present that our editor, William Harrison Haight III, overlooked. What it was, was a pound of limburger cheese, and where he overlooked it, for a very short time, was where it was smeared on the manifold of his Stutz Bearcat when he and his bride began their honeymoon trip. I am not, even now, going to tell you who did it, because Bill Haight is still alive and well and was never that sure of the villain.

In this book Clay mentions that his father was a preacher, and I want to tell you that is like saying Chartres is a church. He was a mid-sized man who stood tall, with a lined aesthetic face that made the sun shine when he smiled. He christened my daughters in the garden, and the consecration endured for years, so that the flowers turned their faces upward, and the weeds did not grow. He was, I am trying to say, some kind of a man, and I hope that some day Clay writes a book that tells how it was to grow up with a father who was a friend of God's.

But that is another book and if I do not get to write a foreword for that, I will buy a copy anyway, which is a way of saying that I expect to get a free copy of this one. With a flowery inscription, even.

There is not, however, going to be anything very flowery in the foreword to this book, because I am just telling you that I have known Clay Schoenfeld a long time, back when it counted, and I know a lot of the places that he writes about.

They are the places like Faville Grove, and Bean's Lake, where there was the biggest tamarack I'd ever seen, and Rock Lake, where Clay and I and every other kid who grew up in Lake Mills learned to swim by moonlight, and to slip a frog off the lily pads of Korth's Bay to attract the great bass on a summer evening. Yes, and the railroad tracks where we learned about pass shooting, and Allen's Marsh.

Those are the places that I think had a good deal to do with the way that Clay and I and a lot of other people turned out; they are the places where a great many things started. Most of those places are changed now, and some of them are gone, but they won't be wholly gone as long as there are people like us who remember them. And Allen's Marsh, just for instance, will live like Camelot, an island in the clouds, as long as there are people to read one sentence in this book: "Then out of some far recess of the sky will come the susurrant sound of wings, and the ducks will be back at Allen's Marsh."

Like Leopold, who taught many things far from the classroom, Clay does not labor over a sentence like that, but tosses it carelessly into an essay as though there were thousands of such sentences to be written and remembered, while truly there are very few.

There are other sentences like that in this book, but I am going to let you find them for yourself. Anyway, in a book that is about the outdoors, and about the way a man like Clay has lived in it and loved it and used it all his life, you may pick out different words for yourself than I would.

He is comfortable, in a classic way, as a member of the natural community, and as a man of rituals that need to be remembered—the historic deer camp, nights in a marsh shack listening to the geese, opening the cabin in the spring. He shares with you, as he shares the diaries of days well spent, days afield with pheasant and woodcock and mallard and teal.

There is something more to be had here than the vicarious experience. In that sense this is really a how-to book, and what you can learn from it is how to live decently and responsibly with the small neighbors with whom we share the planet.

There are great lessons in modest lines about the values of what appear to be underachieving acres, with their wide fence rows, and in unsprayed woodlots, and in dividends lost with progress: "Our sand country currently has acres of irrigated truck farms, but no quail."

This book takes you on many such expeditions, in the field and in reflections, and it is a good companion, because its author is a good companion. He did not mention it in his book, but when he and I were young—and I was much younger—there was a path around Rock Lake, and each summer Saturday every kid up to our time, and for a considerable while after, would pack a lunch and hike around the lake. It was more deeply ingrained in childhood than what Al Hochbaum afterward called the travels and traditions of waterfowl.

Most of us went on, by paths too broad for walking, but such paths run both ways. I am writing this on the hillside that I've come back to, in the shade of the bicentennial oaks that march down through what we used to call Ferry's Woods to the shore of Korth's Bay. And some autumn morning when I am waiting for the sunrise, I will hear the susurrant sound of wings of a passing flock whose dive will tear the dark silk of night, and I will remember, gratefully.

Dion Henderson
Hillside
Lake Mills, Wisconsin
March 10, 1979

Contents

Down Wisconsin Sideroads   9

The Jin'ral and Me   24

Wonderful World of Fishing   48

Hunters' Havens   73

Cabins and Conservation   102

Letters from a Lobbyist   137

Badger Almanac   156

Wisconsin Country   189

Down Wisconsin Sideroads

One Spring day each year you can watch the swallows swarm back to their mud apartments on the side of a red barn at the intersection of two Wisconsin sideroads.

A natural phenomenon such as this packs as sure a message of resurrection as do Easter sermons. But we can't "hear" these important outdoor messages if we stick to the superhighways. To keep track of nature we have to sacrifice speed for scenery and take the sideroads. Driving from Madison to Milwaukee, for instance, we can leave I-90 and take old 30, now called County Trunk BB, from Blooming Grove through Cottage Grove to Lake Mills. We won't get to Milwaukee so fast or so smoothly, but we'll see those swallows--and a lot of other signs of serenity.

Along Wisconsin sideroads, days in May are particularly precious. Spring begins to hold the hills in the folds of a pastel cloak. Drumlins take on a soft tinge of green. Lakes and potholes are horizon-blue again. True, a leafing maple, a covey of migrating meadowlarks, a big full moon over Blue Mound, even all of them together speak in a still, small voice. What is a May hepatica in a day of circling satellites? Yet many of us need, in the Space Age as never before, something of the peace and serenity and detachment that the out-of-doors has to offer. We need them to rout the jitters and clear our vision.

It takes time, this wandering around on sideroads, but the investment is worth it. It was a Wisconsin Pulitzer Prize-winner, Zona Gale, who once championed the advantages of "a serene sideroad existence." What she was saying was an echo of Henry Thoreau, watching a steam engine puffing through Concord, its smoke trailing skyward--as he put it, the smoke "going to heaven while the train is going to Boston."

Few of us would choose, in these challenging times, an isolation like Thoreau's, living apart in the cabin he built himself at Walden Pond. Fewer of us still would have the courage or the genius to make of such a career an immortal success. It is good, then, in our crowded and distracted days, to listen to Thoreau's words. He reported from his out-of-doors that he "heard no bad news." We can hear the same message down Wisconsin sideroads today.

In the spirit of Thoreau, we all yearn for those "old, meandering, dry, uninhabited roads which lead away from town," where our heads are more in heaven than our feet on earth, where travelers are not too often to be met, where our spirits are free, where we can walk and think with least obstruction, and which are wide enough--"wide as the thoughts they allow to visit you."

This is a book about such haunts; about the simple adventures in outdoor recreation that are everybody's for the finding down the sideroads of Wisconsin.

So you will find here a recounting of modest expeditions to field and stream, and some insights into the ways and wise use of the wild. Bass and pike strike hard in these pages, and enough guns go off so that sportspersons should find things interesting; but the emphasis is really more on the stage setting than on the action, so nature fans should feel comfortable.

While this book seeks simply to make good reading for Wisconsin outdoor lovers whatever their faith or fashion, the kind of book to be savored as the seasons turn, yet there is a Leopoldian message between the lines: that the conservation of our natural resources is not only a matter of building Western wilderness preserves but also of building in human hearts a receptivity to Wisconsin wonders close at hand.

Or perhaps our text would be better stated thus, from Isaiah: "Woe unto them that join house to house, that lay field to field, 'till there is no place where one may be alone in the midst of the earth."

In a heaving, tossing world, some may very well give serious question, I suppose, to the relevancy of the out-of-doors. Faced with an "environmental crisis" in every headline, can we continue to practice in good heart such cherished diversions as bird-watching and bluegill fishing? Does the voice of a tanager or the tug of a trout impart any message worthy of the hour? Are we simply engaged in a heedless escape from stress? Or is there in fact some significant meaning hidden in a Spring hike or a Fall hunt?

I believe there are at least three valid reasons for the pursuit of outdoor recreation even in the face of the population-pollution syndrome. One is simply that outdoor recreation is indeed a recreating experience. People have always felt instinctively that they need "fresh air," literally and figuratively. That the human animal demands an occasional change of pace and change of scene there is increasing scientific evidence. Arnold Toynbee has documented the phenomenon of withdrawal and return that has enriched the course of history. Biochemists have discovered alternating cycles of activity and quiescence in cellular affairs that are to be denied only at the risk of health. Psychiatrists are using outdoor activities to calm and cure their patients. Outdoor fans need make no apologies, then, if we take to field and stream now and then. We return better persons.

Exposure to the out-of-doors can take on an inspirational dimension as well. Just as there are no atheists in foxholes, so are there no pessimists on Spring hikes or Fall hunts. The resurrection of the April earth or the fire-dance of Autumn impart a compelling recognition that change is a law of nature.

But the real ecological justification for an occasional retreat to woods and waters is the opportunity it provides to acquire a perception of the oneness of our world. To partake of the natural processes by which the land and the living things upon it have achieved their characteristic forms and by which they maintain their existence, to become aware of the incredible complexities of plant and animal communities, to sense the intrinsic beauty and the creeping degradation of the organism called America--to do these things is to learn a great lesson. There are no country problems that are not city problems, no problems of the inner core that are not problems of the open spaces, no local problems that are not world problems, no world problems that are not local problems, no problems of poverty that are not problems of affluence, no problems of crime in the streets that are not problems of conduct in the home. Insects, birds, fish, mammals, water, soil, wilderness, trees, plants, people, Washington, Peking, Harlem, and Weyauwega are all part of the same scheme, a sort of intricately woven fabric. Snip one thread and the entire cloth begins to unravel; stitch up one tear and you begin to repair the whole.

In short, there is a life of the woods and the waters and the waysides that can mean something. Our lives could be dull and unrewarding without an appreciation of the solitude and the significance of natural surroundings.

This does not mean we become hermits. Hermits are distinguished more by their fear of mankind than by their love of nature. Nor am I suggesting escape for escape's sake. But I am suggesting the value of an escape from wordiness--as a healthy resistance to the false notion that everything of significance can be heard in speech or read from the printed page.

Beyond words there is a life experience that words may evoke but for which words themselves are a poor substitute. In this sense outdoor recreation, away from closed-in spaces and away from crowds, may offer unique opportunities for personal growth. Away from the clutter of words, there is what the physiologists call the wisdom of the body. It is older than any culture. Its controlling mechanisms run deep into every fiber. You swim or you sink.

Most of us may listen too much to others and to ourselves, anyway. At times we use words to the detriment of understanding. To seek the meanings that lie beneath the rhetoric we can go back, whenever we can, to the world of nature, to hear in the stillness of the fields what Mr. Wordsworth called "the music of humanity."

That is why outdoor life stirs people so. It is a healthy return--if only for a brief time and under simulated conditions-- to a life the whole race of humankind once knew. It is Mr. Thoreau cutting a broad swath and shaving close. It is Mr. Frost going out to clean the pasture spring.

Of course it is not enough just to sit like a pumpkin by some local Walden Pond, or to walk unknowingly through a meadow under a scarcely noticed pattern of stars. There are wonderfully meaningful forms in nature, from the microscopic to the galactic, and a way to sense them is to combine reading with direct observation. It is a matter of studying and searching and comparing, and at the same time enjoying the outdoor life on a plane of personal experience.

I guess I'm not so naive as to suggest that every lathe operator with a spinning rod is a potential Thoreau, that every member of the Audubon Society is an Aldo Leopold in disguise, or that every delegate to a state Conservation Congress is a homespun Albert Schweitzer. But let's proceed here on the assumption that exposure to the out-of-doors, however casual or however intense, direct or vicarious, can be a doorway to an ecological understanding of our utter interdependence with our environment and with life everywhere, and to the development of a culture that will secure the future of an environment fit for life and fit for living.

So come along, then, as we travel down the sideroads of Wisconsin in search of those pleasures in outdoor recreation that are everybody's for the finding, and as we talk about conserving those resources that are inextricably linked not only to economic prosperity but to the inner prosperity of the human spirit.

Each Wisconsin sideroad we may follow has a character all its own, sometimes ever-changing, sometimes immutable.

Mineral Point Road, for example, is a link to a certain past and an uncertain future. The road runs straight as a die west from Madison, equidistant between Highways 151 and 14, following a cadastral section line through Pine Bluff to join Wisconsin 78 between Black Earth and Mount Horeb. Straight as a die, that is, except for a half-circle around a perverse rocky knob that apparently defied primitive highwaymen. Or perhaps it was a perverse farmer who refused to permit a right-of-way across his pet forty.

Mineral Point Road is struggling to maintain authenticity as a sideroad. Despite bulldozed curbs and blacktopped surfaces, it still manages to exude some air of bucolic charm as it knifes over drumlins, through alluvial valleys, past old stone farmhouses and country taverns, into sprawling cornfields and vistas of Blue Mound glowing in the summer sunset. But its days as a sideroad may be numbered.

Mineral Point Road has seen a lot of history. Before there was not even a wagon trace, Jonathan Carver was here, marveling at the wildfire-fashioned oak openings that resembled "well-kept orchards." The road itself was first laid out by a young Army lieutenant of engineers by the name of Robert E. Lee, its purpose to carry lead to Milwaukee and settlers to the mines of Iowa County. Henry Dodge and his mounted volunteers rode here, enroute to trail the illusive Black Hawk.

Today Mineral Point Road is making history of a sort again. It is the site of a very special kind of housing development, named, with something less than accuracy, Cherrywood Glen. Most of the Glen construction is off to the south, obscured by oak trees, but the Glen-to-be is evidenced by percolation-test pits in a farm field adjoining the road, the pits resembling nothing so much as fresh graves. Cherrywood Glen is the epitome of urban sprawl. To avoid city building restrictions and attract buyers bent on savoring country air, developers have hop-skipped into Town of Middleton, scavenging woodlots and cornfields to construct a subdivision just beyond metropolitan zoning ordinances and square in the middle of prime agricultural land. The perc-test pits speak to the necessity of private septic tanks in the absence of public sewer connections.

To occupy the resulting three-bedroom ranch houses--with patios--will come, perchance, members of the Sierra Club pledged to saving California redwoods but oblivious to the havoc they are wrecking on the remnants of Jonathan Carver's prairie groves. Next door may be devoted contributors to CARE who ravage the arable acres they are taking out of carbohydrate production. Their children will crowd the one available district school, requiring a new wing, to the end that more farm acres will fall to the big earthmovers to "broaden the tax base." It is probably only a question of time until there is a shopping center at the nearest intersection, its neon signs blanking out the stars--and Mineral Point Road will have become but an extension of a Madison boulevard.

There is no question who owns Mineral Point Road property. Whatever it may say in the records, the entire Mineral Point Road environs today belong to the internal combustion engine.

But Nature may well write the last word in the Mineral Point Road history book. You see, Cherrywood Glen is a long daily commute from the central city, and its "independent" water wells are dependent on long power lines. Given a real energy crunch, the bucolic charm of Cherrywood Glen translates into punitive gas and electric bills. It is not too much to imagine that, in the fullness of time, a latter-day lieutenant of engineers will level abandoned houses, Jonathan Carver's prairie groves will once again attain ascendancy, a Henry Dodge the Tenth will ride horseback down a Mineral Point Trail to barter at a trading post, bittersweet vines will curl around an old sign bearing a tattered inscription reading "Choice Lots for Sale," and septic tank pits will be excavated by curious archaeologists searching clues to a vanished tribe.

The modern Mineral Point Road mentality has not yet migrated west to J. Jones Road in Iowa County. Along its four miles of indifferent gravel there are only four dwellings. One of them is ours--we think. According to the County Register of Deeds, my wife and I duly own 58.9 acres of country property along J. Jones Road. Sometimes we are not so sure. The records in the Dodgeville Courthouse do not intentionally lie, of course. Indeed, they are specific and voluminous. Despite the small acreage involved, it takes a full page of ledger to describe our meets and bounds in the manner prescribed by the Land Ordinance of 1785. That's because our property is a bastard piece, shaped like a frying pan on its side, with a bulbous portion a quarter-mile deep at one end, and a narrow, mile-long handle running between J. Jones and a section line. It all spans 6 forties in two different sections of the Town of Arena, and each partial forty must be separately identified. What is more, no self-respecting surveyor can say simply that our southern property line is the center line of J. Jones Road. Even sideroads can change their courses. So each zig and zag of our road must be described as so many feet at an azimuth of so many degrees.

There may be something esthetically satisfying about owning a nice, square forty, but we wouldn't own anything at all if our piece were not so odd ball in nature. We couldn't have afforded it. As it was, the previous farmer owner didn't place much value on what became our strip of land. It was too narrow to fence all around, and too steep and rocky to plow, so all it had raised for a hundred years was an occasional crop of fence-post or barrel-stave oaks. Eddie White couldn't figure out why anybody would want to buy it, and he didn't want to "hold anybody up," as he put it, but he thought he ought to get its assessed value. That turned out to be $16 an acre. All this, of course, was well before the recreational-property boom in Iowa County. Today, the more odd ball the land around us, the higher its price, if it's on the market at all.

Incidentally, after we put up a cabin on our woodlot, its official description didn't change. This is one of the peculiarities of the country system of land registration and transfer. No matter what's put on or taken off the land, its description doesn't vary from the original. It's as if the land really owned itself.

Despite the fact that our northern border is a section line, our line fence makes a curious right-angle turn at one point, and again at another. It has been that way for 80 years, so under an old common law practice, where the line fence runs now represents our property line, irrespective of what a modern surveyor's transit might say. We think we know what happened. The line fence was originally strung by two neighbors, using dead reckoning. For the most part they went along pretty straight, but here and there they mutually agreed to jig or jog to avoid cliffs. We are the recipients of one such hundred-yard detour, clearly indicated by a band of rusty barbed wire if not in a courthouse ledger. It's all enormously complicated compared to the description of our city lot, which says simply that our ownership of some unidentified property on Madison's west side is insured by a big title company. Somehow we feel more secure with our uninsured country description.

There are times of the year along a country sideroad like J. Jones, however, when one's ownership is suspect. Take a certain 10 days in November, for example, when we are invaded by deer hunters. Our feeling of being violated is overpowering, akin to what it must be like on a Saturday afternoon in the football season if you live on Breese Terrace across the street from Camp Randall Stadium. Despite big, yellow "NO TRESPASSING" signs every 200 feet or so around our entire perimeter, the red-clad army storms across our borders like Guderian's troops going through Belgium.

In a certain seven days in May we are invaded by quite a different army, waving Lilliputian banners of many hues. They are the spring ephemerals--bloodroot, marsh marigold, Dutchman's-breeches, hepatica, spring beauty, violet, wood anemone, columbine, shooting star, wild geranium, trillium, Jack-in-the-pulpit. Almost as soon and as quietly as they have come, the spring flora fade away, leaving a lingering perfume on the morning air.

Scarcely have the Spring blooms withdrawn than we are deluged by a congregation of migrating warblers, manning the treetops of oaks and hickories not yet in full leaf. With the help of Norman Fassett's invaluable handbook, we have come to know the flora, but we cannot identify all the various warbler visitors. They defy accurate analysis by all but professional birdwatchers, despite the assistance of Roger Tory Peterson's guide. Durward Allen, distinguished wildlife ecologist, once wanted to be an ornithologist, but he confesses he "got tired of memorizing the warblers all over again every Spring." Being insect eaters, the warblers avoid our feeders, preferring to exercise their momentary dominion in a most discrete fashion. They, too, depart as suddenly as they come, but they leave behind a rear guard of brilliant kin--indigo buntings, Baltimore orioles, rose-breasted grosbeaks, and scarlet tanagers, who keep us compatable company until a skein of Canada geese summons them southward once again in Fall.

In Summer we share our woodlot proprietorship with a largely unseen nightly chorus: the high trill of leopard frogs and the deep rumble of bulls from the pond across the way, june bugs bumbling against the porch screen, the almost-mechanical whine of myriad mosquitoes, owl talk, the haunting call of whip-poor-wills, the distant drumming of a ruffed grouse announcing his domain, the lonesome baying of a coon hound who recognizes no season, or the humanlike scream of a cottontail rabbit fallen prey to a succesful fox.

Year-round we share custodianship with an array of lichens, some on the north sides of old oaks, more decorating the sandstone cliff sentinels that guard practically the entire length of our property. Geologists tell us these pockmarked rocks mark the shores of a paleolithic sea. When we thrust our heads into a mini-cave aperture, we imagine we can hear the pounding, pounding of ancient surf. The lichens lend a marine-green touch to the stone walls, as if in memory of undulating weeds and waves.

In Winter it used to be that snowmobilers took over our woods, tooling up an old logging trail, the constant, raucous roar of their motors shattering that priceless country commodity-- silence. The gate we put up was no deterrent. The snowmobilers simply pried off chain and padlock. No more. To fill in a garden-patch site, we needed several truckloads of good dirt. What better place to get it than from the center of that trail, where centuries of erosion had deposited six feet of top soil from ridgeline fields. Removing the dirt automatically created a tank trap absolutely impervious to snowmobiles. So silence sits once again in our Winter woods. Silence, and something else.

On the first seasonable Saturday in December, after the deer season is past, we cruise our back fence, looking for dangling wires, checking to see how many signs need replacing, and harvesting a Christmas cedar. Invariably a red-tailed hawk screams imprecations at our intrusion. Our chore completed last year, my wife and I were dropping down from the cliffs to the road when we came upon six fresh deer beds in the "pan" of our panhandle-shaped property.

"Come to think of it," S.S.S. said, "We've hardly taken a single step today but what we were following a busy deer run. It's the deer who really own our woods."

It is curious now to recall, but a primary motivation for our becoming uncertain owners of deer country was not so much to acquire a rustic retreat as to find a secure site for a bomb shelter. It was 1961, and the Berlin Crisis was in full swing. I was in the Army Reserve at the time, and privy to classified information. I knew Truax Field to be a prime target as a key NORAD base with strategic SAGE apparatus. I recognized an atomic warhead aimed at Truax might produce blast effects for a radius of 30 miles. And I presumed main exit roads from Madison would be jammed in case of an emergency alert.

So we went looking for land about 35 miles away, up wind

from Madison, entirely accessible by sideroads, with soil suitable for building a fallout-proof dugout, and encompassing a private spring. If it all seems silly now, it didn't at the time. What is interesting is that the factors that dictated our search led us to a piece of land we wouldn't otherwise have chosen, but that very land has turned out to have plus values for quite different reasons.

A 35-mile drive to recreational property is ideal. It is long enough to represent a physical and psychological break from the city, yet short enough to conserve gas and nerves. Up wind from Madison places you in the driftless hills of Iowa County, immune from the bustle of lakeshores and riverbanks. A 100%-sideroad route offers instant solace from beltlines and semis. Soil suitable for a dugout turns out to be suitable for a basement. Our spring raises fine watercress.

We never did build that bomb shelter. The fad faded, if not the threat. For a time the threat was very real to me, at least on moonlit nights, even in the bucolic peace and quiet of J. Jones Road. It was all a hangover from World War II.

When I had been deposited on the beach at Anzio as an Infantry lieutenant and a recent product of the Camp Ritchie (Maryland) Military Intelligence Training Center, I quite properly drew an assignment as a Regimental Intelligence and Reconnaisance (I&R) Platoon Leader. That may sound like a rear-area desk job, but it was actually hairy duty. The I&R platoon was the regimental commander's eyes and ears. Its leader was charged with finding out what's out front, where, in what strength, with what intentions. One prescribed way to do so was deliberately to draw enemy fire. So an I&R lieutenant and his 29 men lived hazardously. There was a lot of turn over in a WW II I&R platoon.

Come to think of it, it is one of the great mysteries of the human animal that people will actually let themselves get shot at, so long as you call it "war." It is not bravery; that is, it is not the absence of fear. At least in my case I was scared stiff the whole time. It is the surmounting of fear for a purpose, a purpose rendered rational for a variety of reasons, depending on the person involved. I knew some George Patton types who actually seemed to love armed combat, and some regulars for whom it was an honored profession, but for most of us amateur soldiers it was simply the damned job we were stuck with at the moment, and we did it as best we knew how, burying any personal civilian instincts in the fog of the overwhelming peer pressure an Army outfit exerts on its inhabitants.

Sometimes "as best we knew how" wasn't very good. To delineate German machine-gun positions in preparation for our big beachhead breakout in the Spring of '44, I was leading a nightly patrol forward of our lines. So long as it was cloudy we could move about in no-man's-land in relative safety; relative to daylight, that is. But one afternoon I forgot to check the met forecast, and that night, as a bright full moon suddenly broke through the scattering clouds, it caught me and four men upright within earshot of an enemy bunker. Instead of freezing in position as we had been taught to do, we each hit the ground prone, and that movement provoked mad bursts of Schmeizer fire. What is more, every moonbathed bush assumed the outline of a stalking Kraut.

Thanks to a new wave of clouds sweeping in from the ocean, we all made it back in one piece to the regimental CP--almost. Somewhere in Italy I left behind a piece of aplomb. It was to take me 25 years before I could steel myself ever to walk in the moonlight--even down my J. Jones Road. S.S.S. finally cured me. There is nothing like a hot July night, a Wisconsin country woodlot, and a glowing woman to change one's attitude toward bright moonlight.

When S.S.S. and I added a porch to our cabin, we inadvertently created a shelter for the real king of J. Jones Road--a woodchuck. If you have to acceed control of your country property to anybody, a woodchuck is the ideal monarch. He exerts his authority with the greatest of finesse, never intruding on our occasional tenancy. Indeed, we rarely see our landlord. He rests secure in his burrow beneath our porch, only rarely to scurry out on some majestic mission. He may munch on some tender lawn grasses, but he studiously avoids sharing any garden truck. His unobtrusive presence is eloquent testimony to the still-rural qualities of J. Jones Road. As our car backs down the driveway at the close of a weekend, King Woodchuck emerges to mount his throne on our front stoop, silently surveying his J. Jones Road empire. There is no Cherrywood Glen in his ken. For him, J. Jones will be a sideroad forever.

A Wisconsin sideroad, of course, doesn't actually have to be in Wisconsin to share the spirit of Wisconsin. My brother, born in the driftless area of southwestern Wisconsin, has made the Virginia Blue Ridge foothills his adopted home.

Let's let a master writer talk about that star-crossed "Walton's Mountain" country:

> At night in Virginia, across the old fought-on earth, there comes a special kind of darkness. It seeps in from the sea and, carried on the wind of tall dead planets, it drifts across the tide-land. It comes from the sea and it swallows little towns with the old names. Flowing eastward, the night sifts along the rivers of old Virginia, along the James and the York and the Rappahannock. It hovers over the Dismal Swamp and then it goes inland.
>
> Crossing Smithfield the darkness falls on fields where peanuts grow, and even while the chickens cluck apprehensively in their huts at Waverly the night is on them and past them and all of Surry County sleeps. Now the damp smell of night is on Hopewell, reaching toward Richmond, and the sad city of Petersburg is sadder because night is on it and it

is afraid, for night is when the sounds of return of battles lost long ago, and the trenches are unquiet.
Over Richmond, the night goes on, sweeping across its quiet lawns, touching the heads of its dead heroes with damp hands, and goes on to the country beyond. Up in old Amelia County they light the kerosene lamps and Negroes sit in the doorways of their little shanties and they are afraid because the dark night has come in from the sea and brought something old and dreadful and terrible with it. On across the sleeping fields of grass and corn the inexorable night walks and, reaching Charlottesville, it begins to climb and walks on over mountains.

I came on that passage in a paperback novel, <u>Fifty Roads to Town</u>, that I picked up to while away the time a good many years ago in a fog-bound Roanoke airport after visiting my brother in Blacksburg. Even though the author was a then-unknown writer, his lyric qualities impressed me, so I inserted the paragraph in the first edition of a text I was putting together on feature writing. Years laters I heard the very same passage again--in the preamble to an episode on the then-No. 1 TV show, "The Waltons." I was incensed. The TV script-writer had pirated the passage in cold blood, I told my wife, and I trotted out a copy of my text to prove it. Whereupon, of course, she pointed out that the author of the paperback novel and the man responsible for "The Waltons" story line were one and the same--Earl Hamner, Jr.

It just goes to show that captivating Wisconsin sideroad style has a universal appeal--it sells novels, it wins high Nielsen ratings--and it can make you at home anywhere.

Several times a year, my granddaughters Jennifer and Chrissie Meier jog down a sideroad midst mile-upon-mile of wheatfields in eastern Washington near Pullman. We aren't sure, you understand, but we can imagine we are tracing the footsteps of an ancestor who took his lead-miner's poke from Wisconsin to turn it into Western gold or lumber--and who was never heard from again. But he left us a sideroad.

Someday I'm going to take my grandson Joseph Jones Krantz to Pennsylvania along Valley Forge sideroads where Joseph Jones II, Sergeant, New Jersey Line, spent the winter of 1777-8 with General Washington under conditions of indescribable hardship. And I will remind Joe he is here because there was the blood of a great-great-great-great-grandfather in the snow of an Appalachian sideroad.

Someday, too, I'm going to take another grandson, Norman Rogers, II, on a tour of the sideroad net spanning the Blue Mountains between Sydney and Brisbane, Australia. It was here that an ill-trained, ill-equipped, ill-led Wisconsin 32nd National Guard Division prepared to do the undoable-stop the Japanese in New Guinea at the gates of Darwin in 1942. So I'll remind Norm, II, that what <u>National Geographic</u> recently headlined as "Big, Breezy, Bloomin' Sydney" was purchased by nameless Badgers in stinking Buna swamps. My daughter Laurie has already paid a visit to a very special kind of Wisconsin sideroad, one that winds through a mammoth military cemetery in Italy where are buried troopers that helped protect her dad in the hell of '44 at Anzio, their stark white crosses bearing uninviting testimony to collective depravity and individual nobility.

On a 20-foot pole on the front terrace of our J. Jones Road cabin, a Wisconsin flag flies daily, a silent salute to those who have trod sideroads worldwide so that we might trod ours.

A murder took place one year on a sideroad leading to our cabin. The body of the victim lay rotting in plain view of passing cars. Yet authorities issued no warrant for arrest because, in the eyes of the law, no crime had been committed.

The victim, you see, was a hillcrest woodlot, and the criminal code has nothing to say about killing a woodlot. A man can be arrested for beating his dog or sassing his wife, but his woodlot he can put to death without so much as a by-your-leave. A city person will be apprehended for raising chickens or rabbits in a back yard, but a country person answers to nobody for raping a hillside.

Unlike so many outdoor crimes, you can't blame the government for this one. All the forces of federal, state, and county capitols have been mobilized for years to defend woodlots. University professors issue bulletins extolling their values. The state grants a tax deduction for their preservation. Washington pays money for their wise management. But nobody has yet figured out how to manage the people who own woodlots.

For many of us who didn't own it, that woodlot was something special. It was the touch of the wild closest to town.

In the Spring we would search its floor for hepatica and anemones, or listen to a band of warblers in its budding treetops. In the Summer you could wade through the underbrush and start up families of young rabbits. In the Fall it always held a couple of grouse and on one rocky point a splendid growth of bittersweet. In the Winter we would stop our cars and watch the quiet woods fill up with snow.

Most of the woodlot was second-growth red oak and ironwood and hickory, but at one spot stood a bur-oak veteran of age-old fires. To one side was a hidden pond where an occasional wood duck nested. From another point you could look away and away over a fertile valley to the hulk of Blue Mound. Because it was well-fenced, one section held a perched prairie with remnants of native grasses. Thrushes and flickers and tanagers lived along the far edge of the glade.

What will become of our woodlot now? Perhaps it will be planted to corn for a couple of years. The ears will join other ears in government bins. Then, after a history of cultivation has been established, the field will be retired and the government will pay somebody for not growing corn. The topsoil will be gone by that time. Rains will wash it down the steep slopes to speed the atrophy of a nearby marsh, roil the waters of the valley trout stream, and leave only an eroded clay knob. Ragweed will flourish where once there were andropogen and wild plum.

Or perhaps our woodlot is destined to become a subdivision where city folk will seek escape from neon and asphalt by building ranch houses on a naked hill. They will sweat and strain to grow imported sod and trees where once native flora held dominion. Their taxes will go to pay for mammoth storm sewers with expensive covers, and their spending money will go for gas to carry them to a park miles away where somebody else has preserved a woodlot.

It's been said the basic problem of democracy is the continual clash between the rights of the individual and the rights of society. Somewhere in the equation there ought to be something said, too, for the right of a sideroad woodlot to life, liberty, and the pursuit of happiness.

It can be done. With spade, water bucket, and sack of seedlings, we were at work one Spring trying to manufacture an outdoor miracle. We were replanting a barren fencerow. What it has taken 50 years of civilization to crucify, we are intent on reviving. It will be a race between our aching backs and the inexorable course of "progress," and it is by no means clear today that our backs will win. But we are making a dent.

I first saw our fencerow in the '20's. Our Overland Six touring car had mired in the soft sand of what they generously termed in those days "an unimproved country road." While we waited for a friendly farmer with a team of draft horses, we lounged in the shade of the roadside.

The fence itself was an old split-rail, with a wide "turn around" on the field side and an equal expanse toward the road. Such a fencerow could not be burned without losing the fence, and it could not be mowed except by hand and after laborious debrushing. Nobody in the Town of Arena had heard of "clean farming" or "unobstructed rights-of-way" back then, anyway. So the fencerow was the home of lush flora and fauna.

For ground cover there were such prairie remnants as silphium, butterfly weed, andropogen, shooting star, and wild rose. Above were hazel, sumac, haw, crab, dogwood, bur oak, and wild plum. In this haven lived quail and grouse, skunks and weasels, woodchucks, gophers, chipmunks, deer and meadow mice, meadowlarks, field sparrows, indigo buntings, brown thrashers, catbirds, vesper sparrows, mourning doves, and shrikes. All told, 17 major plants and 18 major animals thrived in this typical Wisconsin fencerow of another era. It was an era doomed by gasoline and steel.

Already in the 20's came a boom in land values and the

barbed wire fence, encouraging the clearance of brush and the widening of cultivated areas. About the same time the road was widened to enable cars to pass, and debrushed to prevent snowdrifts. Result? All the prairie species were extinguished by the gradings. The woody species were likewise reduced. Bobwhite and other wildlife went out with the brush. Quack grass, timothy, and clover came in. There were now in the fencerow 10 plants instead of 17, and 12 animals instead of 18.

Next, metal fence posts came along. The non-burnable posts gave the final and complete release to fire as a tool for clearing the fencerow. Burning encouraged quack grass and discouraged brush even more. What had been a 30-foot turn around was now a two-foot edge. With the arrival of an electric fence, no kind of cover could be tolerated at all because of short-circuiting during rains.

By the 1940's the roadside had been "streamlined" to permit easy mowing, and to facilitate mowing the roadside was burned yearly. The steep cutbank was graded down to the angle of repose, and the roadway was gravelled. Relief labor performed the chores, and the bill was paid by the same taxpayer who was financing a public park somewhere else.

All game and fur species were now gone from our fencerow, for there was no cover. The rodents were reduced to gophers and mice. The songbirds, except meadowlark and vesper sparrow, were all out. There were now three major plants, all exotic, instead of 17; and four animals instead of 18. Two of them were injurious rodents. The fencerow, instead of serving as a refuge for rich native flora and fauna, had become only a haven for animal and plant pests.

That is what we have to start with. We can't control the county highway department, but we can give nature a hand on our side of the fence. It will take our tiny pine, grape, dogwood, and walnut a long time to recapture lost ground, but maybe in another 50 years somebody else can rest in their shade and listen to the confident call of a quail cock.

The Jin'ral and Me

With great excitement, sociology professors have announced recently their research reveals many outdoor fans place as much or more value in the camaraderie of field and stream as in the actual taking of trophies. Every hunter or fisher has known that for a long time. The fraternity of rod and gun is a precious society, the fellow-you-go-with a special person.

The fellow-I-go-with is Robert L. Hughes, Associate Dean of Agriculture, Brigadier General USAR, consummate caster, 12-gauge sharpshooter, genial outdoor gentleman, friend. I call him, with proper deference, The Jin'ral.

As if to taste armed combat again, The Jin'ral heads for a public hunting grounds on the opening day of each pheasant season.

It would take a combination of the Little Big Horn, the Peach Orchard, and St. Lo to produce anything like the torrent of noise and confusion that erupts at high noon on the Wisconsin River flats at Mazomanie. The big problem at Mazo is not finding pheasants. The conservation boys obligingly turn 800 or so roosters loose just before the season. Your problem is survival. Upwards of a thousand gunners are apt to jam into Mazo's 4,000 acres, and anything that moves is a fair target. Faced with such a situation, the only way to operate at Mazomanie is in the form of a full-scale military expedition. Even then, things can get plenty fouled up, as I am about to testify.

Seven of us volunteered for a suicide patrol at Mazo one October under the stern command of The Jin'ral. As our forward assembly area The Jin'ral chose a shaded draw near the headquarters buildings. Under a big cottonwood he issued our cold field rations, checked our weapons, distributed ammunition, and gave out the orders of the day.

"The line of departure is that row of evergreens," said The Jin'ral, gesturing smartly with his swagger stick. "After we debouche into the open, we'll make a wide sweep and head north to the river. Colonel Schoenfeld, you will act as the right guide and pace our advance."

I synchronized my watch with The Jin'ral's and moved out. That is the only clear memory I have of the next ten minutes. From the reports of various survivors, this is what happened:

As soon as I hit the pines, a big cock got up, I fired, missed the pheasant, but triggered off the biggest bunch of booming this side of Fort Sill. All along the front the shooting became a steady roar, drowning out completely the cackling of airborne targets. Simultaneously a warden appeared as if from nowhere, yelling, "You can't hunt here; you're in a refuge."

"But, sir," I said, "The Jin'ral told me..."

"I don't care if Commissioner Smith told you. Get out!"

I got. But I couldn't find the rest of the patrol. As I later discovered, it had taken cover in a gully, hiding from the flying lead and from the warden. Crawling on his belly, The

Jin'ral gradually led his command to the south into a cornfield. One of the dogs broke loose and disappeared into the smoke of battle. Undismayed, The Jin'ral ordered his two boys to deploy as skirmishers.

Meanwhile, cut off from my leader, I proceeded as ordered to the north. This course brought me smack through a multiflora hedge into a public parking lot. Reorienting myself by the sun, I struck out toward what I thought was the river, only to find myself right back at our vehicles. Rather than face the shot and shell all alone, I turned on the car radio and ate a second lunch.

Gradually troops began to straggle back from the front lines, dazed by the shock of close combat, shell vests empty, game pockets empty, dog leashes empty. It was a massacre, all right, but not of ringnecks.

Then from the alders to the south there came a blare of whistles and a ruffle of boots as in marched The Jin'ral and his patrol, all accounted for, all in perfect step, bearing aloft no less than six trophies of war. It was one of those moments of truth that a writer must face.

"Private Schoenfeld," bellowed The Jin'ral, "just exactly how are you going to describe this expedition in your next dispatch?"

"That depends, Sir," I said, "on the generosity of the presiding officer at my court martial."

So I was presented with two ringnecks, and you herewith get the facts.

One good shot can certainly make a hunting season. The shot wasn't mine, and it wasn't actually a shot, but it was one of those outdoor events you like to remember, nonetheless.

We were hunting pheasants down at Albany the opening afternoon--The Jin'ral and me and his two sons, Bobby and Michael. The Jin'ral had trained his boys very carefully through the years. They started out with sticks, graduated to toy weapons, and then to BB guns. This was the first Fall they would both be armed with live ammunition, so this was the big test.

Would they know when and how to shoot? Even more important, would they know when to hold their fire?

It's one thing to teach a youngster how to swing a shotgun. It's quite another thing to drill into him the importance of safety first and the rules of sportsmanship. His natural enthusiasm tends to make a beginner trigger-happy. Like curbing a wide-ranging dog you have to lecture and lecture--and then keep your fingers crossed.

We unlimbered along the Sugar River, and the opening-day tension was high as we swung through a cornfield. The four of us converged in a semicircle as we approached the far fencerow corner. Our dog began to make game. Right in the middle of us the first cock of the year got up with a big cackle.

I dumped the bird, but it was the boys that got the praise. Bobby hadn't fired because he was dead in line with me, Mike held off because he was in line with his dad. The freshmen had passed their first big test with straight A's.

At times like this it's the shot that isn't fired that makes the moment--and the memory. That's about all it takes to make a season. That, and the knowledge that a fine crew of young people is beginning to take its place in the field under the tutelage of smart fathers who know that if you take your kid hunting you don't have to go hunting for your kid.

Looking back at a hunting season, I can see it's often the unexpected that sets shooting apart from other sports.

Take a couple of "for examples:"

The Jin'ral invited me to take him out for "a few hours" of pheasant hunting. I thought he would have a couple of roosters tied down for me near town, but we wound up heading 60 miles away to Avoca's huge public hunting ground. Our back-seat guide was John Evans, of Madison, a leader in the Southern Wisconsin Pointing Dog Club.

"Do you mind driving over bad roads?" John asked me, as he directed us off the highway.

"Let's go," I said boldly, never imagining how bad a Wisconsin "road" can be.

John proceeded to guide us cross-country for two miles, over bumpy bogs, through drainage ditches, into alder thickets, and across corduroy bridges--following what John called a road but what looked and felt to me like a poor version of a covered wagon trail. We finally parked plump in the middle of a marsh as big as a township.

John fielded his pointer, said "Let's go," and started out--without a gun. John gets so much pleasure working his magnificent dog he seldom does any shooting himself. We thought we were hunting pheasants, but what we jumped first were quail. We were all so surprised we never even fired. Later in the day, looking deliberately for quail near Lone Rock, we kicked out a ringneck. Despite our surprise we recovered quickly enough to drop him. He splashed in a slough, but our pointers took to the water like duck dogs.

It was again the unexpected that salvaged an otherwise dull day near Waupun. The Jin'ral and me were hunting pheasants in a swamp, but what we jumped was a lone mallard hen. With the whole of Dodge County to range over, that duck took a wide swing and came right back over us.

For the outdoor writer, typesetters can provide the unexpected, too. Like my line about "smoothbore muskets" that came out reading "smoothbore muskrats." Or my recipe for squirrel pie, which came out with one paragraph missing--the one in which I explained you put it in the oven before you put it on the table.

But the most unexpected event for me that Fall was the disappearance of an annoying rattle in the left-rear spring of my car. After harrassing me all Summer, it didn't make even a squeak after John Evans guided us down that bumpy marsh "road."

When the hunters were too thick around Madison The Jin'ral and me liked to say, "Nuts to pheasant hunting," and go in search of quail. So it was that an October afternoon would often find us in one of our favorite haunts--west along the old flood plain of the Wisconsin River, the land made famous by Aldo Leopold in his A Sand County Almanac.
    This is the region the glaciers--and the alphabet agencies--forgot. It was poor soil, no question about that. The clover was sparse, the corn runty. Abandoned farms abounded, dedicated to ragweed, prickly-pear cactus, and lush hedgerows that shrieked of "inefficiency." That was just what Mr. Bob White wanted. Here you would find quail in fair abundance--and no competition from the cordons of hunters for whom only a ringneck is suitable quarry.
    I have a special affinity for this sand country around Arena and Spring Green. It was here that my dad started preaching at the turn of the century. One of my earliest memories is his story of spending a night in a snowbank with a covey of quail when his cutter mired in a blizzard enroute home from a Wyoming Valley funeral. Those quail were still there--or at least their great, great, great grandchildren. Quail could be predictable. Barring a bad Winter blizzard, you could go back each Fall to the same spot and find the same covey. We were on such intimate terms with those sand-county quail families we had even given them names.
    Our first call was on the Cemetery Covey, so named for its preference for a forgotten burying ground where the earliest tombstones said "1851." They were there all right, boiling up out of a thicket of graveyard lilacs. The Jin'ral scored twice with his cylinder-bore, dropping both birds in the middle of the road. I fired wildly and missed clean. Before I could reflush the covey, The Jin'ral had jumped and killed a single that had caromed off to the left. Then we picked up two more from the oak ridge where the bulk of the birds had sought shelter.
    Our next stop was at the Sinkhole Covey. We found their dustbath right away, but two successive casts around the area netted nothing in the way of actual birds.
    "I know they're here," the Jin'ral said, as he plowed into the middle of an alder thicket.
    Even as he spoke the covey exploded with such abandon that we were unable to get off a shot. But we marked them down in a nearby cornfield and followed up quickly. Shooting quail in standing corn is no picnic. Out of ten birds flushed, we got a grand total of one. So we moved on to the Fencerow Covey.
    We hit this flock right on the dime. As a matter of fact,

it was two coveys that year. One bunch of adult birds careened out of the sumacs and across the stubble. Another bunch of immature birds, resembling nothing so much as bumblebees, cut on down the fencerow. We took one out of each covey. The big birds had pitched into a marsh. Since it was late in the afternoon, we decided to try "whistling them up." After a couple of calls, we got an answering "bob-white" from up ahead in a tangle of ragweed. We moved in.

The agronomists and the economists kept trying to figure out how to "improve" the sand country. Some of us hoped they would never succeed. We were happy with its thin stand of corn and hunters, and its occasional crops of quail. But the alphabet agency guys finally won. Our sand country now has acres of irrigated truck crops but no quail.

For some of the sportiest upland hunting in Wisconsin The Jin'ral and me have to thank old Colonel Gustav Pabst, of blue-ribbon fame, who introduced the Hungarian partridge to the Midwest in 1908.

The Hun is a quarry to stir the most jaundiced gunner. He gangs up in coveys like a quail, spots oncoming hunters like a prairie chicken, runs like a deer, rams out like a pheasant, careens off like a grouse, barrels through the air like a canvasback, flairs like a mallard, and melts into the ground like a woodcock.

To hunt Huns the only requirements are a strong back, a weak mind, and an Annie Oakley aim. It takes a strong back to charge over a whole township in pursuit of one errant gang of partridge. It takes a weak mind to look for them in the unlikely spots where they may be hiding. It takes a steady aim and keen eye to bring them down when they jump.

Forty years ago you used to be able to hunt Huns with good success throughout much of southern Wisconsin. Now you have to go to the strip between lakes Winnebago and Michigan.

The Jin'ral and me spent a solid day chasing six Huns near Cedar Grove in Sheboygan County. We kicked them out on a windswept slope early in the morning. After repeatedly marking them down and flushing them, at 4:00 in the afternoon we watched five gray ghosts careen away over the horizon.

His ability to outfox stealthy hunters and to fly unscathed through a charge of No. 6 shot partly explains why the Huns stay with us. Another reason is his ability to survive hard Winters in open country where quail, pheasants, and grouse find no shelter.

Why the Hun should no longer be present in numbers on his original stamping ground around Waukesha while thriving in east-central Wisconsin is harder to explain. One theory suggests that the heavy clay soils of the lakeshore counties have enough of a delayed haying season to allow Hun hens to bring off their broods, while further south hay mowers typically take a heavy toll of nesting birds that no longer can find fencerows in which to set up housekeeping.

Whatever the exact reason for the Hun's precarious survival, it is a most welcome phenomenon. This bird of the European steppes has come to occupy in Wisconsin what the biologists call an "ecological niche" that native species or other imports cannot fill, providing blue-ribbon hunting for strong-backed and weak-minded outdoor fans like The Jin'ral and me.

Some of our game birds are veiled in mystery. Not the least of these is the woodcock.

The Jin'ral and me have never been able to agree on what to call this odd member of the snipe and sandpiper family. He is variously known as American woodcock, wood hen, golden bombshell, timberdoodle, bog borer, big-headed snipe, big mud snipe, blind snipe, whistling snipe, wood snipe, night partridge, night peck, hookumpake, Labrador twister, bogsucker, bog-bird, pewee, whistler, and big eyes.

Replete as he is with so many labels, the woodcock has lent one of his names to a species of dog, the cocker spaniel.

In both morphology and habits the woodcock defies explanation. Its head is too big for its body, and its eyes and bill are too large for its head. It walks with a clownlike waddle and flies with the crazy course of a ship without a rudder.

The woodcock subsists on a diet made up almost exclusively of earthworms, and hence is particularly susceptible to the residues of chemical poisons that the worms ingest from sprayed soil. The bill of the woodcock, incidentally, is unique in that it is hinged in the exact opposite manner from most other birds and animals; the upper, rather than the lower, portions being movable. The woodcock uses its bill to probe into the soft, moist ground where earthworms abound. The Jin'ral and me look for these characteristic "holes."

The sex of a woodcock is very difficult to determine except by internal examination. It is generally considered a migratory species, but apparently not all individuals migrate to the same degree. Some take off for long distances at the first breath of frost; others hang around just ahead of the snow line.

In general, the bird is a woods inhabitant, although the definition of woods must be broadly interpreted to include pine-oak barrens, alder runs, sumac swamps, and even vacant lots on the outskirts of cities.

The food of woodcock is almost entirely animal material, and the bulk of this menu consists of angleworms, as we have said. Transmuted into a broiled bird on toast, however, there seems to be no difference of opinion among epicures that the woodcock is delicious eating. Viewed down a wavering gun barrel, the woodcock's sporting qualities are equally beyond question.

Sir Willie asks very little of man and nature. He has just

two basic requirements: First, a mossy stage from which he can take off on his sky dance in the Spring. Second, a damp dining room where he can bore for food in the Fall.

   The Jin'ral and me found him in abundance in one such favorite haunt one Sunday--along a clean, sweet swale where alders and willows formed a thick, shadowy retreat. We had scarcely waded into the bogs when the first bird of the day got up underfoot with a characteristic twitter, topped the trees in one rush, and then took off in erratic flight. Our brushload 8's stopped him. We marked him down with great care, but his protective coloration made us hunt hard. Before we could find him, a second woodcock fluttered up nearby and careened back out of range through a screen of popples.

   That was the way the day went: lots of flushes, some snap-shooting, some crossing shots, long-range pokes, quartering opportunities, overhead chances--all the bewildering variety of gunning that only Wisconsin woodcock hunting provides. At the end of the afternoon we had collected an assortment of cedar boughs, maple leaves, alder limbs, and dogwood sprays, as well as a comfortable heft of birds in our game pockets.

   All the while we saw not a single squadron of competing hunters, but we were able to commune abundantly with a tinkling brook, a phragmites swamp, and a hidden copse of hazel brush. There are more dramatic forms of game than woodcock, perhaps, but no other species of wildlife is so intimate a part of a mild and mysterious nature. His pursuit makes The Jin'ral and me officers and gentlemen in spite of ourselves.

A sad day for the hunters of Wisconsin is the last day of the grouse, rabbit, and squirrel seasons. Which means that at twilight you have to set aside your shotguns for eight long months.
There's one item of hunting equipment, however, you can't just store in a closet, and that's a hunting dog. All through the off-season you feed him, bed him, and curry his favor-- looking ahead to a handful of weekends next Fall when he can once again perform. Which makes a hunting dog an expensive luxury, at least according to most families. Like a transcontinental bomber or a fire engine, you have to keep him around during months and years of inactivity if you want him on tap for that crucial thirty seconds over a target. If you are unlucky, it will all be for naught. He will miss the scent, or bolt the point, or chew the bird. If you are lucky, however, that thirty seconds can be the difference between a glorious season and a bust.
It was so with me one Fall. My Brittany pup Mac was something less than a distinguished hunting dog most of the season. I was no better a hunter. But he chose one particular afternoon to perform brilliantly before a special audience, and I came through, too.
With us was The Jin'ral. I had chosen to take him down to the headwaters of the Pecatonica River.
We had scarcely loaded up and struck off into the woods when Mac surprised himself and me by coming on a solid point. The Jin'ral moved up to take the shot. Mac held, even when the grouse flushed. The Jin'ral missed. I connected at great range. Mac made a stylish retrieve. A little further down a cow path through the brush, the same thing happened again. I passed it off as a routine performance. The Jin'ral had no way of knowing what a rare phenomenon he was witness to.
Atop a ridge we came on an abandoned hayfield. In normal style, Mac charged off like a bullet, only to swing around in full stride on as fancy a point as ever graced the cover of a sporting magazine. Through no fault of his, the birds got up. They were quail. Working back to the car along a little creek, Mac began to make game in a peculiar way. Soon he was on point again in a half-crouch. This time it was a woodcock, the first he had ever smelled. The Jin'ral missed. I dropped the bird. Mac retrieved.
Now there is a man who thinks the Pecatonica Valley is loaded with birds, magnificent dogs, and crack shots. I'll never tell him otherwise.

If a Joseph and Mary were to come looking for a place to stay in metropolitan USA at Christmastime, chances are they would find a lot of signs still saying, "No Room at the Inn." Homes would be too hectic to hear the doorbell. Schools would be busy staging holiday sideshows. In the centers of trade the travelers couldn't even find a place to park. But The Jin'ral and me know of stables away in the heart of southwestern Wisconsin where weary strangers are welcomed warmly--and where there are plenty of partridge in nearby prickly-pear trees.

I personally get a particular kick out of bagging grouse in Wyoming Valley. This is the ancestral home of the Iowa County Joneses, from whom I am descended. None of the Jones boys ever made much money off the land, but these rugged hills are finally yielding up to a latter-day Jones an even more valuable crop-- the king of American game birds and a sense of the Christmas spirit.

It was a week before Christmas one year that The Jin'ral and me set out for southwest Wisconsin, like not-so-wise men from the east, to get away from the tinsel and to close the partridge season. We found some birds and we also found something of even greater value--a countryside dedicated to peace, and a humble man of goodwill.

We had flushed a bird out of a grape tangle without getting a shot at him, and we followed him across a draw onto another ridge. He flushed wild two more times, leading us further into the woods. Before we realized it we didn't know the way back to our car. I climbed to a height of land and spotted a road far down in a valley. We struggled down to it through thick brambles, only to find it wasn't our road. We walked a quarter mile in each direction trying vainly to get our bearings. Around a bend we came on the sort of buildings you sometimes still find off the beaten track--log house, tar-paper barn, delapidated "rest room." A man was hollering at us from the stable door. At first we thought he was ordering us off the premises, but it turned out he was asking if he could help. We told him we were lost, and where we wanted to get to.

"Well," he said. "You'll waste a lot of time following the road. You go back up onto that ridge, bear to your left, keeping a big cliff to your right, and then get up onto the next ridge, bear to your right for a mile, keep following that nose, and you'll come out right at your car."

He wanted us to come in for a spell, but we decided it was getting too dark.

"You pa'tridge hunting?" he asked.

We admitted we were, expecting to be told we had failed to heed some "No Hunting" signs.

"I've seen a few birds around," the man said. "Good luck. And stop in again sometime."

Our friend's directions were superb. Just as the evening star appeared The Jin'ral and me found our car right where he said we would. But more precious than his guidance or his grouse was the goodwill he gave us. It is always so. The great gifts of this world come in simple wrappings.

I once introduced a beginner to the fine art of waterfowling. Neither he nor I will ever be the same again. My pupil was The Jin'ral. He is an expert on pheasants, but he had never been in a duck blind in his life. I undertook to share some of my profound experience.

Things went wrong right from the start. I failed to orient my student properly, so The Jin'ral showed up at my door in a scarlet hat, a crimson shirt, and white canvas gloves. He did not take kindly to my insistence that he cover himself in an old olive-drab parka.

At the marsh he suggested that I row the boat "because you know the area." I tried to tell him that I couldn't row because tossing out the decoys required a special touch, but he merely reminded me that he outranked me in the Army Reserve. I rowed and he tossed. The resulting set resembled nothing ever seen on sea or land, and I said it would never in the world attract a duck. As things turned out, we had ducks sitting in our decoys all day.

Once in the blind, I emphasized the importance of staying down low and motionless, but The Jin'ral kept standing up to see what was going on around the marsh. I objected, but the ducks didn't. Attempting to demonstrate my most dulcet tones on a duck call, I succeeded only in scaring a flock of blackheads away. The Jin'ral gave one unearthly toot, and the flock swung back.

"They're 'way too high," I told my pupil. "Don't try any skybusting."

"They look in range to me," he proclaimed, and proceeded to drop one.

Far away to the south we spotted a flock of mallards traveling high and fast.

"They'll never pay any attention to us," I announced.

"Yes, they will," The Jin'ral said. They did, indeed. I missed.

Another blackhead gave us a pass. We fired in unison and the bird collapsed.

"Well, I finally hit one," I said.

"Nope," said my pupil. "I'm using 4's and you're using 7 1/2's. A light load would never reach that far."

"You aren't supposed to be using heavy loads," I complained. But my voice was beginning to carry no conviction.

As the sun slowly set over the marsh, I headed home empty-handed and The Jin'ral carried a string of ducks. I've had to take him along again and again.

We get to our blinds early, well before the sun is up, because there is a special magic about a predawn pothole. To the accompaniment of the mysterious noises of the night, we toss out the decoys--a tight knot of puddlers here, a string of divers there, and in between a gaggle of geese.

A mallard hen becomes audibly enthusiastic back in the rice beds, but we cannot make out what she is talking to. A flock of bluebills, pitching pondward, tears the dark silk of the night in one long, rending nosedive, but there is still nothing to see except stars. Then with an unbelievable rush the dark is gone and we are revealed to be suspended in time and space, a trio of waterfowl hunters eye-deep in the marsh like so many muskrats, clinging to the strand of cattails that separates tamarack from tossing waters.

A sense of history lies heavy on such a place. Yearly since the Ice Age it has awakened each fall morning to the clangor of Canada geese and the beating pinions of pintails. In the incredible sweep of millennia which underlies the affairs of nature, our hunt is only a momentary intrusion.

Far to the northeast, winding the oxbows of the Wisconsin River, an arrow of waterfowl cleaves the dawn sky. They appear to be geese. Are they moving steadfastly south or are they looking for a place to sit down? Can they hear us? These are the immemorial questions that lend almost unbearable suspense to the world of the waterfowler. Bob McCabe gives them a tentative toot on his goose call. They seem to answer. He goes to work in earnest. They turn our way, giving tongue to a few querulous honks. The Jin'ral hunkers down lower in his boat and holds his breath. Majestically the flock sweeps high over us, stepping up its conversation.

Do they like what they see? After an agonizing swing to the west they come pumping back. In a pandemonium of trumpets, croaks, and cries they set their wings and glide down, black landing gear lowered and rumps white against the far hills. Out in the middle of the pond they come to rest with a great honking and splashing, long necks and beady eyes surveying the scene with the caution that has brought them safely to this spot from Hudson Bay.

What we see displayed before us is no mere bird. As Aldo Leopold suggested, the Canada goose is the symbol of our untamable past, the cymbal in the orchestra of evolution. His annual pilgrimage is the ticking of the geologic clock. Upon the hunters he visits he bestows an apostolic blessing, and upon the place of his alighting he confers a peculiar distinction. Amid the antiseptic surroundings of civilization, a goose pond holds a paleontological patent of nobility. The sadness discernable in some subdivisions arises, perhaps, from their once having harbored geese. Now they stand humbled, cut off forever from the flow of nature.

Our geese are not with us long. For a moment they conduct a loud debate over the relative merits of staying or of heading for Illinois. The urge to travel wins. With a surge of flapping and gabbling they take off. Their angle of ascent and the direction of the wind are such that they present me with a target as they gain altitude--16 huge honkers spread out in the sky right in front of my blind.

Almost reluctantly I throw three quick shots at the milling mass of birds. Nothing happens. They continue on their way without so much as breaking formation. Soon they are once again nothing but a distant V on the southern horizon, and I am left with the problem of explaining my poor marksmanship to The Jin'ral. But he does not press the point. He senses we have harvested something more substantial than feathers.

Every so often The Jin'ral and me seem to get an urge to win a medal of some kind by exposing ourselves to hostile gunfire. There are two simple ways to get shot at. One way is to join the army. The other way is to go deer hunting. If anything, your chances are better deer hunting.

It was in 1939 that I first became a human target. My unknown assailant was a fellow deer hunter in a Flambeau Valley thicket near Park Falls, Wisconsin. Only his abysmal aim kept me from making the headlines--as a casualty. In 1944, I didn't have to go deer hunting in order to get shot at. I was wintering at an Italian seaside resort called Anzio, and my German nephews were very obliging about bracketing in on my platoon command post. We thought things were rough at Anzio, but from hindsight I can see it wasn't so risky after all. There couldn't have been more than 100,000 troops in the area, Allies and Nazis combined, and that's less than a fifth of the number of armed men that take to the Wisconsin woods every November, each of them bent on slinging bullets with an abandon that would turn a supply sergeant's hair gray.

In 1948, with the war over, we once again sought danger on the Wisconsin front, this time on a battlefield known as Necedah, where three rounds from a .250-3000 de-limbed the cedar under which we were crouching. In 1952, the Korean Conflict took care of my need to ride to the sound of the guns.

For a recent rendezvous with lead the Jin'ral and me chose a peaceful country knoll in Columbia County. We joined the convoys rumbling out of Madison in the predawn hours and managed to find a parking place in an assembly area a thousand yards back of the front lines.

By 6:19 we were on our stand, all set to start ducking. But all in all it was a disappointing morning. There was plenty of shooting all around--we counted 39 shots in the first 30 minutes--but not a single slug whistled our way. We even saw five deer, which wasn't what we were looking for at all. In desperation, at mid-morning, we crashed through an alder swamp and stomped along an oak ridge, but we still didn't draw any fire. Sometimes you just can't win a medal no matter how hard you try.

Sometimes you can't win a buck, either. Either the standard references on big game animals are in error, or the deer around Dane County are just plain dumb.

Reading from the opening lines of Townsend Whelen's book:

"The white-tailed deer is a forest animal."

Well, you can't find any forests around Mount Horeb, but you can find plenty of deer sign, which is why The Jin'ral and me opened the deer season down that way one year. Apparently the deer can't tell a forest from a farmyard.

"There is nothing that will alarm deer as quickly as the scent of man," Colonel Whelen goes on to say. Our deer hadn't read that chapter, either. One trail we got on ran right past a schoolhouse, along a main-traveled road, over a farmhouse lawn, and into a feeding lot.

"If you wait by any runway or feeding ground, you will have a very good chance to see a deer," writes Dr. William J. Long in his book on whitetails. We waited by that runway, all right, but the deer had their signals mixed. They never came down the trail. We did see one farmer, two boys, and a lady hunter.

"When you stalk a deer, change your gait," Dr. Long says. "Every animal is so curious about an irregular sound he may approach to find out about it." This sytem worked very well on inquisitive pigs rooting in an oak woods, but it didn't produce any deer. Those darned deer just hadn't read enough manuals, that's all.

I.H. Bartlett, another famous deer expert, says any man can walk down a deer. He claims "a startled but unharried deer does not run out of the township before stopping." That may be true in Michigan or Maine, but in Wisconsin the deer keep going, at least until they get to a well-posted woods.

"A feeding deer lifts his head two or three times every minute for a quick look around," Bartlett writes, "so move slowly toward him when his head is down." We looked all over the area for a deer with his head down, but we couldn't find one. In fact, we couldn't find one with his head up. However, we did run into some fine Guernseys on a back forty.

"Any sound like coughing, sneezing, or talking will send deer off in a hurry," Colonel Whelen claims. Our deer must be deaf, because the only deer we saw was a doe that stumbled up to us while we were chatting and eating lunch. The Jin'ral and me were so surprised we never got off a shot.

I was one of those who joined the ranks of the Protesters one November. Protesters are a subspecies of humans who have as their rationale an escape from organized society. To distinguish themselves from Conformists, all Protesters wear uniforms, consisting of plaid shirts and soiled pants. All Protesters are also unshaven. All Protesters engage in marches, sit-ins, and other disturbances of the natural environment. Actually there are two types of Protesters. One type is typically found in urban settings like a university campus. This type is commonly called the New Left. The other type of Protester is found in rural habitats like a cedar swamp. This type is referred to as the Deer Hunter.

It was the latter Protest Movement that I joined, along with three other fugitives from the city, The Jin'ral, Robert Hougas, and Harland Klagos, plus three junior-grade Protesters. In true Protester fashion, our first tactic was to hold a committee meeting. We chose as our site the Hughes retreat near Mazomanie. We barricaded the access road and called the meeting to order. The first item on the agenda was a discussion of how best to disrupt the Dane County deer herd the next morning. The senior members of the cell proposed peaceful tactics like sitting-in along various deer trails. As a matter of fact, one of us would have been satisfied with a lie-in at the cabin. But we were shouted down by our junior colleagues, who insisted on a militant march through the hills. We then turned to a more academic subject, Economics 105, described in the catalogue as "Low Hole Card Wild." Here again we senior Protesters were out-maneuvered by the New Generation. Michael Hughes in particular broke up the meeting by pocketing all the legal tender.

A half-hour before dawn the next day found us all heavily engaged in Protesting. With yellow signs on our backs, shouldering weapons of war, and uttering vile curses at blackberry brambles, we violated the peace of the countryside with true escapist abandon. The senior members of the cell tried to exercise some semblance of control over the goings-on, but the New Generation insisted on taking over. It was not Chairman Hughes who shot the first buck, it was young Michael. At least we got him to agree to tag his animal and check it in at the state station. As we told him, even Protesters have to live by certain rules.

Our cell has now disbanded for a year. Each of us has gone underground, posing as just another Conformist. Our plaid shirts are in mothballs. We have even shaved. But come another deer season and The Jin'ral and me will become Activists once again. That is, provided there isn't a law against Protesting.

If you are frequently invited to accompany assorted colleagues on assorted hunting expeditions, it may be because of your good looks or your good spirits. On the other hand, if you are like me, it will be because you are a poor shot. A lousy marksman is a handy gadget to have along on a hunt. He can perform menial tasks like brush-beating and dishwashing, he can be positioned in a marginal spot without risking the efficiency of the expedition, and his poor performance makes everybody else appear expert by comparison.

One year I really began to suspect the role I play as a hostage to the gods of the chase. The last day of the deer season The Jin'ral invited me to go deer hunting with him on his farm. I was flattered. I was even more flattered when he put me on a stand and made the first drive himself. No deer came my way. "I didn't expect to push anything out here," The Jin'ral said cryptically. He then placed himself on a likely stand and told me where to drive. I was only half way on my swing when his shotgun boomed. By the time I got there, The Jin'ral already had the buck dressed out. "Good thing it was my turn to stand," he said. I had the privilege of dragging the deer to the road.

Early the next grouse season I was asked to go along with The Jin'ral and his boys on a partridge campaign. For our assault on a wooded draw, I was positioned in the middle of our line in heavy cover. I flushed feathers but I didn't get a bird. They careened off to the left and right to be taken in the open by my partners. When I complained about the situation, they said, "We planned it that way." The real moment of truth came during the pheasant season when I was again invited to accompany The Jin'ral and his boys. It was Kevin's first hunt, but at 12 years of age he already knew the rules of the game.

"You work through that ditch and I'll take the field," Kevin told me.

I put up a rooster. Kevin and I fired simultaneously.

"Who got him? Kevin asked.

"You did," said The Jin'ral immediately.

"How do you know?" I asked.

"Because with the track record of you and your 12 gauge, the odds are all in favor of Kevin and his 410."

I whimpered like a baby.

My morale had lifted a bit by the time I was invited to join the same crew for the opening of the deer season. We assembled at the Hughes CP near Mazomanie. At H-hour my partners prepared to sneak away.

"Where do I go?" I asked.

"You, Colonel," said The Jin'ral, "will take your car, drive me to my stand, bring my guncase back to the cabin, and fix brunch."

"Can't I even take my gun along in the trunk of the car?"

"Let him take it," said Michael. "He won't disturb anything out there on the flank."

For once my partners reckoned wrongly. Tramping through the woods they saw no deer. Cruising back along the town road, I did. Off to my left I spotted a buck sneaking along the ridge. I dismounted and slipped through the underbrush to position myself in the path of the animal. It was almost as if the deer knew the caliber of his adversary. Fearlessly he came forward and stopped not 40 yards away to stare brazenly at me. I raised my shotgun, took deliberate aim, fired, and scored a direct hit--on a nearby birch tree. With what I guess was a snort of disdain, the buck bounded off, saluting me as he went with his white flag. Somewhere in western Dane County next morning a young buck was telling his harem, "In the case of some hunters, the only thing you have to fear is fear itself."

Someday, perhaps, I will recapture my GI shooting eye, and will then be able to hold up my head in the presence of my fellow hunters. The only trouble is, if that time should come they may no longer invite me along.

As Army Reservists our orders may say that we're to proceed to Fort McCoy for Summer military training, but you can't blame us if we take our fly rods along, because some of the best trout water in the state flows through the McCoy reservation.

As a matter of fact, any fishing expedition pans out better if it's run like a minor military operation.

First comes what's called in GI lingo the "prior preparation." This phase includes accumulating a stockpile of "ammunition"-- bait, that is; picking the day and the hour, after much consultation of almanacs (and family); naming the assault spot (this being an exclusive prerogative of the commanding officer); arranging for chow; cleaning equipment; and getting into proper uniform.

On H-hour minus 18 up at Fort McCoy, The Jin'ral calls a conference. We troop into the barracks and pay attention to orders. First, information on "the enemy" and "friendly forces." Two, the general mission. Three, specific duties. Four, administrative details. Finally, communications.

"The rainbows should be hitting well on the reservation," the CO says. "They're taking worms. Some local boys filled up Thursday."

"We're going to take off tomorrow afternoon at 1630 and fish until dusk. We'll try Squaw Creek first and then work on down to the lake. Randy, you and Clay pick me up on the dot. Wear boots because we'll need to wade. Ace, make sure Benway will be out about 1900 with C rations and coffee. If it's raining, we'll check signals. I'll be on Range N."

Our fishing operations up at McCoy usually go according to plan. We meet "the enemy" and they are ours--nice strings of rainbows and browns averaging half a pound apiece. They lie in the slicks, charge our bait with abandon, and fight hard.

But there's one big catch to going fishing with The Jin'ral. As a junior officer you have to make sure he comes home with the biggest trout. Two other colonels and I tossed back our best fish last year rather than run the risk of surpassing the brass.

I see by the papers where more fishing licenses will be sold this year than ever before in the history of the United States. I don't know of anything more than that statistic that so testifies to something tenacious in the human spirit. Because it takes a peculiar, pesky soul to be a fisher.

First of all, come drought or high water, death or taxes, recalcitrant wives or pleading mistresses, you positively have to participate in opening-day festivities. There is a piscatorial law that says so. The opening hour is not a respectable 12 noon, as in the case with duck hunting. It is dawn. The night before you are always invited to somebody's cocktail party. When you attempt to leave before 1 a.m., people look at you askance and whisper behind your back.

You get up at 3:30, stumble around the kitchen in hip

boots, and fumble around in the icebox for sandwich makings. Somebody yells something from a bedroom. The streets of the city are so deserted they are absolutely unrecognizable. You search furtively for the avenue leading out of town. A squad car looks you over suspiciously, and trails you for two blocks.

As you near your chosen spot, however, the darkness and solitude disappear. Campfires glisten every couple of yards along the bank. Scores of shadowy figures have preceded you.

You lace on a nightcrawler and cast. The reel you had so carefully overhauled conks out. You work for half an hour untangling the snarl. You cast again. Nothing happens. You switch night crawlers. The futile ritual is repeated regularly for an hour. The sun rises but the fish don't.

At this juncture a nattily attired, wide-awake latecomer elbows in at your side. You have to make room for him because he is The Jin'ral, who proposes to use something exotic called a salmon spawn bag--a little nylon sack of fish eggs, which he says he has prepared himself from materials acquired in strange places. He makes one dainty cast--and reels in a trout. He makes a second cast and hooks a second trout. He takes four more in rapid succession. Then he pauses because he sees that you are crying.

"Would you like to trade baits?" he asks.

With a disgusting display of gratitude you take his spawn sack and give him your angleworm. The results are sensational. He continues to catch trout and you do not. Fortunately, you now remember that you have an urgent meeting in town. Trailing clouds of ignominy you depart. On the way back to the city you think up a likely fish story to tell your family and friends:

"The water was too muddy and the wind was too strong. Nobody was catching anything."

"It hardly pays to go," they will say. But you will return. You are a febrile fisher.

As near as I can place the date, it would have been the first Sunday in June, 1927. My father was delivering the Rally Day sermon at the Barneveld Congregational Church, and his eight-year-old son was required to go along.

On this particular day, however, I was not parked in a rear pew. Instead, I was deposited alone at the rude stone bridge where a primitive County Trunk T passed over Trout Creek just north of town. I had a cane pole, a hank of line, a cork bobber, a Carlisle hook, a can of worms, and unlimited hope. It was not misplaced. Before the echoes of the opening hymn died away, the first trout of my life lay flopping on the bank. It was a rainbow, his gaudy pink stripe and inky back testifying that he, too, had been born in Iowa County.

I would like to recount how I remember the fight he put up, or his record weight. I can't. He was a little fish, and he succumbed to some very crude tactics. What I do remember very

clearly of that day is the trimmings: the soft conversation of
the stream, the song sparrows speaking from pasture tussocks,
the breeze in the box elders, the snort of an inquisitive steer,
the passage of a very occasional touring car on the gravel road,
and the appearance of only one other fisher, who gave me a wide
berth according to the custom of the day.

It is so with every angler. One's standard of quality for
an outdoor experience is established very early in life, and a
fishing career from then on is a perpetual search for recapit-
ulation. For many of us, quality is associated with little
country rainbows.

On the trail of a memory, I hied myself last opening day to
that sacred spot, Trout Creek just below Barneveld, in the
company of another fellow knight of the grail, The Jin'ral. It
is a mastery of understatement to say that the setting was not
that of 50 years ago. In place of a meandering brook there is a
man-made lake. In place of a pasture there is a blacktop parking
lot. In place of song sparrows there are transistor radios. In
place of polled Herefords there are people--by actual count, 369
of them elbow-to-elbow around the pond. One of them in particular caught our eye. He was an eight-year-old by the name of
Jimmie, on his first expedition. He was wielding sophisticated
spinning tackle with aplomb. And he was catching fish. Not
just one little rainbow, but a limit of big ones. It did not
seem to bother Jimmie that his trout had been delivered by tank
truck a few weeks before, or that he had the problem of keeping
his line from getting tangled with a dozen others. He was
having a big outdoor experience, Model 1980.

The Jin'ral and me will go no more back to Trout Creek at
Barneveld. For us it no longer offers a quality outdoor experience.
But Jimmie will undoubtedly go back many times to seek its big,
urbanized rainbows. He and they are all part of a production-
line age that has its own measure of excellence. Without question,
with our bulldozers and antibiotics we are manufacturing rainbow
fishing today in surprising quantity. But perhaps some of us
will be pardoned if we still go looking for nothing more than a
boy, a bobber, and a brook.

On the surface, the world of the largemouth bass fisher has
changed a good deal in recent years. For one thing, bass management
ideas have changed, and with them the regulations governing bass
fishing. Time was when you had to wait until June 20th to fish
for largemouths, you could only keep ten-inchers, and the bag
limit was small--all in the name of conserving what was thought
to be a dwindling supply against the ravages of overfishing.
Today the fisheries experts think they know better. They figure
that in the presence of acceptable habitat, prolific bass will
produce enough offspring to withstand even the heaviest fishing
pressure, and that what we most usually have to guard against is
too many little stunted bass rather than too few lunkers. So

opening day is earlier, size limits are out, and bag limits are bigger.

For another thing, bass fishing tackle has changed. Time was when the standard weapon was a ponderous bait rod used to toss a pork rind, a Skinner spoon, a harnessed night crawler, or a live frog. Today the wandlike spinning rod or spin-casting rod are undoubtedly the most popular and most effective bass fishing tools, and a variety of salt water jigs have been modified for deep-running inland use as lures: spoon plugs, jig-a-doos, bucktail wobblers, daredevils, bombers, and silver minnows.

But the really important things in the world of the bass fisher haven't changed at all. July is still the most active month for largemouths. At dusk or just after dark, when faint night breezes condition the tepid air, high-riding lures are still devastating in their effectiveness. A bass churning up from the water to take a surface bait is still an unsurpassed fishing thrill. And there is still that fishing partner who goes along to help--and harass--you with his advice.

The Jin'ral and me were afloat on Rock Lake marsh one evening to field-test some new artificial frogs. Rowing the boat and coaching was Professor Henry Darling. We pupils weren't doing very well. A half-hour of casting had produced only one half-hearted strike.

"Now let me go over this again," said Professor Darling. "Cast softly into a break in the lily pads. Let your bait rest for a count of eight. Then twitch it ever so slightly, and let it rest for another count of eight. Repeat the process as you retrieve slowly.

"You see that open spot over there? Let's try it once more by the numbers."

The Jin'ral managed to execute a cast according to Coach Darling's directions, and he let his green frog ride the surface idly. The rings spread out from the bait, the water returned to its boring calm, and nothing happened. Then, as if on a cue from Coach Darling, a big largemouth exploded like a grenade, took the frog in his flaring jaws, shook it like a dog with a bone, and bore down beneath the surface to weave and lash among the rushes. There are other heart-stopping experiences in the out-of-doors: the roar of a grouse in the winter woods, the rip of canvasback over a blind, the snort of a buck in a pine forest. But nothing really can compare with the savage charge of a largemouth attacking a surface lure.

I would like to report that we boated the bass. We didn't. That's another thing that hasn't changed about bass fishing. You lose as many as you catch. It's probably just as well. There's always a bass left to lure you back to a lake.

The spoon slithered through the lily pads again, trailing its hank of pork rind. Nothing happened.

"I tell you this lake is empty as a bathtub, "I said.

"Didn't that guy at the gas station say we were nuts to be fishing for bass here?"

The Jin'ral admitted I was quoting correctly. The natives were strictly down on this particular lake. Didn't have anything in it except runt crappies, they said. Just plain "fished out."

Yet there we were, at 4:00 in the morning, casting away as if we had sense, all because The Jin'ral had had what he calls "a hot tip."

Once more my spoon sneaked around the rushes, poking and ducking like a spy in a bomb factory. Then a G-man in the form of a largemouth bass swam into the picture, and the first thing I knew a strong arm grabbed the end of my line.

With more instinct than skill I set the hook. That was all the challenge Lieutenant Largemouth needed. He came charging boatward with the abandon of a commando--lunging, boring, churning. I managed to retrieve enough line to keep the chain-of-command clear. When he broke water, shaking his wounded head, I gained ground on him. Finally he was belly up in the net.

"Did you say 'fished out?'" was all The Jin'ral had time to say before we were casting again. By the time the sun was well up we had seven more. Not big bass, to be sure, but bass from a lake which had been written off the list of fishable water.

The secret? Fisheries people at work.

Four years before this particular excursion of ours, a crew of fisheries biologists had gone to work on this particular lake, after getting repeated loud complaints of "poor fishing." What they found was a lake ideal for bass but one in which there were so many stunted crappies that there wasn't room enough or food enough to raise catchable fish. So they netted and trapped the runts and planted bass fingerlings, along with forage minnows. The result? On opening day three years later an angler caught his limit of largemouth in just eight minutes[That's where we came in, after The Jin'ral got his hot tip.

There's a special satisfaction in taking fish from "fished out" lakes. They aren't supposed to be there. They give you the thrill of fishing unknown wilderness waters, and yet they're practically in your back yard.

Yes, sir, give me one of these "fished out" lakes every time--lakes where hungry bass have been substituted for stunted panfish. Thanks to some high-powered research and practical work, there's getting to be a lot of this rejuvenated water all across Wisconsin. Your local conservation warden can direct you.

The Jin'ral and me were looking for a new boat, my old boat having sprung an irrepairable leak last Fall. We discovered, however, that you can't buy a boat any more. You can buy a status symbol that floats, but you can't buy a simple boat.

"I'm looking for something modest," I told the marina salesman, who wore something resembling a dinner jacket.

"Runabout, cruiser, corsair, or sedan?" he asked.

"I think what I want is called a duck skiff," I said.
"I'm not familiar with that name. Would you describe it, please?"
"Well, it's about so long and so wide, and it has a deck at both ends."
"A deck at both ends?"
"Yes."
"Most unusual! I wonder if you aren't thinking of something like this."
He led me over to a craft just a little shorter than the Queen Mary.
"Note the chrome fiberglass lapstrake siding, the Malaysian mahogany trim, and the solid brass fittings," he said. "The galley is fully equipped, the seats convert into bunk beds, and the shower stall is full-size. Just think what the neighbors will say when they see this tied up at your pier."
"But I don't keep a boat tied up at a pier. In fact, I don't have a pier. I just want something I can shove around through a duck marsh."
"Oh, you want a john or a pram. We have this special 18-foot aluminum model with styrofoam floatation. Note the flamenco red permanent finish."
"That would be too hard to camouflage. Don't you have anything about 10 feet long and painted dead grass tan?"
"I'm afraid you're in the wrong store. We haven't carried anything like that for some time. Perhaps a junk dealer over on the river..."
"Let me look at your outboard motors, then. I want something light."
"Now I think we can help you. We have a special on this little utility model. It is only 10 horse and weighs just 45 pounds. Of course, it can't compare in power with our regular models."
"I was thinking of something about the size of my lawn mower."
"You mean a one-cylinder job? Why, we wouldn't think of stocking anything like that!"
"Why?"
"They won't start."
"My lawn mower starts. All I need is something like that for trolling."
"But what would people say if they saw you with a one-lung gadget hanging out of your boat?"
"I try to go fishing where there aren't any people."
"You mean you don't want a motor you can show off?"
"I hadn't thought of it in those terms, no."
"Well, you'd better get with it, guys. If you want to take to the water these days, you'll have to shape up or ship out."
I shipped out but the Jin'ral shaped up. He now owns a cruiser, a pontoon boat, and three giant motors. It has put a strain on my comradeship and his pocketbook.

The Jin'ral and me identified with JFK. You may remember that President Kennedy once said, "We must set before the people the American agenda." High on his agenda was conservation.

In his first year as President Mr. Kennedy sent a special message to Congress on conservation. He followed it up in May of 1962 with the first White House Conference on Conservation since the one called in 1908 by Theodore Roosevelt. One of his last official acts was a conservation tour of 10 states--including Wisconsin--in which he called for a "third wave of conservation" in the wake of the leadership of the two Roosevelts.

John Kennedy sponsored establishing more national seashores and lakeshores, giving the new Bureau of Outdoor Recreation adequate funds, strengthening federal water pollution control programs, speeding up the crash program of wetlands acquisition, trying to get the Wilderness Bill through Congress after a five-year delay, taking steps within the federal establishment to lessen the potential threat of chemical pesticides and detergents to people and wildlife, knocking heads in the federal bureaus to achieve a coordinated approach to "new programs of land steward-ship."

And then came the end.

For The Jin'ral and me, the Wisconsin deer woods were an awful place November 23, 1963. Solitude peered out from silent draws between the ridges. Pine plantations were peopled with ghosts. A great gray cloud blanket hung like a shroud over the western horizon. Chickadees sang a minor strain. Even the cawing of ravens seemed somehow muted. Deer hunters on stands fingered their weapons with a strange nervousness. Deer hunters on drives chanted in hoarse whispers as if they were passing down the aisles of a mortuary. There was no excitement in the occasional shots that broke the stillness, only a gnawing emptiness.

An hour after sunrise there were more red-clad figures clustered around car radios than there were in the woods. By midmorning the forest cabins were full of hunters who earlier had vowed they'd stay out 'till dusk. Nobody said much. It just wasn't a day for talking--certainly not for toting a gun.

It may be hard for some to understand why a hunter especially would feel the events of that weekend like a knife-stab in the gut. After all, a hunter is one who fondles rifles, who takes deliberate aim at defenseless targets, who lives in a small way with a sense of violence. Yet nowhere was the country's grief more evident than in the deer woods.

The answer lies partially in the hunter's deep sense of tradition. Hunter and rifle are as American as Daniel Boone. Since the days of Jamestown and Plymouth Rock, Americans have been shouldering firearms to wrest from the land an increment of nature's crop. Since the days of Lexington and New Orleans, sharpshooters have been marching out to defend the parapets of freedom. What happened at Dallas was an inexpressible desecration of that tradition. Every hunter felt personally betrayed.

The answer lies also in the hunter's sense of the fitness of things. Nothing is so orderly in a fundamental way as a deer hunt. Cordons of people merely perform the functions of nature formerly reserved for screwworms and cougars. The deer hunter revives, in play, a drama inherent in the life of the wild. In the last analysis, perhaps, a hunt is an esthetic exercise, with a sure purpose that serves both human and beast. What happened at Dallas was so utterly senseless that the revulsion cast a palsy on sportspersons' trigger-fingers.

The Jin'ral and me like to remember a quite different time when we were one with John F. Kennedy.

It was the night of November 5, 1960. Radio and television were bubbling with the voting story, and with the report of a weather front moving down from Canada. We bundled ourselves into a car--even though the final returns were not yet in--and headed north for a rendezvous with ducks. I can still hear the ponderous voice of the announcer on our portable radio at dawn the next morning, proclaiming the election of the youngest president, even as northern mallards poured into our blocks.

This is the America The Jin'ral and me like to remember, "in unforgotten Autumns gone too soon."

Wonderful World of Fishing

The lakes and streams of Wisconsin are full of fishers--and pollsters. What used to be the simple pastime of "goin' fishin'" has been exalted in recent years as a phase of something called "outdoor recreation," which in turn has been discovered as a fruitful field of study by a growing phalanx of social scientists. So, if you are accosted on your favorite creek or flowage by somebody making a public-use or public-opinion survey, don't be dismayed. You are about to enter the domain of outdoor statistics.

What the people-watchers are discovering about Izaak Walton's ancient and honorable art just goes to show what any fisher has always known--that fishing has tremendous appeal for a tremendous number of people. In the United States as a whole, the magnitude of fish harvested by angling is on the order of one and one-half billion pounds annually. While the nation's population will about double by the year 2000, the number of anglers will probably triple and the number of fishing days may quadruple. When outdoor fans are asked spontaneously what "usual" leisure activity they engage in "quite a lot," fishing leads the list.

With data like these, the economists and sociologists are able to put their finger on certain aspects of fishing, but they will likely have trouble explaining what the sport is really all about, because its appeal is as much in the setting as in the action, particularly on opening weekend. To get the true flavor of fishing-time we may have to continue to rely on poets. On T.S. Eliot, for instance, speaking of a month that "frees lilacs out of dead land, mixing memory and desire, stirring dull roots with spring rain." On a current <u>Saturday Evening Post</u> commentator, describing "a sudden apparition of yellow, white, and purple crocuses sprung out of the earth violently and so bright they hurt the eyes; inside of one of these blossoms a bee was rolling about in the pollen and performing a microrite of spring." On Edgar Guest, who once wrote in his inevitable way that "the brotherhood of rod and line and sky and stream is mighty fine." Or even on Herbert Hoover, who was not otherwise given to profound statements, but who once said that "before a fish, all men are equal."

Statistics or not, it could be that the great American rite of "goin' fishin'" is somehow our best single avenue to communion with nature and between people.

"I'm not a fisher myself, but I've got a youngster who wants to go. What do I do?" So many people have asked me this question that I take it the problem is universal enough to rate some comments:

First off, I strongly suspect that what some of these parents are looking for is a guaranteed tip on a spot five minutes from the garage where they can drive right up to the bank in the middle of a Saturday afternoon, deposit their sons or daughters, get back in the car without missing more than 30 seconds of the ball game, and then very shortly open the car door so their kids and their monstrous strings of pike can be hauled home to be cleaned by somebody else.

If this is what you have in mind, forget all about fishing and buy your youngster a set of golf clubs. Fishing isn't like that. You see, part of the sustained fun of fishing comes from the suspense of wondering where and when they'll be hitting today, and the patience it takes to sweat out a bite. These elements of the sport are as important to teach your progeny as are the techniques of baiting a hook. What's more, the lure of fishing is deeply entwined with a sense of exploration--to faraway places with strange-sounding names, at unholy hours of the early morning. Your boy or girl is entitled to this facet of fishing, too.

All right, you say you're willing to give it the old college try. What equipment do you get? Much as you yourself may be intrigued with fancy rods, reels, and flies, don't burden your youngster with tackle far beyond his or her ability to manipulate. For the beginner, it's hard to beat a cane pole, 25 feet of ordinary fishing line, and a size 6 snelled hook onto which you thread that old standby, an angleworm. If you want to jazz things up a little, invest in a telescopic steel rod and a cheap reel, but definitely don't load your juniors down with anything more complicated until they're experienced enough and interested enough to demonstrate they're really ready for a bait, fly, or spin-casting outfit. The less gear they have, the more time and attention they can learn to give to watching the bobber, and the water, and the sky--the real ingredients of fishing.

What do you fish for? Forget about game fish at this stage of the game. Your child will be much more happy catching a string of panfish than he or she will be trying to catch a bass. Most veteran fishers got their start on pumpkinseeds and bullheads.

Now, where do you go? The best rule here is, elbow in wherever you see a crowd of fishers. By and large, the best panfishing in Wisconsin is to be had wherever fishers congregate. The conservation people maintain children's fishing ponds in some cities. Or there may be a bullhead-stocked puddle right in your golf course.

Wherever you go, watch how the person who's pulling them in is fishing, and copy the system. Don't try to do any serious fishing yourself. You'll be much too busy threading on worms and untangling lines. And insist that your kids clean the catch themselves. The odds are slim indeed that they'll marry somebody who'll skin perch.

Any parent who introduces a youngster to fishing is laying the foundations for a lifetime of wholesome, satisfying sport. The big thing for teacher to remember is that fishing, like any sport, is reckoned not by the score but by how you play the game.

To be sure, freshwater fishing involves many different techniques for catching many species of fish. A beginner and the uninitiated parent may be pretty confused when it comes to making a first selection of equipment from the wide array of gear now available.

Basically, any fisher wants to present a lure or bait to a fish in its natural habitat, and this means putting the lure far enough away from the angler so one's presence won't be detected. Youngsters sometimes start off successfully with a cane pole, to which a length of heavy line about the same length is tied. With this rig they can fish from bank or boat with worms, minnows, or other natural bait, but they are limited in coverage of water to a radius of about 25 feet--not much in a day of globe-girdling astronauts.

An answer, of course, is spincasting, the finest of all beginner's methods for using artificials, and very hard to beat for using all natural baits.

A spin-cast outfit is not to be confused with spinning, fly, or bait-casting tackle. The typical spin-cast rod is a five- to six-foot hollow glass fiber medium-action pole with large line-guides. The reel is a fully enclosed, bobbin-type affair which is mounted above and in front of the handgrip. The proper line is very lightweight nylon. This rig will throw a wide range of half-ounce lures to surprising distances with no possibility of a backlash, no "thumbing," and no back-cast.

Spinning is more sporty, involving a longer rod and lighter lures, but it is tricky to master. On a spinning outfit the open bobbin-type reel is mounted below the grip.

Fly casting is considered by many the epitome of fishing art, but it is even more tricky to master, involving a wandlike rod, a weighted line, and an automatic reel mounted below and behind the grip. Dry flies will take trout when no other lures will, but they will also take their share of alder branches on the back-cast.

In fishing for heavy game fish, of course, bait-casting tackle is still the standard--a relatively short, stiff rod; top-mounted drum-type reel; heavy braided line. Here, too, however, there is an art to mastering the proper thumbing, and the multi-hooked plug in the hands of an amateur can be a lethal weapon in a small boat.

Whatever tackle you choose for your boy or girl, don't load up on lures until you know where you're going and for what. The spinner that's a killer in one lake can be a clunker in another, and the bug that takes bass can be of no avail on walleyes.

Whatever you do, don't wait until your first fishing trip to give your child his or her first casting lessons. Get him or her to practice on a golf course pond or, if necessary, on your own lawn, using practice weights which can be purchased in any sports shop. The time to learn how to use an outfit is before you go fishing.

If the whole thing seems too complicated, go back to my original suggestion: get a bamboo pole, a hank of linen line, a package of hooks, a lead sinker, a can of worms, and head for the nearest sucker hole. After all, fishing has nothing to do with tackle, anyway, and very little to do with fish. It's the wind in the willows that is the main ingredient.

The ideal bait for the beginner is really the night crawler. It's about time somebody said a good word for the night crawler. Old <u>Lumbricus</u> <u>terrestris</u>, as they call him on the campus, is the real hero on more fishing trips than any other bait, dead or alive. Yet his praises remain largely unsung. So I herewith pay due tribute to the worms (nonhuman, that is) I have known.

Nobody knows exactly how many fishers use worms, and nobody ever will. Dr. George Gallup tried to take a poll on the subject once and got into water over his head. People who gladly admit they beat their spouses or cheat at poker simply will not confess they fish with worms. Dr. Gallup, for instance, could find only 77 avowed wormers in the whole state of Wisconsin. Now there may well be only 77 worm fishers in Wisconsin, but I am inclined to doubt this because I personally know 49 in Madison's nineteenth ward alone. Not that they have told me, you understand. It was a case of my sneaking up on them when they weren't looking. In my frank opinion you can arrive at a pretty accurate estimate of the number of Wisconsin wormers by adding up the total number of fishers in the state.

There is one big reason why so many fishers use angleworms, at least on occasion: worms catch fish.

Worming has another distinct advantage over all other forms of fishing. It multiplies your expeditions by two. You not only go after fish by day but you go after worms the night before. I'm speaking now especially about that king-size worm, the night crawler.

If you have never gone night crawler hunting you have missed an experience. Night crawling is a sport in itself. There is as much technique involved in grabbing a big night crawler out of his hole before he can duck back in as there is in sneaking up on your favorite trout hole. Night crawling is practiced only at night, the darker the better. That old saying about the early bird catching the worm is strictly not so. It's the late operator who gets the night crawlers. A warm, moist night is the best. For equipment all you need are a good flashlight, a pair of tennis shoes, and a tin can.

Picking the hunting ground is important. Just any old patch of grass won't do. Favorite night crawler spots are cemeteries, golf links, city parks, and well-watered lawns. There the crawlers come out on the damp ground and loll around, eating leaves, and making love.

It sounds as though it ought to be simple to walk out and pick up a dozen or two crawlers in 10 minutes, but it isn't that easy. First of all, you have to be very sneaky. Crawlers have no ears, it's true, but they're very sensitive to vibrations. You've got to step carefully or you'll put down every crawler within five yards. Flash your light around cautiously until you

see a crawler shining in the grass. Then flick your beam quickly
to the side a little so that the full glare doesn't fall on the
worm or he'll whip out of sight in a flash. Stoop down carefully
and get set for the coup. This is the crucial stage. One bum
move, you have a fistful of grass, and your crawler is gone.
Every once in awhile you will find two crawlers "necking," as it
were. To take them both at once is the acme of night crawling
skill, not to mention a dirty trick.

The first time you try night crawling you're like as not to
come home empty-handed. In that case you can always grab a
shovel and go dig a canful, but this technique isn't considered
the least bit sporting. (As a matter of fact, it's just about as
bad manners as fishing with worms.)

There are several ways to keep crawlers. You can hold them
in a small box full of dirt and coffee grounds and covered with
damp leaves. You can store them in a big bin sunk in your back
yard. The simplest way to keep them is in an air-tight glass jar
in your refrigerator, preferably next to the freezing unit. They
will stay in a state of suspended animation for two weeks. So
will many a family.

Winter and summer, youthful anglers can fish for perch. Perch
are so abundant in some lakes that even the statisticians hesitate
to hazard a guess. Recent estimates on one lake place the total
at something in excess of six million. There are frequently no
size limits or bag limits on perch. A catch of 25 an hour is
common, and some of these fish will run upwards of a pound in
weight.

If you are a veteran perch fisher, you'll have a select spot
where you go and drop anchor year after year. If you're unfamiliar
with a lake, the best tactic is simply to go where the boats are
the thickest.

Favorite perch bait is worms, although some anglers swear by
perch eyes, perch gills, salmon eggs, and other live bait. A few
purists stick to wet flies or tiny spinners and spoons. Most
perchers use handlines, the better to "feel" the soft bite of the
perch, but you can use any type of tackle. You'll need up to 50
feet of line. Evening is the best time to fish.

Scientists have found that some perch schools have unusual
habits. They move into shallow water promptly at sundown and
settle to the bottom. Here they remain throughout the night,
apparently "asleep." Then, at dawn, they get up and swim slowly
back into deeper water. The older a perch, the more likely it is
to be found in deep spots in a lake. Young perch are typically
found in shallow areas along the shore.

Perch hug the bottom fairly close during fall, winter, and
spring. By late July, as the oxygen supply begins to decline in
the depths, most perch inhabit a layer about 22 feet deep.

Like ordinary fishers, even the scientists sometimes have
trouble locating perch. One July night a crew set up a curtain

of gill nets after dark where perch ought to be by the thousands. Not a single perch showed up. Two weeks later, under what appeared to be identical conditions, the same nets caught 41 perch an hour.

Why the difference? Only a perch can tell you.

About a May morning there is a special quality that can turn time backward. Gentle air, filtered sunlight, scented grasses, and bird song inspire mystic memories of bygone springs when the world was new. Perchance, those memories involve trout fishing. Samuel Johnson may have said that a fishing rod is "a stick with a hook at one end and a fool at the other," but many of us from our youths have preferred Izaak Walton's dictum that "angling is an art worthy of the knowledge and practice of a wise man."

Trout fishing in the twenties meant pursuing quarry with the romantic titles of Lock Leven and Von Behr. Through time and interbreeding, these varieties have now lost their immigrant Scotch and German traits, and the fish is presently known by the pedestrian name of brown trout. There is nothing common, however, about the sporting qualities of the brown, as fishers discover as they open each season. It could well have been a brown trout to which Shakespeare referred when he said that "the pleasantest angling is to see the fish cut with her golden oars the silver stream." The brown is not really brown. It is golden, distinguished by orange or brown spots on the side and by an orange tinge of color in the small, fleshy adipose fin just behind the main dorsal.

Before we knew much about trout management, we used to plant browns as tiny fry in the fond hope that they would survive. Very few did. Then we switched to stocking legal-length browns each spring just before the season opened. They had a rearing-pond pallor and were pretty vulnerable to lures. Now we know better, thanks to a good deal of fisheries research. We plant fingerling browns in the summer and fall. They grow to sporting size and habits on natural fodder, and provide good angling opportunities for several seasons.

Purist trout fishers operate on streams with artificial flies bearing such exotic names as Royal Coachman and Parmachene Belle. But the biggest strings of trout will be taken at night by small kids of all ages soaking night crawlers--in Thomson's words, "beneath the tangled roots of pendent trees." For getting back behind the years there is nothing like a May evening, a bamboo pole, and a squiggly worm. The stream bank may bear the marks of a Public Law 566 watershed improvement project; the water may have gone through two or three Cross Plains kitchen sinks; and the trout himself may bear a tag reading, "Manufactured at Nevin State Fish Hatchery." But the tug on your line is a message straight from a pleasant past.

To Trout Fishers, and they are legion, a trout stream is the cream of America, rating right up there with a band concert in the park and mom's apple pie. I have, for example, a favorite pike hole and a choice perch bar, but the place closet to my heart is a stretch of trout water near Mount Horeb. I guess this is because a trout stream is sort of the whole outdoors distilled into one dram of countryside: water and sky, land and sunlight, combined in a vista small enough for one to grasp. A trout stream is challenge and a trout stream is balm.

Two decades ago we trout fishers were well on the way to losing our streams. Today the deterioration of trout fishing may not yet have been entirely revised, but the process has certainly been slowed down, thanks to the application of modern trout-management principles.

We have learned, for instance, not to dump trout into top-condition streams where natural production is good enough to balance relatively light fishing pressure. On the other hand, we have learned that, in poor-condition streams where natural production cannot match the fishing pressure, we can maintain fishing throughout the season only by scientific stocking.

Stocking techniques are still being refined, but there is agreement on one point: a run-down stream has to be stocked year after year. Hatchery techniques and trout strains are constantly being improved. But put-and-take trout are inevitably so expensive that the trout harvest has to be limited if we are to maintain economical public trout-fishing. Improvement of the stream bed is a better long-range way of improving the trout situation than stocking. Even sounder is a thorough program of watershed management.

Biologists have also learned recently that where conditions are right you can substitute thriving rainbows in lakes and ponds oversupplied with stunted panfish. Such lakes return some four pounds of trout for every pound planted, which is one big reason why wardens and anglers are enthusiastic about "human-made" trout water. Particularly if you have no qualms about using live bait, you will find these lakes productive. Sometimes a small spinner will add extra appeal. On the other hand, if you're an inveterate fly-fisher, tie on a nymph, that leanly dressed fly that is most effective when you let it sink to the bottom, and then retrieve it slowly to the surface.

A trout lake has an appeal all its own. Terns clamor along the shore. A fox barks once, twice, off in the underbrush. The crests of the circling hills are bathed in sunlight. The water is crystal clear, mirroring rocks and trees and sky. You seem suspended in space. For a day, at least, you can shut out the world of civilization and tune in the out-of-doors. There may be some new alarm or excursion every hour in the city, but trout-lake sights and sounds are changeless. They sing a universal song, and every strain plucks some string in our memories of good things.

Some dates stick in your mind like a cocklebur to a hunting shirt. One such date is June 20, which used to mark the annual opening of the bass season. That was back when we thought we had to protect brood bass on their spawning beds if we were to save the sport. Now we think we know better. We recognize it's just as easy to have too many little bass as too few, so we open the season in April. For some of us, however, mid-June shall be forever associated with the proper time to switch from trout and pike to bass.

As all wielders of rod and line know, the black bass is a very special kind of fighter. A trout is a fancy dan. He will feint and spar, backpeddle around the ring, and then close in with a flurry of blows to the head. A northern pike, on the other hand, is a street brawler. He has no finesse, only brute strength. He likes to swing haymakers from left field, or punch you in the kidneys in the clinch. The bass is something else again, a finny combination of Gene Tunney and Jack Dempsey. He can engage in the fanciest footwork to throw you off guard, and then deliver a massive blow to your solar plexus when you aren't looking. He will sulk among the stumps one moment, and come churning up in a wild leap the next.

If you are like me, you cut your eyeteeth on small-stream smallmouths. You tied on your first artificial lure--a Skinner spoon--and skittered it beneath shelving banks and over rocky runs, using a cane pole three times your height. And you have never been the same since a bass as big and black as a medieval knight smashed into your primitive tackle. Now you have probably graduated to lake largemouths, which you pursue with more sophisticated gear, twitching marvelously lifelike plastic frogs among the coontail, or sending plug minnows probing down where sandbars drop off into cool green depths. The result is the same: a bass striking like a right to the jaw to leave you as committed as ever to the pursuit of "the gamest fish that swims."

Whatever the law books say, June is still the time you turn to bass fishing. Maybe it is because of the setting: along a conversing creek, where the scents of mint and clover spread in the first Summer heat to provide an angler's aphrodisiac; or on a quiet bay, where terns dip down to dimple the waters, and pond lilies stay abloom far into the evening. It is in such peaceful surroundings that the black bass lurks, ready for his June jump into your heart.

Somehow or other the idea has grown up that creeks are for trout fishers, but that you have to head for lakes or big rivers when it comes to bass fishing. The fact is you can find some of your most enjoyable smallmouth fishing in small waters.

In the first place, small-stream bass fishing has all the picturesque pleasures that go with upland angling. In the second place, small-stream smallmouths are real fighters. Third, creek bass will keep striking during those times of the year when river bass let you down. The point where a small stream empties into a large river turns out to be particularly productive water.

Small-stream fishing takes small tackle. With a light-bait casting rod you can try half-ounce plugs, weighted No. 1 spinner-and-fly combinations, midget spoons, and metal wigglers. A gut leader helps. With a fly rod or spinning rod almost any lure fits creek water, except that I, at least, have never had any luck with bugs on moving current.

All creek water is worth casting. During the day the bass usually will be lying in the deeper holes under grassy banks, in the lee of boulders, or behind lodged debris. At dusk, fishing the ripples is profitable. The smallmouths congregate there on the feed. A cattle-crossing can be a real hot spot, because the cows will turn up helgramites and grubs as they stomp on the flat rocks, and the bass know it.

In some areas, small streams do not hold bass because the streams are "sick." Excessive erosion from nearby fields has robbed them of their fish-holding capacity. They lack sufficient natural food, pools, or spawning grounds. Dumping in fingerlings won't do any good, but stream management will. Log deflectors can create new homes for smallmouths. Bank cover will increase the food supply. Wing dams can form spawning grounds. Woodlot management and soil conservation practices in the watershed will assure long-term rejuvenation.

Wherever small streams are in good shape, bass anglers are lucky. Here they will invariably take smallmouths, even in

August. These will not be big bass, but against light tackle they will fight hard, and they will furnish sport when river bass won't.

Something should probably be said, too, for a less tangible advantage to small-stream fishing. Rivers may be crowded with bathers and boaters, but your only company along a creek will be an occasional farmer cutting his late alfalfa and the only disturbance the song of cicadas.

Prior to the 1950s, the Conservation Department made fairly regular plants of smallmouth fingerlings. Since then, no bass stocking has been done. The result? Continued good production.

Investigations conducted with an electric shocker show no correlation between year of stocking and year-class strength. As a matter of fact, more fish were turned up from the years in which none were stocked. It is sudden drops in water temperature and siltation of nests during floods that control bass supply, not stocking, biologists have discovered.

Used to be you could keep Sam Smallmouth only if he measured a certain length. Now there's no size limit. The result? Better fishing. The size limit was designed to give a fish a chance to spawn at least once before becoming legal quarry. It didn't serve its purpose because a smallmouth reaches legal length at least a year before he spawns. The new rule does a better job of protecting the breeders because it encourages anglers to keep small fish. According to recent tallies, over 80 percent of the bass in streams are under 10 inches in size at any given time.

When the opening date was moved from June 20 to May 1, a lot of anglers worried that bass fishing would go down hill. The fear was unfounded. It is mainly the male bass that is vulnerable to early fishing, and it takes only a few adult bass to repopulate a stretch of river.

In short, as Biologist Clifford Brynildson has described the situation: "Natural reproduction is very good, and the smallmouth is holding his own in the face of heavy fishing pressure and deteriorating habitat."

"Inch for inch and pound for pound the gamest fish that swims" is the accolade worn by Sam Smallmouth.

If the countless Americans who vacation in August depended entirely for their angling sport on game fish, August vacations would be unproductive indeed. But fortunately, it is August when the bluegill comes into his own. August is the month of the bluegill, and of his panfish cousins--the sunfish, the rock bass, the crappie, and the perch. The bluegill is found from southern Canada (where he is sometimes called the red-breasted sunfish) to the Gulf states (where he is commonly known as the bream).

Although he usually runs less than eight ounces in weight, he frequently gets up to a pound, and weights of three pounds have been reported. His deep, compressed body gives him more leverage on the end of your line than his length and weight would indicate. Buster Bluegill can be told from the common sunfish, or pumpkinseed, by the black spot above the base of the fin just behind the spines on his back, and by the lack of orange on the "ear" lobes of his gill covering. The bluish cast to the lower sides of his head gives him his descriptive name.

The bluegill is very popular with cane-pole fishers and with small kids of all ages, for he readily takes worms, grasshoppers, and even small pieces of perch. Fly rod fishers and spin-casters take him frequently on flies and small spinners. Red and yellow flies seem to be the most effective, and a copper spoon is usually better than a silver one. On the table he is a favorite, too, because his meat is well flavored and relatively free from bones.

According to a recent Wisconsin creel census, more bluegills are caught here than any other species. In fact, they make up nearly half the total catch of Summer anglers in this state. On an expedition in Price County one August I would have drawn a blank if it hadn't been for Buster Bluegill. Bass and pike weren't hitting at all, but I took 32 bouncing blues in three days--some of them on night crawlers from 35 feet of water, others on a tandem of gaudy streamer flies fished slowly near the surface.

The wide popularity of the bluegill used to lead to his being planted in large numbers by well-intentioned but badly-informed sportspersons and conservation departments. When he was stocked in waters in which he did not naturally occur, he sometimes upset the balance of the native game-fish supply. When he was stocked in waters where he was already present, he often overcrowded the living room and produced a race of runts. Now we know better. We plant him only in appropriate waters that need seeding, and we fish him heavily where he occurs naturally. One of the best points about bluegill fishing is the realization that even by taking a string you're not depleting the resource. In fact, you're probably helping improve the balance of nature.

It may be true that, from the raconteur's point of view, big game fish will always be more satisfactory than these pint-sized models. There is no use telling your friends you had to battle your bluegill an hour to land it. On the other hand, not everybody can move quickly enough to pull up when a bluegill yanks down, as many a good pike man has discovered to his chagrin. At any rate, an August day with Buster Bluegill is well worth the spending, and even beginners can do it almost anywhere in Wisconsin.

About few other species of game fish are so many strong words spoken as about the walleyed pike. Conservation departments are damned if they stock 'em, and damned if they don't. The walleye himself is cussed out by anglers, because he refuses to change his habits to accommodate us fishers. Fisheries experts state vociferously that walleye stocking absolutely doesn't pay where brood stock is already established and where suitable spawning grounds are present. But try to tell that to a walleyed walleye fisher just back from a fruitless fishing trip to his favorite pike lake.

The plain fact of the matter is that walleyes are hard to catch.

One reason is that they're a schooling species. You either run into a lot of them, or you don't find any. Another reason is that they're most active in Spring and Fall, when fishing is light, and least active in July and August, when most anglers are out. Generally, too, walleyes feed at night, so if you fish between 8:00 a.m. and 5:00 p.m. your chances of hooking a walleye are considerably reduced. What's more, walleyes are very skittish. Anything bright or prominent ahead of your lure--like a snap, swivel, wire leader, or even heavy line--will cause many a walleye to pass up your offering.

I like to sneak up on walleyes early in the Spring, when the're ganged up below the river dams that block their spawning runs. When Wisconsin water temperatures reach 38 to 44 degrees, the walleyed pike leaves her Winter haven in the depths of lake or river and heads for a gravel bar, there to lay her eggs. This Spring spawning run of the walleye produces superior fishing. Of the walleyes tagged in Lake Koshkonong, for example, more than half are caught in April in the Rock River. Perhaps the most famous Spring-run walleye stream is the Wolf. When the run is at its peak--usually the middle of April--you can hardly see the water for the boats at Fremont, near Waupaca. On the Wisconsin River, favorite walleye spots include Castle Rock Dam near Adams, the "grade" near Okee, and the Prairie du Sac dam. Other anglers prefer the Rock at Jefferson and Ft. Atkinson, or the Pecatonica from Darlington downstream.

You can throw just about everything in your tackle box at these Spring-run pike, but you will probably have your best luck either with spoons or with live bait. On the other hand, some fly-rod and spin-rod persons swear by big, bright bucktails. Whatever you use, be prepared to lose plenty of gear. These rivers are full of snags, and the pike are on the bottom, so you've got to go deep and expect to get hung up regularly.

My best early pike catches are almost always made on minnows-- fairly small shiners. For this kind of river casting it's hard to beat a triangle rig. Get a triple swivel at your tackle store. To one loop, attach a gut leader and the hook. To the opposite loop, tie your line. To the bottom loop, tie about eight inches of line holding a dipsey sinker. This setup keeps you on the bottom, but the minnow is free to work with the current. Even with this device, a walleye can give you the runaround. He's a very soft striker, preferring to mouth the bait for a minute or so before he takes off on his characteristic run. Set the hook too soon and you've lost him. Then's when you reach into your tackle box for a supply of strong words.

What we don't know about walleyes would fill a book. The walleye's nearest relative is the perch. So what makes the

walleye ornery, preferring mild-mannered perch as food? The
original range of the walleye was confined almost entirely to our
major rivers. Now he is found in a thousand lakes. So how did
he get there? Why does walleye color vary so considerably? In
some waters he is dull silvery gray, in others brassy olive buff,
elsewhere golden brown.

Walleyes don't like weeds. They prefer big, open waters
with windswept, rocky shorelines. Unlike bass and pickerel, they
don't thrive where aquatic vegetation is abundant. Why? The
walleye is a vigorous swimmer, capable of overtaking a largemouth
bass, but he depends largely upon unwary, resting fish for food.
Is he lazy at heart? Walleyes live near or on the bottom in
deep, dark waters, migrating only at night to feed on bars and
shoals. Does bright light hurt their big eyes? When she spawns,
the walleye usually prefers a spot where water flows over gravel.
Why, then, do you get spectacular hatches on flooded marsh vegetation
or in still pools in the river bottoms? A mature female will lay
from 35,000 to 600,000 eggs. Why aren't our lakes crammed with
walleyes?

Some years the hatch does well, other years not. For instance,
a lake under study in southern Wisconsin produced 32 yearlings
per acre one year, only 13 per acre the next. The same lake had
a population of 25 adults per acre, while a neighboring lake
carried only 11 per acre. The reasons for these differences is a
fish story that biologists are trying hard to unravel. Male
walleyes become mature when they are two to three years old and
12 to 13 inches long. Females wait until they are four to five
years old and 15 to 17 inches long. Why this difference? We
know walleyes can reach a length of three feet and weight of 25
pounds, yet in actual practice, weights over 10 pounds are rare.
Where do the lunkers hide out? Walleyes invariably harbor lots
of parasites, but diseases and worms are not known to cause
significant mortality. Does the walleye have a built-in wonder
drug?

What's the best way to fish for walleyes? Nobody knows this
for sure, either. You can still-fish with live bait. You can
troll with spinners. You can bait-cast with plugs. You can spin
with little spoons. You can fly-cast with streamer flies.
Walleye fishing is usually most profitable after dark, retrieving
the bait slowly along the bottom. But for some reason, there
will be times when you will do very well with surface poppers at
noon in shallow water.

There is one thing about walleyes on which there is no
confusion: they have firm, white, fairly dry, bone-free flesh
that makes them highly prized on the table. Large fish can be
cut into steaks, medium ones filleted, smaller ones prepared
whole. Broiled, baked, or fried, they are delicious, especially
with a simple lemon sauce.

Perhaps the biggest walleye puzzle is the stocking policy of
many states. Biologists around the country have never been able
to find that planting walleyes does much good, once brood fish

are present. Yet each year conservation departments sprinkle millions of walleye fry and fingerlings around in various waters, in response to the demands of assorted fishers. Maybe this means we know ever less about people than we know about walleyes.

The water lily, a symbol of watery tranquility, marks a favorite hideout of America's fiercest game fish, the huge, voracious--and mysterious--muskellunge. Even though he is big and fierce enough to be king of his watery castle, the musky doesn't act like one. His favorite food is soft-scaled, slow-moving forage fish like suckers. He doesn't roam around much. He prefers a comparatively small home range where he spends a lot of his time sleeping. Oddly enough, the most significant predators on muskies are insects and pan fish. Diving beetles, dragonfly nymphs, bluegills, and rock bass account for staggering numbers of muskies when they are in the fry and fingerling stage.

Finding a musky is a mysterious business. Even in the best musky water there is probably not more than one adult per acre. He will usually be lurking near a drop-off, along a weed bed, in a small bay, or close to shore near a tree stump. But he can also be in 50 feet of naked water. So mysterious are the feeding habits of the moody musky that nowhere can you get any agreement as to the best time of day to fish for him, much less the best month, or the best lure.

There is nothing mysterious about a musky when he decides to strike, however. Charging the lure, he will cut through the water like a surfacing submarine. Once the hooks are firmly set, he begins a wild, gymnastic dash that may take him all over the lake. Flailing and charging, the fish leaps again and again out of the water, standing on his tail, twisting like an eel, changing his course erratically, suddenly sounding in an attempt to snap the line on a sunken log. When the fight is played out of him and he is drawn close to the boat, the battle still is not won, for a musky's barracudalike teeth can eaily chomp through a landing net or a fisher's careless hand.

It is his savage nature and his mysterious habits which have made the musky a trophy fish so prized by so many anglers. To maintain a fishable musky population, musky states have been going through a series of mysterious gyrations that would do credit to the musky himself. Despite a lack of evidence that it does any good, conservation departments hatch, rear, and plant millions of young muskies a year in American waters. The Sport Fishing Institute in Washington has estimated that each stocked musky finally brought to boat represents a state investment of $300.

"From their inception in 1899, these states obviously never dared face up policy-wise to an evaluation of their musky stocking programs," the Institute says. Wisconsin Biologist Leon D. Johnson puts it this way: "Although the stocking of muskies has won wide public acceptance, the benefits are not thoroughly understood."

That pretty well rounds out the picture. There isn't much of anything about the musky that is thoroughly understood by either anglers or scientists--except that this mysterious monster will continue to dominate angler lore for many years.

Musky research has turned up the interesting fact that some of the fabled "tiger muskies" are really not true muskies. They're hybrids--half muskellunge and half northern pike.

How can you distinguish between muskies, hybrids, and northern pike? One way is in the number of mandibular pores, or underjaw holes. The northern pike almost always has ten. True muskies typically have 14 or more. Tiger hybrids are intermediate. Cheek scale is another clue. In the northern pike, scales typically cover the entire cheek. In the purebred musky, only the upper half of the cheek normally is scaled. Here again, half-breeds are in between. Another clue is coloring. The northern pike has greenish-gray sides with irregular rows of small, horizontal, oval, yellowish spots, and a dark, unbroken back. The purebred musky, although he varies a good deal, typically has a solid back and silvery-gray sides with or without hazy broken or unbroken stripes. In the case of the hybrid tiger, the alternating light and dark vertical stripes or bars on his sides are much more distinct. The dark stripes run farther down onto the light belly, and the light stripes continue into the dorsal, or back, area. So, viewed from the top, the hybrid tiger shows what is known as reticulation--light lines cutting into the dark pattern of the back.

Tiger females usually are fertile, but tiger males are sterile. This makes them useful in lake management. The males are being planted in waters which have become overstocked with panfish, to eat up surplus sunfish and perch.

I like to go musky fishing in September, in that lull between tourists and teal. The musky is something special to me in the way of a game fish. He is big, He is vicious. He is found only in select northern waters. His taking requires special gear and special techniques. He lures anglers from all over the country to a handful of famous lakes.

Musky fishers live in a wonderful world of their own. It is a world of king-size tackle, monstrous lures, off-trail haunts, monastic habits, superstitions, and stick-to-it-iveness. To open the door to this mysterious world of the musky, it's best to get a guide.

My guide has these words of advice for musky anglers:

Tackle--"If you are going to be a musky fisher you should have a special rod made for that purpose by a reliable company. The average reels sold to fishers are far too light to use for musky fishing. The musky fisher is better off to use a 24- to 30-pound test line, brand new."

Lures--"I'll stick to big, black bucktails."

Season and Weather--"The best musky fishing I ever had was a week in September. Every day the weather was dull and gray with heavy banks of dark, threatening clouds rolling continously out of the north. The water was never calm, but there never were white caps."

    Time of Day--"From 9:00 a.m. to 4:00 p.m."

    Where to Fish--"Wherever there are weed beds on or near the surface."

    Casting--"Never cast aimlessly, and retrieve your bait slowly."

    Landing a Musky--"Always have a gun, a gaff, a big landing net, or a club. I prefer a long-handled gaff."

    Attitude--"Don't be discouraged or give up just because you don't catch a musky every time you go out. The ways of the musky are mysterious. Muskies are scarce, wily, and hard to hold. Many of us have fished hard for a solid week--with the best of anglers and in good musky waters--without landing a keeper. That's the challenge."

    Muskies are a mystery to the biologists, too. Some states go in strong for stocking muskies. Other states say stocking doesn't pay. The question is really one of economics. How much can a state afford to spend in order to add musky to the take? Resort owners say a musky is worth at least two-hundred dollars. Taxpayers may have a different standard of measure.

    But the lure of musky fishing is no mystery. There is sheer murder in his strike and all the cleverness of a jungle beast in his fight. Get a leaping, lunging, rolling, churning tiger musky on the end of your line, and you'll never be the same again.

"There aren't enough northern pike any more!"

    "We've got too many northern pike!"

    On the same day the conservation people often hear these seemingly contradictory complaints. And they both may be accurate. In some areas the pike population is slipping. In other regions, pike are too plentiful for musky fanciers. So, for state fishery biologists, headache is spelled "pike."

    The northern pike is in tough shape in urban areas because his spawning grounds have been disappearing steadily. Gone are many of the large pike spawning runs that occurred every Spring into marshes and flooded lowlands adjacent to our lakes, because the wetlands themselves are gone as people have "improved" their lakeshores. It is back on shallow, flooded areas where a northern must go early in April to lay its 30,000 to 100,000 eggs in the weed growth, gambling that enough water will remain to permit the young fish to escape to deeper waters. Spawning possibilities disappear entirely where such areas are filled in. The future of the northern in these areas depends on saving wetlands. And he's well worth saving. As a predator, he helps control panfish. As a game fish, he strikes with abandon and fights hard.

    In other regions, on the other hand, some people would be just as happy to see fewer northerns. They're the resort owners and musky fans who prefer our biggest game fish and who see the northern as competing with the musky for food and living space. Whether such competition actually exists no scientist has ever found out for sure, but a good many people think it does. "I resent the northern pike in musky waters," a resort owner told a Wisconsin Natural Resources Commission hearing. "Guests come to my resort for trophy fish and not for meat. The musky is the bread-and-butter fish of the north and must be given every consideration."

So what you think of _Esox lucius_ depends on where you sit, _Esox lucius_ being that elongated bit of underwater meanness known as northern pike. Thanks to some recent field research, we now have some pretty scientific insights into just what northern pike eat, when they eat it, and under what circumstances. The scientists have collected stomachs from thousands of northerns. Their findings are valuable to fish management and helpful to anglers:

The first interesting thing found was that 76 percent of all the pike stomachs were empty. That means we fishers can assume that the majority of pike are ready and willing to dine. What will they dine on? Pike take anything that moves--trout, bluegills, perch, crayfish, snails, crappies, bass, suckers, worms, bugs, and other pike. The only food preference was for the most abundant available item.

Now here's another interesting item: the pike examined ranged from 15 to 36 inches, and the largest food item found was no bigger than a quarter-pound slab of butter. While the length of the food was apparently not a factor in its acceptability, in width the food items were usually one-third narrower than the northern's mouth width. So, say the biologists, "Indications are the smaller baits catch the most northerns." One stomach contained three hooked bait minnows, but the owner of that stomach was caught within a short period of time on a spinner. Numerous stomachs contained two minnows. The lesson is: if you get a strike but miss your fish, bait up quickly and get your line back in the water. _Esox lucius_ will probably be waiting to strike again.

Males were caught as readily as females. Both sexes were caught in equal numbers month after month. A tabulation of artificial baits indicated so many kinds were used to good effect that no significant differences could be detected. Daylight hours were best for northern fishing, with the best angling success coming just before 8:00 in the morning. Northerns caught in the morning almost always had empty stomachs.

Most of these findings check with the experience of pikers. What the scientists couldn't measure was the sporting quality of old _Esox_--the devil-may-care tugging and leaping that makes him so sought after and so respected. That sort of research you'll have to do on your own.

Although it was 30 years ago now, I can still see see it as it came over the side of the boat--pig eyes gleaming evilly, scissor-toothed mouth flaring, spade tail writhing. My record book says it weighed five pounds, but in retrospect that fish has grown at least a pound a year. My record book also says it measured 24 inches, but I'm sure now that's an error by a good half foot.

Whatever the statistics, the northern pike I caught on the Fourth of July, 1934, was the prize fish of my life. Not the biggest, not the rarest, not the tastiest, not the fightingest, but still the best. It is so with all fishers. Somewhere, sometime, we have each taken a fish that has been destined to occupy a very special niche in our memories of good things.

I think I know why this particular northern pike is so special to me. It represents my first personal triumph over society. Every fishing expedition, you know, is really an attempt to escape from the world--from jobs, from routine, from bosses, from lawn mowing. Sometimes we make this escape so successfully that the moment becomes precious beyond measure.

It was so with my Fourth of July pike in 1934. According to the traditions of my hometown in those days, July 4 was the day on which all the school pupils of Lake Mills marched in an annual parade. We assembled in the city park, heard an oration by a local preacher, and then toted flowers to the cemetery. All the family and community pressures of a small town were operating to make me participate in that parade, but I played hookey. For the first time in my life, I said, "To heck with it," and I went fishing.

It was damp and lonely on Rock Lake that morning, I remember, and I was beginning to think the life of a rebel wasn't so hot-- when my prize pike hit my spoon. It was the only fish I took and it was below average in size for those waters in those days. But it stood for something that every outdoorsperson seeks--a private Independence Day.

Since 1934, as it's turned out, I have had to march in more parades than just about anybody in Lake Mills, what with seven years of active army duty. And that may be simply the peculiar retribution that the gods of Independence Day have seen fit to mete out. But I still have my memory of a very special pike. What more can a fisher ask?

In January there appears on Wisconsin lakes that special breed of human known as the ice fisher. Just the reverse of his outdoor cousin the bear, the ice fisher hibernates for nine Summer months. Then in Winter he or she emerges from clapboard dens to be seen in a favorite habitat--a windswept stretch of ice.

Like the bear, the ice fisher can be recognized by a lumbering gait, thick, fur-lined parka, and boot-and-mitten clad paws. Unlike the bear, however, the ice fisher always sports a red face, which is due to frost nip and also to other types of nip.

The ice fisher, like the bear, usually ranges alone or in pairs, and if you should approach a favorite fishing hole they will growl ominously. On occasion, however, ice fishers will cluster in small groups. The scientists who study such matters report this phenomenon occurs when jumbo perch or pike are being hauled in at one particular spot.

While ice fishers would seem to be an indolent lot as they loll on the surface of a frozen lake, they are actually an industrious crew. There is bait to be gathered--grubs from goldenrod galls, worms where leaves have kept frost from the ground, corn borers from stalks of corn left in fields, worms from hazel nuts. There are ice cleats and spuds to be sharpened, sled runners to be honed, tarpaulins to be mended so they can be used for windbreaks, tip-ups which need new lines, hooks, and sinkers.

Such meticulous preparation can pay off. A census of ice fishers on Wisconsin's Lake Mendota, conducted over a Winter, netted an estimated catch of over a million perch. They averaged more than eight inches in length and weighed a third of a pound apiece--a yield of 41 pounds per acre for a three-month period.

There are individuals, of course, who feel that ice fishing is bad business. They write letters to fish and game departments demanding that such and such a lake be closed to ice fishing so that the Summer fishing won't be ruined by the Winter harvest. The fact is that in every case ever studied by biologists, there has been no evidence of depletion of a game fish or panfish population through excessive Winter fishing. As a matter of fact, most lakes can stand a lot more fishing pressure than they now get, Summer or Winter, so the scientists say. Those wise old bears, the ice fishers, knew it all the time.

The human polar bears who dot the icy surface of Winter waters are practicing one of our most ancient sports. As early as 8,000 years ago, a relative of Fred Flintstone invented the "gorge." The gorge was a short length of bone or flint, sharpened on both ends. A line was tied to its middle and bait wrapped around it. The primitive fisher dropped this contraption in the water and waited to pull on the line until a fish had completely swallowed it.

Some time later, the gorge was found to work better if it were carved into an angle and lined with barbs. From 4000 to 2000 B.C., hooks of iron and bronze began to appear. The famous cave drawings of Europe picture early "anglers" using these angles in both Summer and Winter.

The fishing rod first shows up in Egyptian murals dated at about 2000 B.C. The Egyptian drawing is of a short pole, probably about six feet long, with a line the same length. About 950 B.C. Homer has the people in some of his stories using a fishing pole and an ox horn for a sinker. When a fish bites, Homer's angler hoists him out of the water fast. Thus, the practice of "horsing one in" is almost as old as civilization.

Early fish lines were made of braided horsehair or flax. Plutarch instructed in 100 A.D. that "the hair cast next above the hook must be as near white as possible so as to resemble the color of the water." The artificial fly dates back to this period. A Greek wrote how "anglers wrap dark red wool round a hook and tie on to it two feathers which grow under the wattles of a cock."

We get the first clear picture of jointed rods from a "Treatise on Fishing with an Angle" which appeared in England in 1496. The bottom half was hollowed-out hazel. The top half was slender enough to slip inside the lower half, and "this so disguises the rod that you might walk with it and no one would guess that you were going fishing." Apparently so long ago as the days of Columbus it was necessary for the fisher to sneak out of the house!

These rods were 12 to 21 feet long, because the reel had not yet been invented and the only way to play a fish was with a line not much longer than the pole. In wide rivers, anglers began to wade after their fish, although hip boots were unknown. Fishers were cautioned to "pull down your stockings and examine your legs; should they be black or even purple it might perhaps be as well to get on dry land." Modern ice fishers know what that early writer was talking about.

Forty years or so ago, as a reporter for a country weekly, I remember covering a big outdoor news story--the dumping of several ceremonial canfuls of walleyed pike fry into Rock Lake. One of the alphabet agencies had built a federal fish hatchery in town, and the pike fry were our first tangible evidence of the New Deal. Our Congressman came from Washington to preside, the municipal band played, and the Congregational pastor offered a prayer.

That was back in those simple times before professors and pundits began to rock our notions about conservation. As we stood on Sandy Beach we were all utterly convinced that happy days were, indeed, here again, and that every one of those quarter-inch pike would help restore Rock Lake to the heights of walleye waters.

As things turned out, even the prayers didn't do any good, much less the stocking. A couple of years later we were told the trouble was that the fry were too small and feeble, and that if you kept the pike in rearing ponds until they were three inches in length and then planted them, all would be well.

For ten years that was the accepted solution. Then as fish management became a more sophisticated matter, the limnologists began checking to see just how many fingerlings did in fact survive. In most lakes they could not find enough tagged pike to measure, and when they once found a lake with a 13 per cent return they went into raptures.

Now things have swung full circle again. Some boys out in Iowa have reported good luck in stocking little walleye fry by doing their planting in those years in which natural reproduction is poor, and refraining from stocking in those years in which natural reproduction equals the available food supply. A Wisconsin project, involving staggered stockings on three lakes over a nine-year period, is checking out this theory.

Meanwhile, the accepted conservation department dictum is to the effect that "generally walleye fingerling stocking appears unjustified due to poor survival."

A quarter-century ago we were equally confident that musky populations would respond to stocking, too. There are on record a couple of northern lakes where stocked muskies now make up a sizeable proportion of the fish being brought to boat, but the mortality of eight- to ten-inch fingerlings usually is very high, and the survival of two-inch fingerlings is very low to naught. So the biologists have decided there's a lot we need to know about lakes and muskies before we can say with any assurance we have a viable musky-stocking formula.

All these new facts haven't changed many a state chamber of commerce, however. They keep calling for stepped-up stocking of warm-water species in order to undergird the tourist industry. It all goes to prove that at least the sucker population is thriving.

After competing with people and nature for trout or bass in public waters, a lot of anglers start dreaming about private fish ponds. What they don't suspect is that there's one easy way to get crosswise with the government and your fellow citizens, and that's to build your own lake.

The days of the simple pond are gone. Even Robert Frost would need a permit to go out and clean his pasture spring these days. Probably on no other feature of the landscape is there concentrated such a barrage of local, state, and federal regulations as on an artificial pond. The laws and the experts involved are bent on protecting the public interest against the guy who just wants to "throw a little dam across a draw."

For example, let's say you have a fair-sized creek on your property, and you think it would be nice to create a little lake. Don't get your hopes up too high, because if your stream is navigable there are probably all sorts of state court decisions to say you can't harm the flow going to your downstream neighbors. And it doesn't take much of a stream to be navigable. Under Wisconsin law, for example, if it will float a sawlog at low water it is navigable, and the state gets in the picture.

Or suppose you have just a trickle that under no stretch of the imagination is navigable. Once again, don't get your hopes up, because if your creek starts in a spring and empties into a trout stream, trout fishers will call on the Department of Natural Resources to prevent you from warming up their water.

But let's say you are not going to monkey with either a navigable stream or a trout-stream feeder. You just want to dike a little valley and hold back the run-off. All right, in that case the government will not only have no objections, it will help pay the bill.

Yes, properly sited and built ponds are on the list of

approved farm practices under the federal Agricultural Conservation Program (ACP), so you can collect up to 85 per cent of the costs from Uncle Sam. But the Soil Conservation Service must make the plans, supervise construction, and inspect the results. And the SCS boys won't enter the picture unless your farm is covered by a comprehensive soil conservation plan. You can tell the SCS engineers where you want your pond and how big you want it to be, but they won't necessarily agree, particularly if your property is in an area covered by a broad watershed program under another federal law administered, in part, by a couple of other local and federal agencies.

There may come a day, however, when you, Washington, and the county have a meeting of the minds and pocketbooks, your dam is built, the pond starts to fill up, and no major leaks develop. At this stage of the game you start thinking about planting fish. Here you may discover, first of all, that you can't stock fish without a state permit, even on your own property--to protect any nearby public waters. And you have the problem of getting the experts to agree on what kind of fish you should stock for your own good. Some may tell you trout, and others will say bass. In the meantime the neighbor kids may have dumped in a pailful of suckers.

Where do you get the fish? If you agree to open your pond to public fishing, the state Department of Natural Resources may stock your pond for you. But a public fishing hole is probably not what you had in mind. To maintain a private pond you have two alternatives.

On the one hand, you can take out a fish hatchery license and buy your fingerlings from commercial sources. Or you can go back to the federal government and get free fish--provided the SCS approves, the ACP committee approves, the state fish manager approves, and provided the nearest federal hatchery has a surplus of the species you have been authorized to plant when you have been authorized to plant them.

All told, it takes a brave and dedicated person to build a pond these days. But when you take that first trout or crappie out of your own lake, the problems fade away.

If Joe Johnson had lived, he would probably have compiled a book like this. Joe had a knack of putting earthy words down on paper--so you could just about smell the shadowed pines at a bend in the river, or hear the spent wings of a downed grouse as they beat on a woodlot floor. He won a writing prize at the University of Wisconsin in 1940, and a couple of Johnson poems appeared in one of those little anthologies back in 1941.

But that's all. Joe is dead. He was the recon officer for a heavy weapons company in the 8th Division. A land mine blew up his jeep early on the morning of June 27, 1944, somewhere south of St. Lo, France.

Some of us are publishing a little volume of the poems and

sketches which a battalion chaplain found in Joe's musette bag. In his fashion, Joe speaks for all those men of field and stream who went on the Big Trip and never came back. Joe says what all of them felt: that you carry with you in your heart forever a little bit of your outdoors. And your outdoors in turn retains a little bit of you.

As Joe wrote:
> Come what comes,
> If you want to meet me in the years ahead--
> You will find me where men tent together;
> Along a stream the first shy days of any Spring;
> And where the cornshocks march in ordered rows
> Against the hazy sky of every Fall.

There's a sort of a story behind this particular verse of Joe's--a story which I hesitate to tell, because I can't for the life of me decide how much of it is true and how much is pure fancy. Some of it happened, I know, but whether the rest of it is even possible, only Joe can say for sure.

It all began 45 years ago, when Joe and I were growing up in southern Wisconsin. Around the calendar we hunted and fished together whenever school was out--and sometimes when it wasn't. We had a favorite trout stream. It was a little creek that rises in a spring up near Mount Horeb and flows down toward Black Earth. I never have heard of an official name for the stream. Joe and I just called it Memorial Day Creek, because we fished it faithfully every thirtieth of May. Joe was in love with all of outdoor Wisconsin, but I think he liked our creek best of all.

Joe and his stream were a lot alike. A man and his trout creek do grow together somehow, know what I mean? It is beautiful there on a fresh May day with the wind rustling the new leaves on the willows and red-winged blackbirds cheering from spires of alder. Joe's writing was like that. The trout are mostly browns, not big fish but scrappers that lie in the narrow slicks and strike hard. Joe must have soldiered like that, too. The valley is as peaceful and remote as a cemetery, and, come to think of it, the whitened aspens sort of look like tombstones. I guess Joe would feel at ease there right now.

I can still see Joe as he would creep up to a likely spot on his hands and knees and maneuver his fly rod into position. Joe always fished as steady as the current. He would work a single hole for half an hour. As he cast he was always whistling "I'm Always Chasing Rainbows." That was sort of Joe's song, you might say. It was popular in the twenties, you may remember, and Joe liked it. He was still whistling it on Memorial Day of 1941. We were seniors at the university and we drove out from Madison just to keep our annual date with Memorial Day Creek. He didn't know it at the time, of course, but that was the last time Joe was ever to fish Memorial Day Creek. At least so far as I can say for sure. The next month we went in the Army. We went to Camp Grant together. Joe was sent on to Camp Livingston one afternoon. That's the last time I saw him alive. He's buried in St. Corneille

Military Cemetery in France.

    I get back to Memorial Day Creek occasionally. As a matter of fact, I was there one recent May 30. I got to the stream about four in the morning, before the sun was all the way up. It was dark and misty, and if I hadn't known every foot of the valley, I wouldn't have been able to start fishing right away. So I was surprised to find somebody already working the opposite bank.

    The fellow was down on his hands and knees, casting under a low-hanging willow, and I couldn't make him out in the half light except to see that he seemed to be wearing an old set of Army fatigues and GI boots. He didn't say anything and I didn't want to disturb the fishing, so I didn't say anything either. Presently, I heard him playing a heavy fish, and then he tramped on downstream, whistling as he went. I worked on up to the spring and back again. By this time the sun was up and the mist gone. I had taken three nice trout and I would just have soon showed them off to somebody, but I couldn't find the fisher I had run into earlier. He had evidently quit for the day.

    It was not until that evening that I made anything peculiar out of my encounter with that fisher in the mist. I had stopped at Joe's home, and Mrs. Johnson had given me an infantry notebook full of Joe's poems. I was reading them over and I came to these haunting lines:

        If you want to meet me in the years ahead,
        You will find me...
        Along a stream the first shy days of any Spring...

    All the old thoughts of Joe came rushing back as I read. You know how it is. Something triggers your memory: Joe shooting squirrels in Ferry's Woods with his .22. Joe catching frogs in Weber's Meadow. And mostly, Joe coming down along Memorial Day Creek, with a string of trout at his belt, whistling as he cast.

    And then I remembered: our creek that morning in the dawn. A fisherman on the other side. And the tune he was whistling was "Chasing Rainbows."

Hunters' Havens

I wind up the grouse season each January, tramping alone through the Iowa County hills. A solitary partridge hunt is not an even contest. The odds all favor the grouse. It was so one Sunday. The score of the game was Grouse, 11; Me, 0.

On such an afternoon you begin to wonder why you hunt at all. There is, of course, the popular motive for hunting provided by parlor psychiatrists: that hunting is a frantic demonstration of masculine virility in an otherwise feminized world. There is the more sophisticated explanation that hunting symbolizes an urge to escape modern mores and retreat back across the bridge of millennia to play once more with the artifacts of our evolutionary youth.

Undoubtedly many of us are still possessed by primordial spirits. Unquestionably, the freedom of body and spirit encompassed in a hunt enables us to shed certain societal pressures and walk, for however brief a time, in the open, on ancient quests. From this perspective, hunting today is the one great basic adventure for millions of ordinary, town-bound people who yearn for personal participation in some kind of frontier confrontation with the great forces of the universe.

Some nonhunters challenge the basic morality of hunting, questioning the right of a reasoning species to prey on other species for sport. It is true that some hunters are interested solely in the full game bag as a token of adulthood and tribal acceptance, but most hunters outgrow this blood urge and come to seek much deeper values. We invest, for example, our quarry with character and worth. To some degree we adapt ourselves to the creatures we hunt, and so acquire a measure of their freedom and sagacity. Particularly, we steep ourselves in the setting of the hunt, in what Charles Nordoff once termed "the spirit of the place."

Much more than a lust to kill, the hunter has a rage to live. We may never have heard the word "transcendental," but we sense its meaning. When such a person hunts, it is very difficult to regard the act as an overt offense to the dignity and spirit of game. Rather, it may be a personal testimony to the dignity and value of the wild. The consummate offense to wildlife in our day is not hunting, but the extirpation of habitats by an indifferent technology in which game is wiped out, not by humankind's passion but by a single-minded devotion to a material world in which wild creatures have no place.

Indeed it is the hunter today, more than anyone else, who feels most deeply humankind's interdependence with our environment, and who has demonstrated a responsibility for that environment and its maintenance by paying special taxes to support habitat improvement. It is hunters who will continue to take the lead in cushioning the impact of modern culture on our natural resources, using the most effective political and scientific tools at their disposal. Thus may well be fulfilled Thoreau's prophecy that "in wildness is the preservation of the world."

There is nothing that will so cut a sportsperson down to size as to take a pup bird dog on that first hunt. You have hunted grouse for years, and this is your dog's baptism of fire. So you are prepared to play schoolmaster. Yet inside of half an hour it is you who are learning the lessons. You are also prepared to excuse the mistakes of your neophyte partner, but it turns out you apologize to him for yours.

This particular day began in proper perspective with me directing Mac into a promising woodlot. He began to act "birdy" almost immediately, and soon came on point in the neighborhood of a downed oak. The point lasted only five seconds, whereupon the dog charged ahead. I called him back and reprimanded him with an alder switch for breaking point. He took off again, and I repeated the process. A third time he bolted, and this time I followed in disgust. Fifty yards away we flushed the bird, which had obviously been running--something Mac had figured out from the start. I made amends by giving Mac a piece of dog candy.

We came to the far edge of the woodlot, and I ordered Mac to stay in the heavy cover. He insisted on cruising the adjacent clover field. I called him in and gave him a stern lecture on the fact that you never find partridge in the open. He looked at me with a sorrowful expression--and proceeded to go right back out into the field, where he shortly put up two skittish birds. I was so surprised I didn't even fire.

Along the edge of the field Mac began to make game again, and came on point staring up into the crown of a hickory tree where a squirrel was scolding away. I wielded the switch again, because there is nothing that so irritates a grouse hunter as a dog that prefers to trail squirrels. The pup let out a yelp--and a grouse flushed from the tree.

By this time I was beginning to get the message--that Mac instinctively knew a lot more about grouse hunting than I did. So I let him have his head while I concentrated on getting a shot. Mac soon gave me an opportunity in a popple thicket. I missed. So long as I live I shall never forget the look of pure disgust in his puppy eyes after watching that partridge sail away unscathed.

I promised to do better, but after a half-dozen more flushes, I had acquired only a bag of ironwood twigs and oak leaves. I explained to Mac the great difficulty of getting on a bird in southern Wisconsin early in the season, but he appeared singularly unimpressed. A bird finally flew into my charge of No. 8's. Mac retrieved the grouse as if he had been doing such chores for 20 years. We quit while I was ahead.

King of the Autumn wild game crop is John Q. Pheasant. All over October's landscape you will see cordons of hunter subjects paying homage to King John in his cornfield courts. John may be an importation from the wilds of China and the hedgerows of Europe, but he has become a favorite monarch in the hearts of many, many Wisconsin gunners.

Not the least of our delight in King John comes from the amazing amount of lore--both fact and fancy--which has grown up about him.

For example, popular fancy long dictated there were two magic ways to encourage pheasants--to sprinkle new stockings over the countryside each year, and to kill off predators. We now know more about pheasant facts of life. Whenever King John goes down, it's typically due to the collapse of his castle. You can't drain more marshes, cultivate more hillsides, graze more woodlots, and burn more hedgerows without winding up with less pheasants. On the other hand, wherever agricultural practices tend to manipulate food and cover factors in King John's favor he responds with bumper broods.

When it comes to hunting tactics, one fancy you will hear now and then is this:

The only place you can find King John at the height of the season is hidden away down in the thickest marshes and sloughs. This is true at times, to be sure, yet on at least three recent occasions I have filled my bag by striking out alone along secluded upland fencerows and woodlots, whence the gaudy fellow had retired when the pressure got too hot down in the dogwoods. Many pheasant hunters will tell you, too, that the place to start hunting is in the cornfields. This is true if you go afield early in the day. John will indeed be on the feed until eight or nine o'clock. But, if you strike out after lunch, you're going to find very few birds in the corn. They'll be on their loafing grounds--in the marshes, fencerows, and alfalfa fields.

Still another popular fancy is the one that endows King John with superhuman intelligence. He's undoubtedly smart, but he's still a birdbrain.

I remember a case in point last Fall. Our dogs had made game along a brushy ditch that led from a barren field down into an alder swamp. We were moving down the ditch toward the swamp. According to all the laws of instinct and intelligence, that cock should have gotten out and made straight for the swamp. But did he? Not on your life! He doubled back over our heads, landed in the middle of the naked field, and ran off like a racehorse. We were so surprised our shots went wild.

Or does that just go to prove King John really is superclever?

Be that as it may, King John is unquestionably big and handsome when alive and tender and succulent afterward. He may be simple to hit when he barges up from under foot, but when he crosses or tops the guns at full speed he can easily be missed, as many of us know to our chagrin. His pursuit leads you neither into the painted fairyland of Autumn woods nor across wide sweeps of unfenced prairie, but through a tamer country of fen and farmland where, against a dun background of frost-seared corn and sedge, his own silvered wings and burnished breast strike the brightest note of color. Here, where the grouse finds no sheltering woods, where overgrazing and the plow have forced the prairie chicken out, where the quail fights an often-losing battle against long, hungry Winters in a stripped country side, John Ringneck finds some way to live.

It is good to be able to salute him as king of field and fencerow.

If a House Un-American Activities Committee should ever decide to investigate game birds, the grouse will undoubtedly be the last to be subpoenaed. Like a feathered Dan'l Boone, the ruffed grouse is 100 per cent American. There is even some question whether or not "GOP" did not originally stand for "Grand Old Partridge."

The ring-necked pheasant may be a spy from China, but the ruffed grouse is a native. Indeed, he is found only in North America, where his range is greater than that of any other non-migratory game bird. I have flushed him from coast to coast, across Canada and into Alaska, and south to Arkansas and northern Georgia. In some places he is known as woods chicken or mountain pheasant, but these pseudonyms are our invention, not his. Nowhere does the ruffed grouse pose as a secret agent. He announces his presence with enthusiastic drumming in the Spring and noisy take-offs in the Fall.

Quail and doves are so groupy and predictable you might accuse them of following some avian party line, but not the grouse. He is the soul of independence. Like a settler who moves on when he can see the lights of his neighbor, the grouse is intolerant of big crowds--human and otherwise. He is no denizen of exurbia. He wants land, lots of land given to trees and undergrowth. Even here he is rarely found in densities exceeding a bird per four acres. He seldom flocks up. When things get too jammed, he pioneers new territory on early Fall "crazy flights," or his population collapses with a dramatic slump.

Geese and ducks require fancy, government-supported habitat, but the grouse is happy to hang out on anybody's back forty. Despite his kinship with the wild, he actually has proven very adaptable, like any good citizen. Being a bird of young-to-middle-aged forests, and having an especial liking for edges and interrupted woodlands, he has been greatly benefited by the younger stages of forest succession which have followed lumbering and fire, and by the patchy openings which are made in the woods by small-scale farming. His greatest numbers are thus not in primeval areas but in regions where there is some human activity, a relationship which is maintained despite a hunter take which runs into the millions of birds nationally each year.

It is just as well that the ruffed grouse is not likely to arouse HUAC suspicions, for he is a tough guy to take testimony from. Despite his being so widely distributed and so well-known, he is little understood. Aldo Leopold called him "this baffling bird," because of the extreme difficulty of learning much fundamental about a species that cannot be trapped or banded in quantity and that cannot be bred freely in captivity.

What we do know about him, however, furnishes some pretty sound clues on how to conserve him. He is a brownish, fowllike bird about the size of a bantam hen--larger than a Hungarian partridge and smaller than a pheasant. The dark, partially concealed ruff on each side of his neck gives him his name. His fan-shaped tail distinguishes him from his cousins, the sharptail and pinnated grouse. The sexes look so much alike that only an expert can tell them apart by the length of the central tail feathers. There are two color phases, red and gray.

The ruffed grouse saga rightly begins in the early Spring woods, when there is to be heard that distinctive sound of a feathered motor boat, the drumming of the cock, perched on an old log, beating the air with his wings so fast they appear blurred even on a slow-motion movie. Some drumming is undoubtedly done for the pure pleasure of it. We have had a grouse drum in our woods all night in August during a soft rain. But at heart drumming has its utilitarian purposes. It serves first to announce to other cock birds that this is private territory. And it summons harem hens to the breeding grounds. Drumming cover, containing one or more logs, must be widely dispersed over the range, because each male exercises complete control over his territory. Where logs are not well distributed, game managers fell them.

Once he has performed his male functions, the cock bird keeps to himself; meanwhile the female seeks nesting and brooding cover. An ideal partridge nursery is a low, dense canopy adjoining openings containing a variety of plant and insect life. Where underbrush is in short supply it is important that cows be fenced out of the woodlots. On the other hand, where openings are needed, light grazing can actually help produce openings, or they can be built with axe and bulldozer. Nursery cover is of critical importance. It is during the relatively short period when cover is required that we lose approximately 75 per cent of the grouse crop each year.

The hen grouse lays 10 or 12 eggs in a simple ground depression under a rock or at the base of a stump. So long as she is motionless, she is surprisingly secure, because she apparently gives off little scent at this season of the year. I have seen a good pointer pass without pause within a few feet of an incubating grouse. The worst nest marauders are often the squirrels, chipmunks, and skunks who accidentally stumble by and sample the eggs.

After three weeks or so the chicks literally run out of the eggs, fluff off, and hide with their mother in the brush, feeding almost entirely on a variety of insects and worms. Cold, wet, weather that depresses the bug population in late May or early June thus can have a marked effect on the Fall grouse supply. In ten days to two weeks the surviving grouse are making short flights. By mid-July they seek molting cover. Rank growths in moist areas are especially attractive, provided there is a dusting ground nearby. By the time they reach pullet size, the young grouse already have the capability of a noisy flush.

No sound of the woods is more startling than the thunderous roar of beating pinions with which a partridge rises, sometimes almost from underfoot, scattering the leaves like a whirlwind, and tearing its way through rustling branches, winning distance and concealment in one breathless rush, leaving the hiker or hunter staring with open mouth and fast-thumping heart. It is not necessary for the partridge to rise with such bluster, however. He can flush, fly, and alight as quietly as most birds.

When he is full-grown the grouse is primarily a plant eater-- leaves, fruits, nuts, seeds, buds, and catkins. This diet is the main clue to his likely Fall whereabouts--feasting on clover along an old logging road, eating apples in an abandoned orchard, sampling berries in a dogwood thicket, budding birch at a forest edge, scratching for seeds along a woodland path. Except in the years when the population is at an utter low, shooting does not seem to be a serious threat to the grouse population. In general, hunters simply crop part of an ample supply.

With the coming of Winter, grouse cover must be of the type that will provide food, protection from extreme weather, and roosting places safe from predators. Now is when you find him in a downed hickory, high up in an oak, underneath a young evergreen, or even immersed in a snowbank. The most critical point in the adult grouse year is that period between the end of Winter cover and the burgeoning of Spring growth, when food is in short supply and yet when nature demands the vigorous exertions of mating. It is then that the delicate balance of habitat may tilt for good or ill. The kinds of foods most apt to prove valuable at this critical time are leafy plants such as clovers and strawberry, and species which retain fruits over Winter and yet do not grow to a height that exposed these fruits above the snow. They should be planted on south-facing slopes, properly interspersed with the cover.

Regardless of how modern management may raise the average level of grouse abundance, its numbers will apparently continue to fluctuate. Good years will be followed by lean, and lean years by good again. Poor brooding seasons, outbreaks of diseases, and great increases in predators have variously been blamed for the grouse cycle, and doubtless they all make their contributions; but the total story is still untold.

There is no mystery, however, about why the grouse furnishes difficult hunting. Eternal vigilance is the price of obtaining a shot. Where the cover is dense the grouse may disappear in a flash, or there may be only a roar of wings to indicate his presence. In hilly country, as you toil up one slope, the bird careens down the other. Or he may allow you to walk past and then zoom away behind your back. You may find a place where partridge abound one day, and on the next you may hunt the same spot all afternoon and not flush a single bird.

It is fortunate, actually, that the grouse is so difficult a quarry. Otherwise you would not hear in the March and April woods that sound of distant thunder, the perennial drumming of a partridge cock, fulfilling that fine prophecy of Thoreau:
"The grouse are sure to thrive, like true natives of the soil, whatever revolutions occur."
To be a good grouse hunter, with a dog or without one, you have to learn to recognize the "birdy" spots. Here are some tips passed on to me by hunters who consistently bring back partridge:
First of all, put out of your mind the fiction that grouse are denizens of the deep woods. Grouse need lots of wooded Lebensraum, true, but they live in young forests. More accurately, they are a bird of the edge, and they are seldom far from streams, swamps, or moist lowlands. Don't waste your time in heavy timber stands where most trees are 30 feet or more in height. And except for slashings and thornapple thickets, you'll have better luck hunting in or near lowlands or draws, not on the tops of ridges.
A good general rule of thumb, according to Walter Palmer: keep within sight of tag alder and you'll find grouse. Often there will be highbush cranberry, chokeberry, and dogwood thickets near alder, and clumps of individual lowland popple trees. This is the picture of good grouse cover. Add to this some small openings having clover and dandelions and you've got the best.
To get this type of cover in some regions you will have to find ungrazed woodlots, because it will only be where big herds

of cattle are fenced out that you will find growth lush enough to shelter grouse. In other regions just the reverse is true, and you will want to look for scattered cows to find wooded areas sufficiently broken up to attract grouse.

The late Professor Aldo Leopold had two favorite grouse clues. One was a spring. A typical spring becomes choked with moss, which forms a boggy terrace, he once wrote. He called these terraces hanging gardens, for out of their sodden muck the fringed gentians lift their blue jewels. He would move systematically from one hanging garden to another. Another of his clues was "red lanterns"--blackberry leaves, red in the October sun. Along little boggy streams the blackberries burn richly red on every sunny day from first frost to the last day of the season. Every partridge has a private solarium under these briars, he said.

Perhaps the best guide to grouse country is to recognize the partridge love of independence, his desire to be different. It works like this. In a run of tag alder and popple you may notice a single evergreen. Work around this tree carefully, because it is different from the other cover. One more balsam-fir tree in a stand of pure balsam doesn't mean much, but a single tree located in another cover type seems to appeal to grouse. Uprooted trees also provide variations: hiding places under the tops, and mounds of bare earth for dusting. Other examples: windfalls, slashings, bulldozed strips, or any place where the ground or the vegetation has been disturbed, as in a very lightly grazed woodlot. Set your hunting pace and direction so you'll be able to swing past these birdy spots. Usually it is easiest to hunt alone or with a partner because you've got more flexibility to change direction. Grouse hunting is not for the gangs that drive pheasants.

If your partner is a dog, there is one essential requirement: he must range close in. Add a light gun, light shot, and you're in for a day of the sport that is fondly rated as the finest the Wisconsin uplands have to offer.

But grouse don't always obey the "laws" I've just laid down.

Take, for example, the idea that grouse are always to be found in tag-alder sloughs. I once wasted a whole day tramping the bottom lands of the Twin Parks Watershed, only to flush one errant jacksnipe. Walking back to the car along a bone-dry ridge, I found the partridge. And they weren't in downed treetops, either. They were spread out in thin cover in the heart of the woods.

Another favorite concept is the gully idea. According to this theory, you will always find grouse in the hill country in the draws. This didn't work, either, one day. After combing every gully around my cabin, I finally mounted to the fringes of a ridgetop field and kicked up the birds.

Grouse are supposed to be intolerant of humans, but they can be as civilized as a chicken. Take my experience one Saturday morning. I struck out through the most remote regions of the

Town of Arena without hearing a single roar. Tired and disgusted after three hours of hiking, I took to a town road. Walking blissfully down the middle, I began to jump birds right at the roadside. Even I can hit grouse when they fly down an open right-of-way.

This is great stuff, I thought, and attempted to repeat the performance the next week. But the birds had deserted the roadside. Where were they? In the blackberry tangles in the draws.

During the deer season one year I ran into a spot that was loaded with grouse--a sidehill copse of hazelbrush. When I went back with a shotgun they were not to be found. Now they were in a thicket down along a creek.

Partridge hunting makes liars of us all. A good friend told me of a hot spot where he had collected his three birds in short order, and I told him of a hollow where I "always" flush birds. I couldn't find any grouse where he sent me, and he couldn't find any in my hollow. We no longer speak to each other.

The remarkable thing about grouse hunting is that it gets better instead of poorer as the season progresses. When the leaves are stripped from the trees, you have a decent crack at a fleeting partridge. When it's cold and windy, you can skip lots of territory and move from one windfall to another. And when there is snow on the woodlot floors, you can track a running bird.

What's more, while ruffed grouse may disappear from the roadsides, they maintain their numbers back in the brush throughout the season. That was the conclusion of Vic Reinders, nationally known Waukesha trapshooter and professor of chemistry at the University of Wisconsin-Milwaukee. Reinders based his findings on five-year records from his diary.

Professor Reinders hunted grouse nearly every weekend. After the second or third week of the season, he usually did not find any birds in spots easily accessible to hunters, but he continued to find birds in cover that wore an inch off his pantlegs each season. Complete records of grouse sightings from the first week to the 11th, for five seasons, permitted Reinders to say: "The number of grouse flushed per day when hunting in the brush does not decrease significantly as the season progresses."

Reinders concluded the grouse population was in no danger from over-gunning in long open seasons. The reason why is that grouse are so darned hard to hit. It will come as great comfort to all amateurs to know that even a national trapshooting champion was unable to bring down all the partridge he flushed. For a five-year average, Reinders and his hunting partners bagged only 37 percent of the birds sighted. Their record was poorest early in the season, when leaves on the trees made shooting tough, and it improved later.

Not too many gunners go after grouse in Wisconsin. The hunters are intimidated by hills, brambles, and a target that refuses to do today what he did yesterday. For those who do practice the fine art of grouse gunning, nothing in the out-of-doors can compare with a sunny afternoon in the Winter woods, and that moment when the stillness is broken by the roar of Summer thunder.

We were coming down out of the hills in the January twilight--twelve-year-old Billy and I. It was very still, so still our feet made a great crunching in the frozen snow. Billy's steps were shorter than mine, but he managed to keep up.

When we slowed down, cutting through the bogs of a pasture, Billy looked back at the wooded bulk of the ridge darkening against the pale sky.

"Uncle Clay," he asked wistfully, "you can't get back behind it, can you?"

"Behind what, Billy?"

"Why," he explained earnestly, "behind your good times. Behind what's happened. Get right back behind it and do it all over again, just exactly the same. You can't do that, can you?"

I chewed a minute on my cigar before I answered:

"Well, no, Billy, we have to admit we can't get back. Not exactly. But say, Billy, there's one way you can come so close to it you can hardly tell the difference, and that's squirrel hunting, like today. Sammy Squirrel doesn't change. He keeps going strong. You'll always be able to get back--with him!"

I think I was dead right. I can prove it, to my satisfaction, at least, any winter afternoon by stopping the car at the foot of the ridge that runs up from the Mineral Point and Northern right-of-way.

I can stroll into those Iowa County oaks--and skat! There's Sammy Squirrel scooting for a den, a streak of red ducking behind a trunk, just as he did when I was a boy.

The railroad itself is gone, and the zinc works, and most of my boyhood chums. But a couple of them I can expect to meet on the ridge, with .22's in the crooks of their arms, getting happily back behind the years--with Sammy Squirrel.

There are lots of us squirrel hunters in Wisconsin. Scratch a pheasant fancier or a deer stalker, and ten to one you'll find a squirrel shooter underneath. More hunters probably have cut their eye teeth on squirrels than on any other game, and we still delight in getting back behind the years with the quarry of our boyhood days. We shoot upwards of a million-and-a-half squirrels a year even in such "civilized" states as Wisconsin, Illinois, and Michigan.

As a matter of fact, we're shooting more squirrels now than we ever did, because modern trends in agricultural land use are creating better squirrel range. Contour farming and the various soil-conservation practices associated with it tend to increase the amount of "edge" between cover types and to create small, irregularly shaped, ungrazed woodlots--just the thing for Sammy Squirrel. Small oak-hickory woods are prime squirrel habitat. Here you will find as many as three or four to the acre, provided the mast crop has been good. In short, effective, long-term squirrel conservation stems directly from sound field and forest management. Predator control, artificial stocking, and even closed seasons contribute nothing.

Most squirrels are taken with shotguns. And who would deny that a blur of rusty fur leaping high in the crown of a white oak is a tough target? But I suspect the .22 rifle is really the ideal squirrel gun, all things considered. Its use calls for more patience and skill, and pays off in keener sport and cleaner meat.

Whatever the weapon, it's always good to get back behind the years--with Sammy Squirrel.

There's big news from the hazelbrush country: rabbits are on the rebound.

For the past few seasons there's been pretty thin pickings for bunny hunters. Rabbits have been at the low point in their mysterious cycle. Now the rabbit population is beginning to bounce back. Hunters are finding cottontails in good numbers where there weren't many before. I have lots of rabbit signs in my Arena woodlot for the first time since 1961.

According to the devotees of fox bounties, rabbits and other game species were doomed when state bounties on predators began to be removed. Just the opposite has happened. There are more rabbits today then there were at the peak of fox hunting. Just what causes these dramatic ups and downs in the rabbit population, biologists don't know. Probably a lot of natural factors pyramid to produce the swings.

How can rabbits bounce back from practically nothing? Well, they have very large litters, and they usually have several litters a year. The litter size may be as high as six, and Molly Cottontail may raise as many as five families a year. Under favorable conditions, a pair of rabbits will raise 16 offspring to adult size in a single season.

The average cottontail lives less than a year, even if he's not shot. A rabbit in his third fall is extremely rare. From 75 to 85 percent of the cottontails shot each season are new rabbits. Rabbits don't move often or far. They generally spend their entire lives in an area of 20 acres or less. Living on such a restricted range, each rabbit gets to know his home territory intimately. That's why he can "hole up" so fast when you jump him. His home may be a natural cavity in stone, earth, or wood, or an old woodchuck den. He may use it even while the woodchuck is there, deep in Winter sleep. Br'er Rabbit likes a den below ground in Winter. In Fall he uses a grass or weed shelter called a "form," a nestlike cavity made in vegetation, often under a woodpile.

When all the tumult and the shouting are done and said about ducks and deer, it is the cottontail rabbit which remains the number 1 target of Wisconsin gunners. For example, last year

Wisconsin hunters shot no less than a million-and-a-half bunnies. If you exclude squirrels, that is considerably more than the take of all other game species combined. Undoubtedly, more outdoorspersons hunt rabbits than hunt any other quarry.

Only two worries haunt bunny hunters today: will the rabbit populations follow a cycle of ups and downs; and will the beagle be ruined as a rabbit dog?

Some game managers believe the rabbit population inevitably swings from high to low and back again every ten years or so. Other biologists say that sound rabbit management and favorable land-use practices can keep the bunny population on an even keel. Hunters wonder who is right.

The merry little beagle has been the favorite dog of rabbit hunters for many years. Now the beagle has become America's number 1 house dog. What this rise in popularity as a pet may do to the species as a hunter has sportsmen concerned. In the past generation sportspersons have seen two excellent hunting breeds ruined as hunters when the house-dog and show-dog fanciers took over--the Irish setter and the cocker spaniel. If the beagle is to maintain his hunting nose and his hunting temperament it will take great vigilance on the part of breeders and buyers.

The flourishing of Peter Cottontail in the face of plow, axe, steam shovel, and gun is a major outdoor miracle. The bunny has proved to be one of those rare native species which actually thrives on civilization and intensive farming practices. Why this may be so is indicated by recent research in Massachusetts, where the cottontail was found to prefer his vegetables with lots of minerals.

Massachusetts wanted to learn what effect fertilization can have on land which is known to be lacking certain minerals. Two test plots were established. One of these was treated with only muriate of potash; the other got calcium, nitrogen, phosphates, and potassium. The cottontail showed a three-to-one preference for the plants grown on the land which had the full treatment. In other words, when a farmer fertilizes his fields heavily he is going to grow more rabbits as well as more corn and hay.

Peter Cottontail has been around these parts for a long time. He not only furnishes top sport for generations of hunters. His way of life suggests certain lessons to a sizzling and thundering world. The wolves and the cougars are gone, but the rabbit remains and multiplies. The passing of the wilderness and the spreading of cities have not defeated the cottontails. The crack of guns and the loosing of dogs have not been able to dent the supply of these quiet natives. In early Winter mornings there is still to be observed in any woodlot or hay meadow around a city this spectacle of reassurance--a blur of brown and white as a bunny dashes pell-mell for his briar patch.

Like a Grant County game warden put it to me, "Bunnies are a bonus that goes along with good farming." The warden had stopped us near Fennimore, checked our licenses, and inspected the three rabbits in the trunk.

"Nice bag," he said. "Where'd you get 'em?"

"Down at Bennett's--John Bennett's--near Lancaster," I said.

"Well, I'll be darned." The warden scratched his head. "I can remember when even a crow would have had slim pickings on that farm. It just goes to show how the game comes back when you stop farming to the hilt and start saving the soil."

He was right. Ten years ago it wouldn't have paid you to tramp John Bennett's acres all day. Last Fall it was different. I had left my daughter and the Bennetts stringing late beans around the kitchen stove and had struck out alone across the lower pasture. I hadn't taken five paces past the fence when I bounced the first cottontail of the day out of a clump of June grass. He went tearing away from under foot and my first shot missed. The second tumbled him, however, as he broad-jumped across the field, heading for a swale. I gutted him on the spot. He was big and fat. Soil conservation had paid off already.

I moved on down the field, quartering back and forth so as to cover as much likely ground as possible. This solo style is not the best way to bag bunnies, I'll admit. Efficiently done, rabbit hunting calls for three or four gunners and a brace of good dogs. But when your ticket to a farm reads, "Nobody else allowed," and you don't have a handy beagle, why you can still find rabbits all by yourself. The trick will lie largely in deducing where to look, then hunting methodically until you strike game.

That particular morning I figured that because the night before had been warm and clear, the bunnies would probably be resting out in the open where dawn had caught them on the feed. I was right. The second cottontail was hunched down beside a milkweed stalk in pasture cover so short it seemed impossible he could have been concealed at all. One instant there was nothing before me but close-cropped grass, and the next second a dab of white and brown was streaking for a thick fencerow. He got there, too. I shot 'way behind him.

Beyond farmer Bennett's pasture was a cornfield. After a rough night or late in the season, corn shocks are likely bunny hideouts. Today I did not bother to kick at them, walked on, instead, to a hayfield where Mr. Bennett had deliberately left strips of unmowed timothy.

After an hour spent scuffing through these havens I had two more rabbits in my game bag. They had sat very tight, as bunnies so often do, waiting until my boot was poised almost over their heads before taking off in long, frantic bounds.

I circled back to the farmhouse then, pausing for a smoke on a cedar ridge from where you can see to the west the line of the Mississippi River. My bag felt pleasantly heavy, and I sprawled down in the shade of a reddening sumac, inconspicuous enough that a foraging titmouse was unaware of my presence. Indian Summer held the far horizon in purple haze. The air was still. Below me stretched John Bennett's contoured fields--clover alternating with grain, the gullies grown up to brambles, cows fenced out of the woodlot, brushpiles stacked in fence corners--natural rabbit country where 10 years before had been "mined" farmland with the soil eroding away and the game disappearing with it. Yes, bunnies are a bonus.

There is quite a crowd at Camp Randall Stadium in Madison, Wisconsin, each Fall Saturday, but it is small compared to the 500,000-plus Wisconsin citizens of all ages, sexes, and conditions of servitude who will take to the woods the same season in pursuit of some 800,000-plus Wisconsin deer. That there are plenty of deer to shoot in this second half of the twentieth century in mid-continent America is one of the marvels of nature. That there are plenty of deer shooters left in this day of plastic plumbing is one of the marvels of humankind.

The lure of the deer woods is compounded of many factors: the camaraderie of the camp, the challenge of the drive through a strange swamp, the almost unbearable suspense on a stump to the flank of a well-trod run, the sheer beauty of a sleek gray coat and a white flag disappearing into a copse of aspen, the skill of the well-placed shot. But the special magic that surrounds the relationship of deer and people may very well stem largely from a subconscious realization that here are two species of the animal world that have been pitted against each other from time immemorial and that have carved out success stories together.

Like humans, the white-tailed deer is a creature of the edge. That is, he thrives best in the brush where woods and fields join. Plow up his openings and level his forests and the deer population slumps. But give him a nice combination of woodlots and meadows and the deer will rebound with alacrity. Just so we are coming to see that humans need edge if we are to flourish. Crowd us into cities or spread us too thinly over the plains and we have problems. But give us environmental variety and we respond with a cultural irruption.

It is in their periods and sites of stress that we see most clearly the kinship of deer and humans. Ranging freely in Summer over well-balanced terrain, the deer thrives. Jam him together in a Winter yard, and he eats himself out of house and home. Ranging freely between city and country, Wisconsin people thrive. Jam us together in an urban inner core with no escape hatch, and we react with violence.

Half a century ago, axe, dog, gun, and trap seemed to have spelled the end of the Wisconsin whitetail. Then a combination of accidental habitat changes and purposeful hunting regulations began to produce a situation in which we literally have more deer today than there were in pioneer days. The return of the deer has been accompanied by the return of the deer hunter. Where less than 25,000 took to the deer woods in the twenties, we can confidently look forward to more than half a million Wisconsin deer hunters in 1980. Other states tell the same story. People and game have not generally flourished together. The whitetail story is different. Whether we can survive as well is another question.

Only yesterday the deer was a wilderness symbol that had faded forever with the virgin forests. With no thought of being contradicted, the Wisconsin Game Commission announced, for example, that "deer are destined to cease to be a game animal in Wisconsin." Then almost overnight the white-tailed deer were back with us across the state. Today the Wisconsin Department of Natural Resources says, "In our major deer ranges we have all the whitetails we can use."

How and why the comeback? There are many reasons, of course, not the least of which is the fact that the deer has a superb set of senses whetted by eons of pursuers. The whitetail depends first on scent, then on hearing, and probably least on vision.

A whitetail's sense of smell is phenomenal. He can sift your scent from the wind at great distances when humidity and terrain are favorable. That's why smart hunters make every effort to work upwind, and refrain from smoking.

A whitetail's great ears can catch the smallest sounds. A wary deer exhibits many of the listening traits of a cottontail rabbit, warping his ears in any direction. Deer have the uncanny ability to detect the difference between a human footfall and that of a wild creature.

In semidarkness when a hunter sees with difficulty, a deer can see very well. Although the deer is color-blind and may often ignore a stationary object, he can detect the wink of an eye, so amazingly perceptive of movement is he, especially of any slight, rapid movement, for quick moves are often associated with predation, as he has come to know.

With these razor-sharp senses the deer cultivates one of his most important resources--an intimate knowledge of his home. A whitetail has a very limited range; with the exception of the rutting season he may live most of his life on a square mile or less, and he becomes very familiar with every brook, thicket, gully, and covert on his home range. Thirty-nine Michigan deer, including nine bucks, were known to live in a mile-square enclosure from which they could not escape--an area of hardwoods, swamp, and open pine barrens. Six experienced hunters went into that square mile in clear weather with an ideal tracking snow. It was almost four days before one of them even saw a buck.

The white-tailed deer first picked his way across the Asian-American land bridge in the Middle Micene period. That was the first golden age of the deer, and the ancient plains and forests of North America swarmed with them. Despite droughts, glaciers, saber-toothed tigers, and even the first human hunters, the deer adapted and thrived. Forged by the stresses of some 15 million years, the whitetail has evolved into a large, strong, graceful animal of singular beauty, fecundity, and sense. A half-century ago he was almost decimated by axe and plow, but now he has bounced back with all the resilience displayed by his ancestors.

The second golden age of the deer is here.

To those of us who grew up in the "good old days" when deer were as rare as jobs, big game hunters bore the stamp of heroism. They were intrepid souls who made long treks 'way up north, emerging a fortnight later with fierce new whiskers and hard-won venison. But their star has faded.

There's much to be said for wilderness trips, but the average deer hunter is likely to do as well near home. You'll save money and time. You also know your home country far better than some distant swamp, and you just can't know a deer range too intimately. Most important of all, you'll be able to scout the deer range well ahead of the season and maybe even have a trophy pinpointed for opening day.

Knowing deer range and deer movements is vital to hunting success. It's smart to begin your local deer hunt in early Fall, checking the lay of the land, talking to landowners and getting to know them, and finding deer runs and crossings. In your late-Autumn fishing, watch sandbars and mudbanks for deer prints. On your squirrel and pheasant hunts, watch for pawings on the acorn ridges, and skinned saplings in the swamps where bucks have shadow-boxed with new antlers.

You can do a lot of scouting on weekends and evenings before the season. Drive slowly along remote roads as soon after rain as possible, watching for hoofprints on road shoulders that may indicate major deer crossinga and travel routes. Early drives-- at dawn or shortly thereafter--will often pay off with sightings of deer at the edges of pastures and meadows. When you see such deer, thoroughly scout the surrounding country. Deer are great creatures of habit, and often leave well-defined trails between their midday bedding grounds and their dawn feeding areas. If you find such a heavily-used path, be there in ambush on opening day. Make it the first dawn, because deer swiftly change their living patterns when they're hunted, and your hot spot can cool off overnight.

Don't expect to see many deer during your pre-season scouting. Look for deer signs, and talk to people who may be out regularly-- farmers, creamery truck drivers, rural mail carriers. Learn the land. Watch for lumbering activities and newly-cleared land, cropfields and small isolated patches in timber or near creeks. Know drainage patterns. County plat maps can be helpful; they show abandoned roads and railway spurs, remote creeks and ponds, and locations of farm buildings. When you pencil in woodlot and field patterns on such maps, adding boundary lines and farmers' names and all reported deer sightings and signs, you have a valuable reference.

Backyard bucks may be worth any effort it takes to get them. Living in conjunction with civilization and agriculture, with a better variety of good food than wilderness deer, they grow into fine trophies and prime rations. Nothing can build antlers and sweeten venison like clover, alfalfa, young corn, and the succulent browse of rich valleys. You can go farther, and grow fiercer whiskers, but you probably won't find better bucks than the ones at home.

Of all our animal colleagues, you would have to agree the white-tailed deer has made a signal success out of civilization, as we've said. If you stop to think about such things, it is really quite remarkable that in a day of I-highways, there are vastly more deer than there were 50 years ago. What may be even more remarkable is the fact that in a day of supermarkets, those 500,000-plus Wisconsin citizens go back in the boondocks annually on the trail of a buck. Given favorable weather, the annual deer harvest can exceed 100,000 animals. So flourishing is the Wisconsin herd that a take of that magnitude won't hurt a bit. In 1924 only 7,000 deer were shot, and the season was closed entirely in 1925.

The whitetail is a Wisconsin old-timer, his bones being found in the earliest Indian refuse heaps. It is quite probable that in prehistoric Wisconsin deer ranged over the entire state, but north of what is now Wausau he was not found in great abundance. The virgin pineries of northern Wisconsin were, in fact, not exactly a haven for game of any kind. Pierre-Esprit Raddisson, who cruised the Lake Superior shores in 1658, wrote the earliest deer hunter's lament: "It is a strange thing when victuals are wanting, work whole nights and days, lie down on the bare ground, the breech in the water, the fear in the buttocks, the belly empty, the weariness in the bones."

It was in central and southern Wisconsin, where the woods gave way to oak openings and prairie, that the whitetail flourished, for he is a creature of the brushy edges between forest and field. With the coming of the white man, the deer's southern haven in Wisconsin did not last long. Axe, plow, gun, dog, and snare made heavy inroads. When the first State Legislature convened in 1850, the "deer problem" was on the agenda.

Meanwhile the first lumbermen were creating openings in the north, and the deer population jumped. After the Civil War the railroads ran "sports specials" to Wausau and beyond. But by the turn of the century massive clean-cutting operations and devastating fires had wiped out the northern range. When the first Conservation Commission was appointed in 1927, there wasn't much in the way of a deer herd to conserve. Then nature and people began to team up. The northern cutover became one vast sweep of saplings, as reforestation and fire prevention programs took hold. In the south, game and farm management practices favored the creation of more edge. The deer bounced back, slowly at first and then with a rush. Now the sound of hunters' guns can be heard from the shores of Green Bay to the foothills of Dane County.

A lot of people take credit, and rightly so, for the current health of Wisconsin's deer herd. Something should be said, too, for the whitetail himself. The cougar and the wolf are gone, but like the cottontail, the deer continues to thrive. His wariness, his adaptability, and above all, his good will, have paid off.

The deer hunter deserves recognition, too. Ever since the days of James Fenimore Cooper's characters, deer-slayers have epitomized the American way. Roaming the frontier as wild and free as their quarry, they have represented that rugged individualism that has been the essence of a muscular young democracy. A deer hunt today has really very little to do with shooting a buck. It is a desperate attempt on the part of urbanized, computerized humankind to recapture the soul of our primeval past. But the price the deer hunter pays for the quest is staggering. We come closer today to representing a character out of Orwell's 1984 than we do Daniel Boone. No other American is so hedged in by restrictions as is the modern deer hunter.

First, deer hunters today are told to buy a special tag, which we then must display in the middle of the back like a human auto license. We are told to buy special clothing, at least 50 percent of which must be blaze-orange. We are told when we can go--on three to 10 precious days in November, between prescribed hours. We are told where we can go--to certain counties or deer management areas. We are told what we can use--a rifle, a shotgun, or a bow, of certain strength, again depending on the area. We are told how we can hunt--no elevated platforms, no shooting from a road, no carrying an uncased gun in a car. If we are lucky enough to shoot a deer we must register the animal at a state checking station before we can bring it home. The only thing that isn't regulated is the number of hunters allowed in a certain area, and that regulation is just around the corner. Not only must the modern deer hunter thread a way through manifold human-made restrictions; we must also combat the immutable laws of human health. Our chair-bound physique is suddenly called upon to exert itself in ways known only to the pioneers. The price is a rash of heart attacks.

According to all the theories of sociology, there should be no more deer hunters. Fear and frustration should long ago have confiscated the sport. No other human activity is so subjected to harassments. Yet the fact remains there are more deer hunters today than there were 50 years ago. There can be only one explanation for the survival of deer hunting. To drive away from the city, to get out of a chrome-trimmed car, to fade into the woods, there to see a gray ghost of yesterday drifting through the brush--this must constitute a primitive, heart-pounding thrill that can surmount any hazard civilization can place in the way of its search. Far from representing freedom, modern deer hunters represent regimentation. But their spirits remain unquenchable. In this phenomenon there may be a profound lesson for anyone who thinks we can change the American character.

There is at least one less whitetail buck in Iowa County, Wisconsin, today than there was last year. He hung for a time from a tree in a back yard in Madison--an ancient and honorable symbol of the hunter's prowess, or a despicable example of human rapacity, depending on your point of view.

For the millions of folks who eschew deer hunting, the

annual assault of red-clad gunners seems at best a foolhardy expression of primitive impulses, and at worst an utter abomination. To the thousands of deer hunters, on the other hand, their pursuit of the wily whitetail is inexorably linked to life, liberty, and the pursuit of happiness.

Admittedly, as deer hunting is practiced by some, it bears only passing resemblance to an outdoor sport. There are carfuls of goons who roam the back roads, dismounting only on the off chance that a buck is spotted racing for cover. And there are cabinfuls of poker players who only occasionally emerge to sit on stumps well out of the wind.

When it is rightly done, however, deer hunting is the epitome of the sporting life. Deer hunting, you see, does not really pit a human against an animal; it pits a person against oneself. It is in the deer woods that modern humankind comes hard up against the choices that have gone into the making of the human species.

Will you succumb to weary leg muscles, or will you follow the spoor of a wounded deer, combing the area in widening circles, until absolutely all hope is gone?

Will you occupy a stand in front of another hunter, or will you position yourself so that not even your scent wafts down a runway where another person is standing?

Will you sit wart-like on a stump, oblivious to the world of the woods, or will you relish watching grouse, porcupines, jays, chickadees, and all the other little folk of the forest?

Can you stalk so quietly that you are conscious only of the beating of your heart, or will you introduce out-of-place events like the rasp of a match or the flash of a handkerchief?

Will you wait for a clear, close shot into a lethal spot, or will you fire at shadows or, even worse, at the sound of hoofbeats?

Will you pull your share of the work of the hunt, or will you complain about snowy tree limbs, cold feet, and a growling belly?

Will you really try to match wits with a buck, or will you stomp home to quarterback the Packers from a couch?

It is in these Thermopylaes of the human spirit that a person takes the measure of oneself. If he or she overcomes these hurdles of the hunt, the deer shooter wins an important contest. He or she may also be awarded an incidental prize--a trophy rack of antlers for the fireplace mantle.

For hundreds of thousands of Wisconsin folks, the good life is linked inextricably with the sights and sounds of wildfowl. Almost any Fall or Spring night you can hear it--the querulous, clarion call of migrating Canadas. At first it may be so faint and indistinct as to be mistaken for the background static on a distant radio. Then, as the long line whipsaws high overhead, a wild chorus from a hundred straining throats proclaims the turn of the seasons in a song as old as time, yet ever new.

Winging steadily in flying wedges and wavering lines, the

leaders calling the tired stragglers on, their eerie chant ringing across the breadth of wilderness and metropolis alike, the Canadas call to us. Listening in the dark we mark these nomads of the night as they journey down the trackless sky trail. Our minds are moved by the old riddle of bird migration; our hearts are stirred by a compelling kinship with nature.

The Canada goose, like perhaps no other outdoor denizen, has had the power to inspire a concern for conservation in human breasts. A generation ago the Wisconsin chapter of the infant Izaak Walton League was formed to restore Horicon Marsh. Slowly the area was converted from a thistle-infested waste to a pulsating slough. And the geese came back. The masses of big birds milling each fall over Dodge County represent more surely than a moon missile a triumph of humankind. For one species to protect another is really a new thing under the sun, as Aldo Leopold once observed. We have saved geese. In that fact rather than in Commander Glenn's rocket may lie some evidence of our superiority over beasts.

Tradition has it that geese in the Temple of Juno once saved the city of Rome. In 390 B.C. the Gauls attacked and drove the Romans to a steep, rocky hill known as the Capitol, which was used as a fort. One night the counsel Manlius was awakened by the cackling of the sacred geese. Rushing to the wall, he saw that the Gauls had almost climbed it. His shouts and the noise of the geese alerted other defenders, and Rome was saved.

The sights and sounds of Canada geese in the skies over Wisconsin likewise alert us of the twentieth centruy. There is a profound message in the music of migrating Canadas. It says, as Stewart Udall has written, that "our conservation challenge today is one of quality--purity of surroundings, and opportunity to stretch, a chance for solitude, for quiet reflection." The message of the geese reminds us as well that Henry Thoreau's decision to "live deliberately"--to absorb the natural world around us, not merely through the senses into our physical being but into our deepest thoughts, to scorn artificiality and find richness in simplicity--that this is the nutrient of a great culture and a more peaceful world order.

So as we save the geese the geese save us.

The federal and state law books may say the duck season officially opens in October, but for all true waterfowlers the season really opens in September. Bob Ellarson and I usually perform the initial annual rites of the duck hunter, appropriately enough, on Labor Day weekend. The rite is known as "fixing up the blind."

No matter how sturdily you build a blind in the first place, the amount of annual maintenance is staggering. For example, the insidious power of ice in the grip of wind and wave is something to behold. It can be counted on to snap off a six-inch-thick tamarack post like it were a match stick. Changing water levels can render the floor of the blind either a foot under water or three feet above. A muskrat will likely have strewn his debris over the seat, or worse, undermined the whole structure. Coons and birds of prey will have left their refuse. Human predators will have defaced your signs. And last season's flourishing garlands of cattails and sedge will, of course, have been stripped clean by marsh gales.

After shoring up the basic edifice with due ceremony and swearing, you turn to the ritual of cutting, bundling, and tying on a new covering of camouflage. We have made a science of it. In the first place, you cut your vegetation at a spot well removed from the blind, so as not to disturb the natural surroundings. To facilitate forming sheaves, we construct a special sawhorse in which to cradle the bunches of grass and bullrushes while we secure them with binder twine. Each year we leave this frame cached in the marsh, and each year we have to build a new one. But we don't really care. It is all a part of the ceremony. So is tying the rushes to the snow-fence sides of the blind, an art known only to duck hunters. No one arranging the centerpiece at a fancy dinner exercises such sophisticated care. From the perspective of every possible on-coming bird, the outline of the blind and its inhabitants must be perfectly concealed. To double-check our artwork, we row out and take a look before we tie on the last batch of bundles.

With the blind reconstructed and camouflaged, the duck hunter now engages in the most solemn part of the pre-season ritual--assuming a shooting position in the blind, and praying. The power of this pre-season prayer is equal only to the power of shoving ice. In no time at all, the sky is filled with ducks, imaginary yet no less real. Far off to the left we seem to make out the first flock as it rises off the lake and comes winnowing over the railroad tracks. They are mallards. Gracefully they trail along the far shore, swing past the south corner of the marsh, and then turn toward us as they see our mythical decoys. For a moment they hesitate, and then they are on us with a rush. We stand, aim our imaginary shotguns, and fire. Then we paddle out as if to pick up the downed birds, turn to admire our handiwork, and then slowly row away, meanwhile keeping an eye peeled for more imaginary mallards. The ceremony is complete. It is almost as compelling as opening day itself.

For the duck hunter, the kickoff of the duck hunting season is a combination of Christmas, New Year's, and Yom Kippur--requiring much advance preparation. By telling tall tales around poker tables, and by repainting decoys and replacing anchor chords, the duck hunter keeps in mental shape even in Winter. Throughout the Summer months one reconnoiters the haunts of local puddle ducks.

When it's September, you can find the duck hunter camouflaging those blinds with rushes, and painting boats that shade of ineffable beauty, "dead grass tan." Off to the store to buy school shoes for the kids, the duck hunter spends most of the time trying on hipboots.

The dedicated duck hunter also practices on a duck call, to the consternation of family and neighbor's dog. To them, the sounds produced in the basement resemble nothing ever heard on sea or land, but to the hunter they bear a remarkable similarity to the feeding call of the female redhead (a feathered redhead, that is).

As Opening Day approaches, true duck hunters are unable to sleep, except at office desks. On The Morning they will rise at 2:00 a.m., after having catnapped since midnight. Were a boss or a first sergeant to get them up this early, they would either resign or go AWOL, but since the act is voluntary they consider it one of the major attributes of American democracy, and they will fix with an icy stare anybody who says they are nuts. The bag for the season will cost a minimum of $20 a pound, not counting blood, sweat, and tears, but the duck hunter pays the bill with aplomb in exchange for the priceless pleasure of seeing a flock of blacks poised over a set of blocks.

How duck hunters have developed, nobody has ever figured out for sure. One theory holds they are a throwback to a race of amphibians that never successfully made the transition from water to dry land. Duck hunters themselves claim they represent the climax stage in man's evolution, because of their manifest kinship with the sky as well as with the ground.

The forces of humankind and nature do not always cooperate with duck hunters, and they at times grow somewhat discouraged. Harassed by restrictions on their guns, their hours, and their bag, rooted out of house and home by federal drainage projects and commercial preserves, plagued by the vagaries of the weather, ridiculed by their associates, ostracized by their families, it could be that the true duck hunter, and not the duck, will become America's vanishing species. If the trends that try such people's souls continue, it is not too much to imagine that inside of another century of civilization the remains of America's last duck hunter will be found only behind glass in some historical museum.

Indeed, maybe the government has been going about things all wrong. Instead of collecting $10 from every duck hunter for the protection of ducks, perhaps Washington ought to collect $10 from everybody else for the care and preservation of duck hunters. Surely it would be an evil day for America were a certain day in Autumn not to signal the assemblage of assorted duck hunters in isolated swamps, their dumb tenacity testifying to something special in the human spirit.

A duck hunt, you see, is not just a simple sporting event. Rightly done, it is a ritual, as complete with secret incantations, special garments, and sacred scriptures as the most elaborate rites of an exclusive fraternity.

Performed properly, the ceremony opens at 6:05 p.m. of a late Fall evening, with the TV weather reporter tracing on a map the course of a big "front" moving down from the Twin Cities, preceded by rain and followed by falling temperatures.

At 6:10 your phone rings. It is the High Priest of the Hunt--the friend who has a private pothole.

"Did you see the forecast?" he asks. This is the password. You give the countersign: "I sure did." Then the High Priest utters the magic words, "Let's leave at seven."

That is the signal for collecting by the numbers the biggest stockpile of combat gear this side of the Suez. Station wagon loaded, you flee the suburbs in frantic haste, like a couple of refugees deserting a doomed city. The rain beats a tatoo on the windshield, and the wind sends cascades of sodden leaves across the glistening road. You don't talk much, because idle conversation might break the spell of the ceremony.

You turn off the highway onto a county trunk, then onto a town road, and finally onto a slippery lane. In a patch of woods you cache the car and head down through the swamp, your flashlights making only a feeble dent in the blackness as you slosh along in knee-deep muck.

The rain has stopped now, but the wind keeps up its high-pitched litany in the tamaracks, punctuated once by the gabble of snow geese waving unseen overhead.

After an agonizing half-mile hike you stumble up to a quonset hut. The stubborn padlock finally yields to a special muttering, and you enter the mystic domain of the duck hunter--the marsh shack. Lamps are lit, stove stoked, alarm clock set, all according to a routine as immutable as a baptism.

You sleep only fitfully, disturbed by the night sounds of the swamp, and you are up making breakfast before the alarm goes off. You have to crack a film of ice on the water bucket. It will be a good day for ducks.

In the strange half-light that precedes the dawn you load the skiffs and shove off. Largely by instinct you paddle toward your assigned blind. To toss out the decoys you assume a kneeling position. This attitude of prayer is a vital part of the ritual. As if in answer to your supplication, a brace of bluebills bursts by. It is still too early to shoot.

Off to the east the dawn is wrestling with the night on a mat of low-hanging clouds. The result is a blood-red draw. A shot 'way off in the distance marks the opening hour. You hunker down in the cattails and scan the sky.

A hen pintail is looping low, straight for the decoys. With a desperately anxious bid for companionship, she plops in, is motionless for a long time, seemingly exhausted. You stand up and she takes off, frantically wingbeating for altitude against the wind that threatens to carry her back into your blind. You fire and she folds up with that total abandon that makes the deed seem preordained. You push out for the retrieve.

It never fails! No sooner are you out of the blind than a flight of blackheads comes in right over the blocks. They must have swept down from up the river, behind you. Your first consciousness was the wing-sound as they went past, low-pitched and soft, yet somehow instantly audible over the roar of the wind and the splash of the waves. There is no way to describe such a sound--a little like the tearing of old brocade, yet that fails to suggest the excitement it arouses. No other noise comes so close to stopping your heart, save the unexpected flush of a grouse in the suddenly broken silence of a deep woods.

A person hunts less for birds than for such moments.

A bunch of baldpate is fooling around high over the trees on the far shore, wheeling, dropping with that old broken-wing flutter, catching themselves, flaring, soaring--the only ducks that give you the impression of taking to the air for the sheer joy of flight. All the other species fly so purposefully, with such grim determination, especially canvasback. You think of the enormous effort that a duck has to expend to live out the pattern of its life. What evolutionary process could possibly have impressed the necessity of a yearly migration over such enormous distances?

From the right, a train of mallards interrupts your reverie. They turn in, circle your set twice, set their wings for an instant-- and then suddenly flare, rocketing up as if they had been shot at. You give them your most plaintive chuckle on your call. They respond nicely.

Cautiously they look over your set again. As they pass, you give them another seductive chuckle on your call. The leaders seem not to hear and keep climbing, but a half-dozen others veer off, make a wide swing, and then cup their wings and come sideslipping down as if pulled by an invisible cord.

Right out in front of you they lower their big orange legs, brace their wings, and splash in.

This is the climax of the duck hunter's ceremony. No matter how many times you've been initiated, it is always a breathtaking experience. No other outdoor event is so fraught with primeval drama. For one awful second there is nothing in time but you, a little stretch of windswept pothole, and a huddle of wild waterfowl. For a magic moment you look right into the eye of nature.

The firing of your gun is strictly anti-climatic, like the benediction after a sermon. If you are like me, as like as not you do not hit anything anyway. At least that's what happened one morning. I shot three times, greenheads vaulted into the air all over the place, and not so much as a feather was left behind.

I didn't really care. The ducks had fought a good fight, and I had kept the faith.

In the top drawer of every sportsperson's memory there's a Very Important Place. For one person, it may be the bass lake where a 10-pound largemouth shattered line and hopes. For another, that V.I.P. may be a stretch of trout stream, where educated brookies tested tapered leader and temper. It may be a cornfield that was alive with ringnecks; a special squirrel woods; or a section of cedars where a big buck was bedded down.

My V.I.P. is a potato patch. At least, that's what it is now. But once upon a time it was a marsh, when conditions were right, the best duck marsh I knew. We called it Allen's Marsh, although I guess it is known to others by other names--a thousand acres, more or less, of marsh grass, dogwood, and smartweed in Jefferson County. In an ordinary year, Allen's was too dry for ducks, but in a wet Fall it would become a regular mallard motel.

Some of us will always remember, for example, the year 1936. That was the Summer of the big drought, you'll recall, when the temperature hit 100 degrees for ten days straight and the dust of the Dakotas lay thick on Wisconsin porches. But on August 17 the rains came--and came. Swamps and potholes that had been baked to a flint filled to the brim and overflowed into cornfields, grain patches, and pastures. Then there followed teal, shovelers, widgeon, pintails, mallards, and blacks by the hundreds to feed and loaf.

That was in 1936. It was the same in '39 and '40, and even in 1941, when I hitchhiked back from the Seattle port of embarkation for one last shot at Allen's before shipping overseas. But that was the end. The drainers came and the ducks went. Today Allen's has plenty of well-engineered water courses but no waterfowl, plenty of potatoes but no pintail.

Hopefully, however, the saga of Allen's Marsh may have a sequel. Under a wetlands reclamation program, areas like Allen's are being purchased and reflooded by the state. So maybe there'll come another day when we can hunt my V.I.P. again. A dawn wind once more will stir through water-logged sumacs, over phalanxes of willows, across bog-meadows heavy with dew. Then, out of some far recess of the sky will come the susurrant sound of wings, and the ducks will be back at Allen's Marsh.

At least once each duck season I make a sentimental journey to where it all began for me near Allen's Marsh on Rock Lake at Lake Mills. Sometimes I am lucky enough to be the guest of a native in his blind on the marsh, and sometimes I just take potluck walking the railroad grade that separates marsh from lake. In a way it is bad to go back. There are a lot of ghosts around an old hunting spot.

Sometimes I think I see Archie Buchanan walking down the tracks. Archie took me in tow in 1933. With him the duck season began the first of August. It was then that we would pile into his Model A and cruise the back roads, watching for ducks using hidden potholes. It was innocent sport, but the Jefferson County warden wasn't sure. He overhauled us once and searched every inch of the car, looking for contraband game. As a pillar of the town, Archie swore me to secrecy, and I've never violated that trust until now.

Archie introduced me to Allen's Marsh, where you sloshed a mile through the muck and then waited in a copse of dogwoods while long lines of mallards whipsawed overhead. Archie also showed me his special technique of lying prone on a blanket on the Rock Lake beach when the bluebills were working overhead. But Archie is gone now, so the railway embankment is lonely.

Sometimes when I go back I think I also see "Bits" Heimstreet standing up in his blind on the point of the island, the same blind where I was first exposed to duck shooting over decoys. It was so foggy that morning that we took an hour to find our spot, and it was 10:00 before we could see to shoot. When the mist cleared the birds were there--pintails and blacks and baldpate, sitting in the blocks. But we didn't spray them. Big "Bits" made me get up and say, "Get out of here!" Then we started firing as the ducks flushed.

Archie and "Bits" died in their beds, but some of the Rock Lake ghosts didn't. One is somewhere in the Pacific near Wake, one in a stinking Buna swamp, one at St. Lo, and another at Netuno. Their names are inscribed with gold stars on the plaque in the city square, but I can't find them where they would like to be--on Rock Lake marsh.

So it is bad to go back. But it is good, too.

There is the same weatherworn bridge which makes such a natural lookout for spying on the life of the marsh. There is the blue-winged teal that cannonballs by just as did his ancestors. And there is the pair of whistling swans that invariably occupies Korth's Bay. Waterfowl don't change. With them you can recapture youth.

Along the grade you can meet yourself--in the form of a youngster playing hookey from high school, toting a double-barrel as big as his hopes. You talk to him about the red sprays of sumac and the golden spires of tamarack. You show him how to tell a bluebill from a redhead. You point out how a wood duck cranes his neck when he flies, and how a hooded merganser will decoy without caution.

You talk and you wait and you watch together, and the years wash away like the waves. There is banging from Shultz's Bay to the north. Far out over the lake you spot them, low on the water--a gaggle of ringnecks. Will they give you a pass or will they swing off? It is a question as old as your years yet as fresh as your young companion's eyes. They keep coming. As they near the grade they start to climb, but they're in range.

"Now!" you say, just as you once were told, and two guns speak together. The lead bird collapses.

"Who hit him?" you are asked, and you say, "Why you did!"

Rock Lake has spawned a new duck hunter.

"Daddy, will you take me duck hunting with you someday?"

"Why sure, Laurie," I said.

It was easy to say yes, because it was an evening in mid-July and even though I was painting decoys in the basement, the duck season seemed a long, long way off.

But time has a way of passing, even for a duck hunter, and a 10-year-old daughter has a way of remembering just about everything. So it was that Laurie called my bluff in the middle of the season. Cornered like a mouse, I said, "All right, we'll go tomorrow afternoon." (An afternoon is no time to go duck hunting, but you can't drag a youngster down to the blind at dawn.)

No sooner had I made my promise than I was beseiged with invitations to adult excursions. To each I had to give a very reluctant, "Sorry, I have a date." When Laurie and I trudged down to Blank Lake, I was feeling very much a martyr to the cause of fatherhood.

"Today is going to be a total bust," I thought. Little did I know what was in store. First there was the test of wits that only a 10-year-old can subject you to. Try giving intelligent answers to questions like these, sometime:

"Why doesn't a duck boat have seats, daddy? Why is it painted all blotchy? Why don't you paddle straight? Why are decoys called decoys? Why do you put them where there aren't any waves? Why do ducks have to land into the wind?

"How can you tell a duck? How can you tell a mallard from a mudhen? How do you know my great-grandfather wasn't an Indian?

"Why do you call it a seagull when it's flying over a lake? Why am I called Laurie? Why is size 7 shot smaller than size 4 shot? Why is a 12-gauge bigger than a 16-gauge? Why are scaup called bluebills? What is a choke?

"Why are ruddy ducks rare? Why is the blind tilted? Why didn't you build it level? How does a muskrat know which is his house? How long do we have to sit here? Why do you use a duck call when it doesn't sound like a duck to me? Why can't those mallards hear us? If they could hear us, why would they be dumb enough to come over here?

"Why are your feet warmer than mine? Why did we separate the decoys into two bunches? How do the ducks know where you want them to land? Why don't you use a pistol like Marshall Dillon? Why do those basswood seeds look like little propellers? Why are cattails and bullrushes the same thing? Was Moses a duck hunter, too?

"Who are those men in the next blind? What is a spoil-sport? Why doesn't the shell go through the barrel? Where does the shot go when it doesn't hit anything? Why doesn't the lake fill up with lead? Why didn't we bring more sandwiches? How does a thermos bottle work?

"Why, what, how, how, what, why..."

Feeling like a guy testifying before a Congressional committee, I would never have seen those canvasbacks if they had not ripped past with a jet-plane roar. They were riding a 30-mile-an-hour-wind, but they heard my call.

"Get down," I told my young partner, and she hunched up like a veteran.

At the far end of the lake the cautious cans climbed to 500 feet, circled for one suspended moment, and then headed back. Far out in front of our blocks they started to sideslip down like satellites, cupped wings whistling, white breasts gleaming, racy heads looking us over.

"Take a good look, Laurie," I whispered. "Not everybody has a chance to see wild canvasbacks at close range."

With a final rush they were on us, and we stood up together. The bull can in the lead looked as big as a Piper Cub. I got off only one shot and never came close.

"Golly, Dad," Laurie said, "that was really something, wasn't it?"

"Yes," I winced, "but I missed."

"That's all right. He'll be something to come back to."

That was all there was to the day but that was enough: a trophy experience with a trophy companion. It was, indeed, really something.

Cabins and Conservation

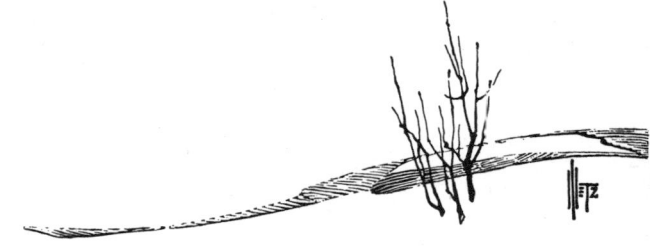

There is a quiet revolution taking place on the landscape, characterized by more and more city folk fleeing to the Wisconsin countryside to stake out little private preserves.

Iowa County is typical of what is happening. When I bought my Town of Arena woodlot and put up a cabin some 20 years ago, I was one of only a handful of city slickers in the area. Now I am surrounded by expatriots. Further to the west, in the Twin Parks Watershed between Governor Dodge and Tower Hill parks, the density of urbanites is even heavier. Other clusters of "second homes" are growing near Blue Mounds, Avoca, and Bear Valley. What is going on in Iowa County is being duplicated in almost every county within a hundred miles of metropolitan Wisconsin. The Montello lakes, the Baraboo hills, the McCann valley, the New Glarus glades, Waukesha county, and other areas are feeling the effects of the silent sprawl of the city.

The results are mixed. More and more "No Trespassing" signs are taking lands out of the domain of hunters and fishers. Land prices have skyrocketed; rural real-estate salesmen never had it so good. For example, an Iowa County forty that wouldn't have brought $100 an acre a decade ago sold for $1000 an acre last week. Carelessly planned developments have turned trout streams into slums. Lonesome haunts of ducks now echo to the roar of motors. Raw, red roads now slash through hillsides once reserved for partridge. Deer try to thread their way through cottage yards where once there were sloughs. Carpets of shooting stars and violet are now ordinary lawns.

On the other hand, some of those adults and youngsters who now have a place where they can "get away from it all" are discovering a new kinship with the out-of-doors, a new sense of stewardship, and a new way to work up a sweat. Eroded croplands are being converted to grass. Evergreen plantations are restoring a touch of green to sand barrens. Stream banks are being shored up, ponds created, and springs made to bubble again. Disheveled farm buildings sport coats of paint. Birds and sunsets are being watched by people who never saw them before. Pump handles are being worked by business executives, and floors swept with a broom by society matrons.

It is all a part of our new affluence. Where once we dreamed of two cars for every garage, now we must have two garages for every car. It is quite possible that the person we elect as President in 1996 will have been born in a log cabin--a prefabricated cabin, that is. Nobody can predict the net result of the back-to-the-land boom. It may contribute to a dull, gray homogenization of life, with the line between city living and a country retreat so thin as to be meaningless. Hopefully, it can be the makings of a humankind-land ethic, under which significant numbers of Americans practice a decent respect for our natural heritage.

President Johnson once said we should forget about the good old days and count our blessings. While this is two cliches in one sentence, he had a point. One blessing certainly worth counting is a cabin in the country. It means you no longer have to choose between city and country life. You can have both on a modest scale. What was available only to the landed gentry at the turn of the century is now within the grasp of the American middle class. Fifty miles or less from many of our main population centers, much land is empty, beautiful, and for sale. As a matter of fact, the more rural people leave for the cities, the more places they leave behind for city folk who have the money to fix them up.

A cabin in the country is the key to a number of blessings. People built cities in the first place for safety. They wanted to get away from the danger of remote places. Now the lonely countryside is safer in some ways than the cities. People went to the cities also for conveniences and services. Now, at least in rural Wisconsin, it is far easier to get somebody to fix your well pump than it is to get a plumber in an emergency in town. Call a plumber on the party line, state your problem, and the plumber comes, visits, tells you about local troubles--and does the job. Above all, a cabin in the country represents privacy and beauty--the two most precious things parents can lend to their children in this plastic age.

"A nation," John Burroughs observed, "always begins to rot first in its great cities, is indeed perhaps always rotting there, and is saved only by the antiseptic virtues of fresh supplies of country blood." America may have indeed reached this point in its story. Philosophically we need the country. Commercially, country land--ten acres or so, a cabin, and a spring that is both bold and true--is the best buy around. Capital, cattle, cheap fertilizer, barbed wire, and flagstone patios have transformed open spaces. But there are still some hillsides, coves, and valleys ready to serve as private parks. They are, as Lyndon Johnson said, one of the blessings worth counting.

To those of us blessed with cabins in the woods, Spring is the season of the year for the performing of that delightful ceremony known as Opening Up the Shack. We have paid visits to the cabin throughout the winter, of course. An oak grove in January has a certain austere beauty, but it is comparatively barren of life. Come May, however, and a woodland welcoming committee is on hand.

Not all of its members are friendly. One year, when we opened up the cabin, we found a freshet gushing through the living room. It was our own fault, actually. We had failed to provide for proper drainage. Another year our spring was bone dry, the result of 22 months of below-normal precipitation in Iowa County. The pond across the road was half its normal circumference. We had to tote our water from another spring down the pike.

Our woodbox may be inhabited by a family of mice. They scurry in all directions, squeaking complaints like the denizens of any area in the path of an urban renewal development. The icebox interior is likely covered with orange "gunk"--the result of a pop bottle that cracked when the temperature hit 13 below. The eavestrough is plugged where a squirrel piled his discarded hickory-nut husks.

But most members of our woodland welcoming committee are friendly. There are the young pines on our perched meadow sporting a spanking green against the dun grasses. There are the oaks themselves, living up to their red names by displaying the tiny, wrinkled, dark-pink beginnings of leaves. At their feet are violets, hepaticas, wood anemones, and May apples in profusion.

The chairman of the welcoming committee is a ruffed grouse. For six years in a row, he has set up his headquarters on an oak log 30 yards back in the brush from our cabin doorstep. Whether it is the same grouse or not, I don't know for sure. The odds are against it, grouse life being pretty hazardous. On the other hand, there are few places safer than a woodlot in which I am the only shooter. I sneaked up on my neighbor one morning as he was performing his immemorial ritual--strutting and drumming to announce that this was his territory and his alone. With a bongo-beating of wings he made the ancient hills echo a signal as old as time.

Few bird and animal instincts are as innate and as prevalent as the territorial instinct. In species after species, an individual or a troop stake out a piece of real estate and call it their own. Interestingly enough, it was not a scientist who helped define the concept of "territory" in birds. It was an Ohio housewife, watching song sparrows through her kitchen window.

Nature, by instilling in the bird or animal a demand for exclusive living space, insures two consequences: first, that at least a minimum number of individuals in any population will be able to breed in relative security; and second, that the surplus will be cast to the literal and figurative wolves who will trim the population to a size the habitat can support.

Those of us who go out into the country to buy a lakeshore lot or a back forty may think we have some very advanced economic and cultural motives for so doing. In reality we are simply reacting to the territorial instinct that our ape ancestors acquired on the African veldt. So my grouse neighbor and I are really very much alike. He will defend his territory against any partridge invasion. I put up big No Trespassing signs. He booms the story of his fine territory to all passing females. I put up a cottage as a status symbol.

It will be interesting to see which territory lasts the longest, mine or my grouse friend's. The odds favor the grouse. As Thoreau put it, the grouse is sure to thrive, like a true native of the soil, whatever revolutions occur. The grouse has not discovered bombs or biotics with which to defend his sovereignty; in fact, his lease on life as an individual is tenuous. But as a species the grouse is marvelously adapted to the world as he finds it. The same may not be true for us humans.

We are, after all, a comparatively minor and recent species. Our lease in the world is precarious. There is no impossibility, in the coming of time, when a planet loaded with woodlots and grouse may spin forward upon its interstellar journey without a person aboard.

What I was sold when I purchased my 60 acres of Iowa County, Wisconsin, was a "useless" panhandle of woodland, crags, and perched prairie, unattended for a hundred years, lying between a section line and a town road, too hilly to have been grubbed out and cropped, too long and narrow to have been fenced and pastured. What I actually bought was a priceless historical library, a reserved seat in the theater of plant and human succession.

At one end of my outdoor library shelf is a magnificent veteran of the prairie wars of 200 years ago--a big bur oak, its wide-spreading limbs testifying that it has stood there since the pre-pioneer days when southern Wisconsin was characterized by orchardlike groves of oaks lacing a magnificent stretch of grassland.

Jonathan Carver has left us a vivid word-picture of the virgin Wisconsin prairie. In October of 1783 he ascended Blue Mound where he gained "an extensive view of the country." "For many miles nothing was to be seen," he wrote, "than lesser mountains, which appeared at a distance like haycocks, they being free from trees. Only a few groves of oaks covered some of the valleys."

How did occasional bur oaks survive the repeated onslaughts of prairie grasses and prairie fires? Their thick crust of corky bark which covers the whole tree, even to the smallest twigs. This natural insulation was their armor. It won for them a place in the southern Wisconsin savannah.

With the coming of settlers and the plows that broke up the plains, the prairies were robbed of their immemorial ally, fire; and seedling black and red oaks forthwith romped over the grasslands to establish the thick woodlots characteristic of southern Wisconsin today. But my bur oak still stands, its open arms defying encroachment, a living monument to what John Muir called "Wisconsin's sunny oak openings."

At the other end of my outdoor library is another remnant of yesterday--a rare copy of the prairie itself. Perched on a steep side hill, unreachable by scythe or mower or cow, renewed occasionally by fires set to burn adjoining brush, this unique museum of natural history bursts forth each spring and summer with a bewildering array of antiques--like bluestem, tall stalks of compass plant, and clumps of cutleaf silphium spangled with saucer-sized yellow blooms resembling sunflowers--samples of the thousands of acres of lush grasses that once tickled the bellies of the buffalo.

For these valuable "volumes" in my Iowa County library I can thank the fact that my woodlot lies in a backwash of progress. The soil is thin. My neighbors are the despair of the county agricultural agent. Their roads are poor. Their fencerows are not clean. Their lowlands are not drained. Their woodlots are only indifferently grazed. As between going fishing and going forward, they are prone to prefer fishing. They are, hence, ideal "curators" of valuable flora.

I am not as smart as they. On the advice of the county forester, to whom any open space is fair game, I began to plant evergreens on my perched prairie. On the advice of a university ecologist, I am now sawing down our pines before they shade out my grasses. Almost anybody, he points out, can grow Christmas trees. It is given to me to preserve a prairie.

Had I been blessed with a lot of money, I would doubtless have bought a fancy farm in the mistaken idea that I would thereby get back to nature with a flourish. As it was, I had only enough collateral for a bastard piece of rural real estate--and wound up with a minor version of the Marshall Field Museum.

A favorite country neighbor of ours is that very friendly and exceedingly smart cock partridge. By accident we built our hillside shack within 35 yards of his courting log. This did not harass our grouse friend one bit. He drummed for us all summer, sometimes during the day and once in the middle of a night shower. One afternoon I managed to crawl to a point where I could watch him strutting. He performed until he sensed my presence and then he walked away as if to say I was violating the rules of woodlot etiquette. Come the hunting season and our grouse drummed no more. Nor could I flush him anywhere in the neighborhood. We were sure he had run afoul of somebody ignoring our No Hunting signs. But with the shooting at an end, Pete Partridge showed up again on his favorite log, as noisy and as cocky as he was in June. A neighbor such as this, who knows when to be chummy and when to be discreet, is a precious neighbor indeed.

Two of our woodlot neighbors are even more retiring: the possum who rustles ponderously through the leaves at night, and the coon who leaves only his baby-finger tracks to disclose his whereabouts. Most discreet of all are the deer who drift through nearby thickets like rust-colored clouds.

Of a more gregarious nature are the ubiquitous chickadees and jays who vie with gray squirrels for our attention--and food. They are the sort of neighbors who never hurt your feelings.

We do have some wildlife neighbors of questionable character-- little freshwater shrimp that abound in our spring. With them we have made a truce. They are free to thrive outside just so they don't infiltrate our water bucket.

Important as are your brute neighbors in picking a place in the country, they are not so crucial as are the human natives. If you are unfortunate, you will find a section of country inhabited largely by fellow escapees from the city, and this can be frustrating. If, on the other hand, you are as lucky as we have been, you will find yourself in contact with people who are pleasant and considerate without benefit of a phony course in psychology.

To the west of us are the Whites, who have farmed the rugged hills of Iowa County for three generations. They have given us the run of their 600 acres, and have even built a small lake a stone's throw from our shack. What's more, they invited us into their deer-hunting league, which is a sign of friendship above and beyond the call of duty. To the east of us are Ernie and Albert Peterson, experts in all manner of woods lore, who pitched in and helped us put on our roof.

These and other new-found farmer friends have two priceless attributes. They know when to visit, and they know when to leave. Which is more than you can say for a lot of denizens in suburbia.

One of my farmer neighbors out in Iowa County held an auction the other day. He is going out of business. So another farm dies, a farm that has been in the same family for four generations. In my township there have been a dozen such demises in the past few years, and there will be more. In Wisconsin, over 2,100 farmers quit last year. The figure will be higher this year. What we are witnessing is a quiet revolution in land use.

There are a number of reasons why my neighbor decided to quit. In the first place, Town of Arena is marginal farmland. The soil is second-rate, the hills steep, the bottomlands narrow. You work more than average to produce less than average. In the second place, the costs of farming have risen astronomically in comparison to milk checks. Hired hands are simply not available at all, and the machinery you have to substitute is extremely expensive. More to the point, the style of farming that would work in Town of Arena is not acceptable to today's generation. You can't practice grandfather's subsistence farming any more. A world given to status symbols and agricultural bulletins will not let you do your own butchering or churn you own butter. You must pose as a big operator or nothing at all. But the straw that is tipping the scale in more and more cases in Iowa County is the phenomenon of the city dweller out roaming the back roads looking for recreational property. The kind of money he is offering for beat-up real estate is very hard for a native to resist.

So short a time ago as 1960, when I helped pioneer the trek to the hills of southern Wisconsin, you could pick up a woodlot for less than $20 an acre. Now a hillside with a rock outcrop and picturesque birches will go for more than $1000 an acre. As a matter of fact, wooded back forties are bringing more than cropland. The poorer the farm from a strictly agricultural point of view, the higher the price today.

What all this means to the economy is now only dimly seen. The farmer who calls it quits may find an adequate job in town, or not. The city dweller who buys the land may husband its resources, or not. The farmer who goes to the city to build a new life may wind up in the company of fellow ex-farmers drawing unemployment checks. The city dweller who goes to the country to get away from it all may wind up suddenly in a variation of suburbia.

One thing is sure. Our instrumentalities of government are catching up with this new trend only very slowly. Iowa County, for example, still does not have a zoning ordinance worthy of the name. But industry is catching on. You can now order a cabin from a catalog and buy a wood range at the corner hardware.

My great-grandfather Jones came to Wisconsin in the 1840s and took out what they called a patent on a farmstead in Wyoming Valley along what is now Highway 23 between Spring Green and Dodgeville in Iowa County. It was not on the main routes of trade and it was marginal farmland, so, with all of Wisconsin to choose from, you might wonder why Great-Grandfather Jones picked Wyoming Valley. One reason was because he was poor, and Wyoming Valley land was cheap. Another was because he was poor, and Wyoming Valley land was cheap. Another was because he was something of a plunger, and there was talk about rich veins of lead underlying all of Iowa County. And a third reason was because he was escaping from the warrens of New Jersey, and there weren't many lights in Wyoming Valley. (In all of these characteristics, Great-Grandfather Jones was probably pretty typical of many of his fellow Wisconsin pioneers. After all, our ancestors weren't generally the pillars of eastern society. They were more apt to be the ne're-do-wells, the drifters, the dissenters.)

Great-Grandfather Jones didn't stay in Wyoming Valley very long. He planted a few crops and a few sons, and then the wanderlust caught up with him once more. He headed west in search of open space and gold, never to be heard from again. To his descendents, Great-Grandfather Jones didn't leave much of anything in the way of material wealth, but some of us did inherit his aversion to crowds, which is one reason why, I guess, I frequently retreat from Madison to our woodlot cabin not far from the original Jones homestead in Iowa County.

My trouble is there are a lot of Jones boys around today, and they're all retreating to Iowa County. The members of the Madison Press Club got a preview the other night of what is in store for Wyoming Valley, thanks to a mammoth "recreation development." Already constructed are a restaurant, the only one ever designed by Frank Lloyd Wright, an 18-hole championship golf course designed by Robert Trent Jones, ski trails, ski lifts, and a ski lodge. To be added to the 4,000-acre multi-million-dollar sports, resort, and residential development are a marina, motels, a 300-room convention hotel, riding stables, tennis courts, permanent residences, weekend cabins, a shopping center, and even light industry. In the words of the principal entrepreneur, the project "will bring to reality many of Frank Lloyd Wright's concepts of a 'Broadacre City,' a decentralized community that will preserve and enhance the natural beauty of the Taliesin area." To fill up this new city, there will be nine million people within 150 miles of Wyoming Valley by 1980.

When things got too crowded in Wyoming Valley for my Great-Grandfather Jones a 100 years ago or so, he picked up and went to California. Where do I go today?

My solution, if you can call it that, is to stay put and husband my tiny bit of what's left of wild Wisconsin territory. You can say the adventuresome Jones blood has peetered out, or that I've learned to make do with things as they are. Whatever, with luck the lights won't intrude on J. Jones Road for awhile yet, maybe not even during the lifetime of my grandson, Joseph Jones Krantz. At least I can bequeath him this Thoreau dictum:

"If you want inner peace, find it in solitude, not speed; and if you want to find yourself, look to the land from which you came and to which you go."

In terms of one's relationship to our government and our fellow citizens, the city dweller who also owns some rural property lives in two worlds. The city is the world of the big stick; the country is the world of the big carrot.

For instance, let's say I'm tired of shoveling snow from my city driveway, so I propose to move my garage forward flush with the street. In order to proceed, I have to get a city building permit, but I can't, because the law says I must comply with a 30-foot setback for all structures in a residential district. I can add a side porch, but only if it does not extend too close to my lot line. I can plant a tree, provided it isn't a cottonwood. I can put up an eaves trough, but only if the discharge doesn't encroach unnaturally on my neighbor. If for sentimental reasons I wanted to erect an outdoor bathroom, the city health officer would be on my trail. If I tore down my house and put up an apartment, I'd be in real trouble with the zoning authorities. Or let's say I hunger for fresh eggs, and install a couple of ambitious hens in a backyard pen. The police come and confiscate the chickens, in compliance with a city ordinance. I am allowed to keep a dog, but only if he lives in a pen and never barks.

I'm not complaining, you understand. I appreciate that all such laws are designed to protect the integrity of urban areas; that is, to preserve the equity of the community in what is otherwise thought of as private property. The net effect, of course, is to make a city person's home something less than a castle.

Now take the situation with our 60 acres in the Town of Arena. Here I am lord of the manor. I can chop down trees at will, graze meadows to a nub, plug up springs, contaminate streams, erect shacks any place, bulldoze ditches, dynamite cliffs, and otherwise play havoc with the landscape. To try to keep me reasonably civic-minded, the federal government dangles various payments in front of my nose in exchange for my engaging in "conservation" practices; but there are virtually no local laws to assure that I really maintain a decent respect for the quality of the environment.

Now I am complaining. It is high time that we rural landholders cease to be beyond the reach of zoning ordinances. We are custodians of irreplaceable natural resources in which the public at large has a heavy stake. I should have no more right to wreck my woodlot willy-nilly than I have a right to tear up the sidewalk in front of my house.

Some people picture countrypersons as crybabies who get unnecessarily exorcised when sportspersons go tramping through their fields in quest of public game. Others say too many hunters are oafs who shoot down No Trespassing signs and pillage crops.

The argument really started about the year 1002, I believe. Up to that time in England, following the ancient Roman custom, all game was considered "common" property. Then King Canute the Dane got the idea it would be nice to have a private game preserve. So he fixed himself up with a "chartered forest" where only he could hunt.

William the Conqueror and his successors "did daily increase these oppressions by making more and more forests in the lands of their subjects, to their great impoverishment," until the major part

of the kingdom was converted to one big royal preserve. This and
similar abuses led to the battle of Runnymede in 1215, after which
the victorious barons exacted from King John the famous Magna Carta,
including among other things a decree that the king held all wild
game merely in trust for the people.
    For awhile then, in England, everybody could hunt and fish
wherever they pleased. But this custom conflicted with another
Magna Carta principle--the sanctity of private property. So in 1500
Henry VII forebade the taking of pheasants and partridges on other
people's land without the permission of the owner. James I in 1600
extended this edict to all shooting on all land.
    The colonists who settled in America carried with them these
two English Common Law concepts, that "while the state has an ownership
of the wild game within its borders, no other person has a right to
go upon private property to take game." Thus was the stage set for
the battle of the signs.
    I guess I occupy a sort of middle ground in this debate because,
while I am primarily a city guy I am also the proud possessor of 60
acres of beat-up woodland where I raise partridge. As a city guy I
like to hunt on other people's property, but as a "farmer" I like to
post my own land. In fact, I have the biggest, gaudiest signs in
Iowa County, Wisconsin.
    The signs don't do much good. Some city slickers tramp my
acres whenever they feel like it, set up tents, start fires, chop
away at birch trees, knock down fences, shoot birds, and rip ruts in
driveways. So I sympathize very much with my farmer friends who are

revolted by ill-mannered intruders. On the other hand, some sportspersons stop and ask me for permission to hunt, and are careful not to leave gates open or stampede the cows. So I sympathize, too, with the hunters who are understanding.

The solution, I think, is really a very simple one. If it is fair for city folks to tramp over private farmland, it must be equally fair for farm folks to come into town, hold picnics on private yards, run their cows on the courthouse lawn, and plow up waste areas like a football stadium.

There would have to be a prescribed season for all this, of course. You could have a two-day any-barbecue season on city lawns, a 30-day season for cattle-grazing in between legislative sessions, and a 110-day season for growing corn. Farmers would be required to wear red clothes, of course, and purchase licenses.

All this would strike me as a very fair exchange. For example, Farmer Jones would raise a couple of bushels of barley on Sportsman Smith's front terrace. In turn Sportsman Smith could harvest a couple of grouse and pine trees from the Jones acres. Naturally we would need a large new state department to administer this Fair Exchange Program (FEP), and that would go a long way to solving the unemployment problem.

If we can't work out a democratic compromise on this whole problem, we'll just have to go back to Runnymede.

Back a hundred years ago or so, when I was a boy, every self-respecting farm and even every small-town household kept chickens; and February was the time of the year when we culled the flock. On an appointed Saturday morning the whole family would help single out the surplus roosters and the over-the-hill hens for a mass canning operation.

There is nothing like the crude execution of a Rhode Island Red to bring a small boy face to face with the thin, mysterious line that separates life from death. One moment the fowl is resting quietly on the chopping block. Then the axe descends, and the headless body takes off over the yard in one last paroxysm, a fitful series of gyrations as if in frantic search for what is forever lost, finally to lie utterly still in a patch of red snow.

"Why does it do that?" I can remember asking. My father would say, "It's the death rattle." And I would wonder at the phenomenon of a dramatic flash of activity that signals not a beginning but an end.

There are human institutions, I have since discovered, that recapitulate in their life cycle the decapitation of a chicken. We are witnessing such developments in many Wisconsin counties. My county board, for example, is struggling bravely to enter an urbanized twentieth century. At the moment the old forces of agrarianism would seem to have the upper hand, blocking even any mild attempts at integrated land use planning. Some might think what is at hand is a viable populist revolt against the city, but what we are actually seeing is the death rattle of an an era. The spokesmen for township and village enclaves are having a last say, but it will be to no avail. Their world is as dead and gone as the backyard chickenhouse.

What is at stake, of course, is a practical means of achieving environmental quality conservation, redevelopment, and maintenance in America. The problems of water pollution, air pollution, urban sprawl, traffic snarl, disappearing fields and forests, waning wildlife, increasing litter, noise, and blight do not confine themselves to township, village, and city lines. They can't be tackled by geographic bits and pieces, nor can they be tackled one by one. They fit together in a matrix of people and practices that will respond only to comprehensive county and regional planning.

Planning is sort of a dirty word in the same quarters; it is said to smack of regimentation. In other quarters planning is looked upon as a panacea--some kind of snake oil good for all the social ills of man and beast. The truth is somewhere in between. Planning is no better than the people who do it and the codes that enforce it; planning does involve a loss of autonomy on the part of individuals. But the alternative is even worse--a headless slide into increasing contamination of the countryside and decreasing physical and cultural beauty.

Wisconsin country lies today between two worlds, the one thrashing in its death throes, the other struggling to be born. What we probably need is a political Bart Starr to call some signals.

There are now a little over two million acres of Wisconsin county forests, more acres than in the state and national forests combined in Wisconsin. The lands are located in 27 northern and central counties. Held primarily for the production of timber, these forests have also been open to the public for hunting, fishing, camping, and other recreational use.

The land involved actually belongs to every Wisconsin citizen. The term "county forest" is somewhat of a misnomer. Title to a county forest area may technically be held by a county, but state taxpayer investment is far heavier. For example, each year the state general fund pays out to the counties 10 cents per each acre of county forest, and the Natural Resources Department's forestry fund pays out another 10 cents per acre. In addition, the Department invests in county-forest technical assistance and in county-forest protection from fire, insects, and diseases.

Where does this money come from? From you and me. So a more correct name would be "taxpayer forests."

The story back of these forests is a dramatic case of the general public coming to the rescue of distressed areas. Back in the very early days of the Depression, after Wisconsin's forest lands had been cleaned out by loggers, hundreds of thousands of acres of cutover were reverting to the counties as tax-deliquent property. Thanks to enlightened guidance from university economists and extension agents and state foresters, the state said, in effect, to these counties:

"We'll bail you out if you'll re-forest these areas, and you can repay us when you have a harvestable crop of timber."

During a recent biennium, the gross value of timber sold from the county forests of Wisconsin was over a million dollars. Thousands of families now depend upon employment in county forests for their livelihood. With sharply increasing urban populations, the recreational escape-valve values of the county forests are becoming even more important.

One of the greatest assets owned by the people of Wisconsin today is the land nobody wanted yesterday--the 2.5 million acres of state and county forests. Once these areas were cutover, burned-over timberlands and abandoned farms, as we have seen, and many of them reverted to the government for nonpayment of taxes over a period of the last half-century. Now this vast public holding is an increasingly important source of raw material for industries, as well as a public playground which is being viewed with growing interest by the one-quarter of the nation's population which lives within a day's drive of Wisconsin.

With population pressures, hunting pressures, fishing and boating pressures; needs for pulpwood, lumber, and other wood products, and more deer food; more hunting clubs and "No Trespassing" signs; more requests for research areas, natural areas, wilderness areas, hiking trails, horseback trails, highways, power lines; winter sports, dump grounds, grazing, gravel, sand leases, easements; requests for land exchanges, cottage sites, pipe lines, artillery ranges, air bases, even warbler preserves; and the perennial cry to "get the land back on the tax roll"--with all these pressures and needs and more to come, the Wisconsin state and county forest picture has changed from the land nobody wanted to the land everybody wants.

A forest isn't just a bunch of trees. It is a mixture of trees of many species, sizes, and ages; of large and small openings; of edge, bogs, and marshes; of grasses, wild flowers, and shrubs; of lakes, streams, and watersheds; of soil and rocks; of birds and mammals; of resort development and wilderness. It is a productive area in terms of crops of timber and some wildlife, and even of the extraction of minerals, and it is a place for recreation in many forms: hunting, fishing, camping, bathing, hiking, canoeing, horseback riding, sight-seeing, berry picking, skiing, loafing. It is also a place for nature study and biological research.

To the extent that we recognize these parts and uses of our forests, and manage for them in a balanced program which brings out the fullest economic and social benefits without destroying the resource--to this extent we are practicing total wise use. Multiple use doesn't mean every use on every acre, of course. While some uses can exist on the same general area at the same time, others require exclusive zones. We don't want a gravel pit in a campground, for example, a plantation on a swimming beach, a dump in a deer yard, or a timber harvest in a nature preserve.

The land everybody now wants will have to meet the needs of two people in the future where it is now providing for one. This means state and county forest management programs in Wisconsin must be intensified considerably. It will take public understanding, public zoning practices, and public money.

One of the biggest outdoor news stories of our day is the efforts of the state of Wisconsin to buy or lease public rights to land. Faced with mounting populations and shrinking living room, we are desperately trying to reserve for ourselves and our descendants a bit of marsh here, a lakeshore there, a spot of streambank in the next valley, or a woodlot over the hill.

With such activity making current headlines, it is interesting if not instructive to recall that some 150 years ago the situation was just the reverse. In 1833 the government was trying just as hard to sell and give away land as it is now trying to get it back. Picture, if you will, the Wisconsin of 1833--36,000,000 acres of public domain, not yet a territory in its own right, miles of prairie and swamp and oak opening and pine forest and leaded hills dotted with only a few feeble settlements and farms, Black Hawk and his Indians only recently hounded from the river valleys, the Illinois boundary just surveyed.

To open up "Ouisconsin" to settlement and development, not to conserve it, was understandably the public policy of the time. It was not to be until the turn of the century that the first halting steps would be taken to ear-mark public preserves. Wisconsin's first federal land office opened at seven-year-old Mineral Point in 1834, and enjoyed literally a "land-office business." There came the squatters to claim their quarter sections at $1.25 an acre or less. There came the loan sharks offering five-year mortgages at 28 percent. There came Moses Strong with $50,000 of Daniel Webster's money to speculate.

Despite what today we would call a multi-media advertising campaign, the land didn't move fast enough to suit the government. The vast public domain was burning a hole in the pocket of Congress. Veterans were given plots. Some 20 percent of the state's acreage was turned over to railroads like the Beaver Dam, Fox Lake, and Northern. The Homestead Act awarded free land to sod-breakers and stump-burners. The Morrill Act awarded free land to colleges of agriculture. Ezra Cornell located 385,000 acres around Eau Claire for the state of New York.

Some pioneers didn't even wait for the land to be sold or given away. Farmers cut fence posts and hop poles in government woodlots. The Washburns, Thorps, Sawyers, Stephensons, and other lumber barons invaded the Wisconsin pineries, cut, and ran. By 1893, it was almost all over. Wisconsin Professor Frederick Jackson Turner, analyzing census data, could no longer find a frontier. To be sure, remote tracts still remained on the public books, but in southern Wisconsin the government was out of the land business.

Eighty-five years later we are trying to buy back little smidgens of what was once one vast public park.

As opportunities for old-time outdoor recreation decline, outdoor fans introduce substitutes. Sometimes we substitute targets, sometimes sports themselves.

One of the first substitute targets to be introduced was the brown trout. Even before the turn of the century, it became clear that our native brookie was no match for what was happening to our streams. All sorts of human-made intrusions caused gravel spawning beds to disappear and water temperatures to rise. So early fish managers introduced the brown trout from Germany and Scotland. Not being so fussy about his habitat, the brown trout has thrived. Today we seldom even think of him as an immigrant, so Americanized is he. Another very successful second-stringer is the ringneck pheasant. When native prairie chicken and quail populations virtually disappeared, we stocked the ringneck. He filled what the scientists call an ecological niche. Today the pheasant is a principal upland game bird, and his hunters are legion.

With the increasing disappearance of rural open spaces in which to roam, we are presently seeing on a mass scale the substitution of the sport of golf for old-time outdoor diversions. Courses are being developed on the outskirts of our cities for the growing numbers of yesterday's anglers who today are wielding nine-irons instead of fly rods. For the veteran outdoorsperson, golf has certain limitations, to be sure. The landscape is well manicured, not wild. You have no bird or fish to blame if you do not score well, only you yourself. You habitually play with a foursome, so you cannot strike out alone and return with a tall story. But golf at least gets you outdoors easily and regularly, and it allows you to identify yourself with those new folk heroes of America, Jack Nicklaus and Arnold Palmer.

What is more, golf has some soul-satisfying rewards of its own. It is deceptively simple and endlessly complicated. It requires complete concentration and total relaxation. Especially in the spring of the year, when the first warm sun presses down on your shoulders, when the grass has just been mowed for the first time and sits there damp and green, with its fresh-cut newly fertilized smell filling the air, when the sky is a deep blue roof punctuated only by an occasional puff of cotton, a golf course is as intoxicating a place as a stretch of trout water. What the hunter finds in the flight of a mallard the golfer finds in the flight of a good drive-- the white ball sailing up and into that blue sky, growing smaller and smaller, almost taking off in orbit, then suddenly reaching its apex, curving, falling, describing the perfect parabola of a good hit, and finally dropping to the turf to roll some more.

Unreconstructed outdoorspersons still look down on golfing as a poor substitute for less formal, more rugged outdoor receation. But you can say this at least for golfers--they pretty much pay their own way. Maybe when bird-watchers and bass fishers start paying a dollar or so for every round of their sports, we'll begin to make a dent in the acquisition of adequate open space for them to enjoy.

Those of us with cabins in the woods or cottages by the shore are often asked, "How often do you get out there?" As if you measure outdoor recreation with a speedometer.

We can either say, "Not very often," or "All the time," and both answers would be true.

A country retreat is an escape hatch from neon lights and

parking meters, a previously prepared position to which one may withdraw from the pressures of office and yard, an innoculation for urbanitis, a shelter from subdivision fallout.

And the interesting thing is, you don't actually have to go there to get the effect. Just knowing your cabin exists, remote and still, like a private Shangri-La, is freqently all the fortification you need.

I remember the other day, for example, I was immersed in one of those countless committee meetings that are supposedly the hallmark of the democratic process. My colleagues were droning on and on, the chairman was exercising no leadership, and I had an almost uncontrollable urge to walk out.

I didn't have to. I just made a mental trip to the country. The buzz of the conversation became the soft bubbling of my spring, and the occasionally strident participant became a red-headed woodpecker hammering away at my bur oak.

Another question frequently put to us countrypersons is, "What do you do out there?" As if you measure outdoor recreation with a pressure gauge.

We can either say, "Not much," or "A lot," and again both answers would be right.

We countrypersons relax. We resist the temptation forever to be tinkering. Instead, we submerge ourselves and our city nerves in the leisurely life of field and stream.

Out at my Iowa County cabin, for example, I am very busy preserving a native woodlot. The secret to preserving a woodlot, fortunately, is to do practically nothing. You plant nothing. You cut nothing. You do not even pick flowers, because when you disturb a flower you disturb a star. About all you do is keep the cows and fires out.

In the meantime you sit in the sun in the Spring, or lie in a hammock in the Summer, or cruise the golden hills in Fall, accomplishing a good deal by doing very little.

Out at our Jefferson County cottage, for another example, I was also very busy in a way. I sat in a flat-bottom rowboat about 30 yards off shore. I listened to the lap-lap of the waves, smelled the evanescent fragrance of water lilies, watched a foraging gull, and occasionally, only occasionally, pulled up my line to see if a bluegill had stolen my worm.

Meanwhile my mind was on a voyage of discovery--to the sheep pastures back of Mt. McKinley, to a seaside resort at Anzio, to Nigeria, Thule, Cairo, Phoenix, and Butte.

This is the meaning of outdoor recreation--Wisconsin-country style.

The person who most made Wisconsin cabins and conservation synonomous was Aldo Leopold.

Thirty years ago, in 1949, a year after Aldo Leopold's death, there appeared his little book titled <u>A Sand County Almanac and Sketches Here and There</u>, much of its setting the Wisconsin outdoors.

A number of publishers had rejected the almanac concept; Oxford

University Press decided to give it a try. The first printing made no "best seller" lists. The book was ahead of its time. We now know, however, that manifold paperback <u>Sand County Almanacs</u> have become the bibles of the environmental movement of the seventies. and that the author is now recognized worldwide as the leading exponent of what he called "a land ethic." Probably no Wisconsinite today is so widely known and so identified with Wisconsin as is Aldo Leopold, unless it would be "Old Bob" La Follette.

Unquestionably Leopold was a scholar and expert practitioner of forestry, game management, and ecology, but it is as an exceptionally sensitive, subtle, courageous writer on which his most universal and enduring fame rests.

What is not widely known is that <u>Sand County Almanac</u> was no one-shot proposition. It was the culmination of over 30 years of prolific, penetrating writing. The Leopold by-line had appeared over 300 times in scores of journals and magazines, untold times on mimeographed reports and statements, and on the cover of a distinguished text on <u>Game Management</u>.

Indeed, much of <u>Sand County Almanac</u> is literally a refinement of lines, paragraphs, and even whole essays that had appeared in print between 1925 and 1947. For example, the seminal chapter in <u>Sand County</u>, "The Conservation Ethic," actually traces back to a remarkably precient article contained in <u>The Journal of Forestry</u> so early as 1933, the same journal that had carried Leopold's first published plea for wilderness perserves in 1921.

According to files in the University of Wisconsin Archives, the first Leopold article to break into print was called "Game Conservation: A Warning, Also an Opportunity," in a 1916 issue of the state magazine <u>Arizona</u>, Leopold being a young U.S. Forest Ranger in the Southwest at the time. The title was prophetic; he would be promoting the cause of wildlife conservation all his life. Before Leopold came to Madison as Associate Director of the USDA Forest Products Laboratory in 1925, the Leopold pen had produced over 50 other articles on such diverse topics as "the behavior of pintail ducks in a hailstorm" and "pioneers and gullies." Many other writings had appeared in <u>The Pine Cone</u>, the newsletter he created for the New Mexico Game Protective Association.

Once in Wisconsin, from 1925 to 1948 Aldo Leopold was to draw much of his raw materials from intimate tramps on his sand county acres near Baraboo, from his deep-digging researches as a pioneer professor of wildlife management at the University, and from his quixotic adventures in the state conservation bureaucracy, seasoned with personal excursions continent-wide and even overseas. Samuel Taylor Coleridge once said the mark of genuis in a writer is the choice of a remote subject. If that is so, Leopold was the exception that proves the rule. He never wrote about anything he didn't know first-hand. Like Henry Thoreau, he made his country cabin take on cosmic significance.

His death did not silence the Aldo Leopold pen. Collected and edited sympathetically by his oldest son, Luna, unfinished Leopold manuscripts and field notes were published by Oxford in 1953 in a sequel titled <u>Round River</u>, a book that never quite caught on yet that contains some of the finest examples of Leopoldian prose. A later (1966) edition of <u>Sand County Almanac</u> does, however, include some of the best of <u>Round River</u>.

What is it that makes Leopold so compelling as a writer, AD 1980?

First, I think it is that, as a scientist, he is so impeccably accurate in his observations on environmental phenomena. His is not the dilettantism of some "nature writers." Nor is he tunnel-visioned. He sees the trees in detail, yes, but he sees the forest, and beyond the forest the galaxies.

With all his taxonomic and ecological preciseness, Leopold is simply a master of the language. He is not dry nor didactic. He can be read at the level of simple pleasure, the same pleasure he obviously took in polishing his diction as if he were fashioning an osage-orange bow. In his evocation of Wisconsin sights and sounds, Leopold is especially appealing to his fellow Badgers, yet his sketches here and there range from Mexico to Canada, so his fans are worldwide.

Third, Leopold has something profound to <u>say</u>. He combines the savvy of the ecologist with the charm of the poet to produce psalms that are at once a call to arms and a benediction. He melds the courage of Nehemiah with the passion of Job. He takes on all comers, yet always with a scalpel, never a meat-axe.

The quality that most makes Leopold live today, however, is probably the plain fact that he was not really writing for his contemporaries. Like Lincoln at Gettysburg, he was looking far down the century to a time when a new generation might identify with his "ecological conscience."

And so it came to pass.

Is there any one piece that best illustrates all the luminous Leopold qualities? My candidate is "The Song of the Gavilan," a lilting essay that made it into the austere <u>Journal of Wildlife Management</u> in 1940, possibly because its author at the time was president of the society sponsoring that scholarly journal. From one perspective, "Gavilan" is an ecological treatise, a "lesson in botany." From another, an exciting deer hunting expedition, yet marvelously crafted like a fine painting. From a third perspective, a gentle yet lethal dart aimed at some of Professor Leopold's university colleagues. Above all, "Gavilan" leaps ahead to address a generation that would understand "the good life on any river will depend on the perception of its music", and will not depend merely on "an indefinite extension" of more people, more inventions, and more science.

Like Leopold's skein of airborne cranes, his writing combines "the sound of hunting horns, the baying of the phantom pack, the tinkle of little bells." How does one achieve such unique expression? I think Leopold supplied his own answer in his observation on "A Man's Leisure Time," a delightful commentary on hobbies. For Aldo Leopold, writing was not a chore; it was a hobby--and "a hobby is a defiance of the contemporary; it is an assertion of those social values which the momentary eddies of social evolution have contravened or overlooked,...(and) a good hobby must also be a gamble...a...revolt against the commonplace.... Nonconformity is the highest evolutionary attainment of social animals."

That such essays, interred like mummies in musty journals, were resurrected like elijahs to delight and inspire millions--this renaissance is a signal tribute to a sparkling writer, a loving family, and a publishing house with guts and foresight. Nothing so presages the eventual universal acceptance of the Leopold ethic: "A thing is right when it tends to preserve the integrity, stability, and beauty of the biotic community; it is wrong when it tends otherwise."

Integrity, stability, beauty--the essence of Leopold, A., Wisconsin writer.

As Aldo told me shortly before his death:

"When it comes to conservation, we sportsmen remind me of my dog. If my dog runs into another dog too big for him, instead of dealing with the other dog, he deals with a tree bearing his trademark. That way he salves his ego without exposing himself to danger.

"Just so we sportsmen often deal with bureaus and laws and programs, which are the <u>symbols</u> of our conservation problem, instead of dealing with the land and its products and ourselves, which <u>are</u> the problem."

That was the consensus of a man who spent a lifetime in conservation as a sportsman, forester, game manager, and teacher. And when you stop to think about it, maybe he was right. Maybe the trouble with the woods and waters has been simply the fact that a generation of citizens forgot that there's an "I" in conservation. We were content to say "Let George Government do it." We merely voted, petitioned, and wrote checks for bigger if not better bureaus, in order that our own responsibilities might be laid in bigger if not better laps. We hadn't asked ourselves to pitch in personally. Something had been lacking in our understanding of what conservation really means.

Professor Leopold had a name for what was lacking. he called it "the ecological conscience," or the ethics of community life, a realization on our part that George can't do it all and that there is something everyone of us can do. I'm not talking now about routine things like obeying the game laws and snuffing out cigarettes in the woods. I'm talking about some pretty deep-seated understandings and ethics.

Fortunately, conservation citizenship is catching on. All over the country we're learning to put an "I" in conservation.

Yes, you don't have to be a world-famous ecologist-writer to contribute to conservation. I want to chronicle here the contributions of some people who have made major dents in the sweep of environmental degradation: a forest ranger and his wife, a hermit, a small-town postman, a minor state bureaucrat, a housewife-outdoorsperson, and a very young representative of a new generation.

For a special breed of citizen, the deer season is the signal, not for a ten-day outdoor binge, but for an excruciating period of hard work. He is the field person employed by the state Department of Natural Resources. It isn't just the wardens who police the deer shoot, although they take the lead. Fish, game, forestry, and park personnel are also mustered to the woods to cruise the back roads, man the check-in stations, and perform all those manifold chores associated with managing the assault of humans on whitetails.

Conservation commissioners and directors and their lieutenants may come and go, but it is the field people who stay to keep the outdoors green and gamey. I was the fortunate guest the other day of one of the real veterans of the woods wars, E.E. Davison, former forest ranger in the Crandon, Wisconsin, area. Davy has been a Conservation Department man since the early 1930s. Most of that time he has spent right in Forest County.

Davy has been shot at by poachers, scorched by fires, nipped by blizzards, reviled by local hot-stove-league experts, and harassed by Madison bureaucrats. He has had his chances to move up or out, but he has chosen to stay in his green field uniform--manning watchtowers, grubbing out lanes, reseeding the slopes, subbing as a warden, stocking fish, and always practicing that lifelong learning that is the mark of the professional man. Now he can look around and know that he has helped mightily in bringing his north country back from a scarred moonscape to a land of rich timber and tourism production.

On his own time through the years Davy has been a lumberjack, and in the course of his cruising he has come by a good deal of tax-deliquent property. It is only poetic justice that this land is now worth a small fortune, particularly the frontage and the islands he owns on Lake Lucerne. The reason this once-discarded land is now worth a lot of money is due to a significant degree to the DNR Davisons who have devoted their lives to the day-to-day chores of Wisconsin conservation when the rest of us were just writing or talking. But the real heroes of the story are the wives who keep the home fires banked while their men are in the woods. There are a good many ten-day widows scattered around Wisconsin each November-- women like Frances Davison. She has backstopped her husband every step of the way, in season and out.

The Davisons now live in the handsome stone home they have built on a prime overlook on Lucerne. When you peer out their living room window at sunset, you can see the last rays of light filtering through mature spruce and maple and aspen to glisten on blue waters, and you can expect to watch a doe as she comes delicately down for an evening drink. The sight is a far cry from the Forest County aspects of yesterday, when you could drive for miles through fire-blackened cutover. You can see something else through that living room window on Lake Lucerne. You can see what it means to make a success out of life.

Without a doubt Postmaster Harry Nohr of Mineral Point was a superb outdoorsman, weaned as he was on the savvy of Indians in northern Wisconsin. As Gordon MacQuarrie once said of him:
"Turn him loose anywhere in his native heath, which is Wisconsin,

and given matches, an axe, a fishhook, and some string, he'll never go hungry or cold. He is a true countryman, a species almost extinct."

In quest of quarry, Harry came to roam far afield--to the Dakotas for pheasants, to Canada for mallards, to Montana for trout, to Florida for sea bass. But it was his experiences in southwestern Wisconsin that made him more than a sportsman. He was a conservation statesman.

To understand Harry's conservation bent you have to understand the hills and valleys around Mineral Point. Long before it was readable on the rest of the Wisconsin landscape, here was a living textbook on environmental degradation. This was lead and zinc country. The first miners came from Cornwall and Wales in the 1820s, and the "badger" dens they dug are still in evidence. Their pit mines pockmark a thousand hills, the seepage yet turning some creeks to orange. When most of the mines peetered out, farmers followed; and before soil conservation practices could catch up, most of the topsoil was deposited in the Mississippi delta. In the absence of wildlife habitat, much of southwestern Wisconsin approached a fish and game desert 40 years ago.

It was all there for Harry Nohr to see, and he recognized the script. He also decided to do something about it. Harry found his vehicle in the Wisconsin Conservation Congress, an advisory body to the (then) Wisconsin Conservation Commission. He got himself elected as a representative from Iowa County for eight terms between 1942 and 1953. For six of those years he was Iowa County Chairman. For five years he was a member of the statewide Executive Conservation Council. As Vice-Chairman of the first WCC Rules Committee, he established procedures that still obtain. In 1949-51 he led the WCC's Upland Game and Wildlife Habitat Committee.

Reading the minutes of the Congress is to recall Harry Nohr at work as a conservationist who looked far beyond the minutae of season lengths and bag limits to the gut issues of wildlife ecology and land use reform:

September 1948--Argued in favor of an any-deer season in southwestern Wisconsin "to keep the herd from degrading the habitat."

December 1948--"Some of the finest streams in southwestern Wisconsin are being ruined by pollution and erosion. Regulations should require controls. I want to get the barn locked before they steal the horse."

February 1949--Testified before a State Senate Committee in favor of increasing the cost of hunting, fishing, and trapping licenses, with the revenues going to fund research and habitat improvement.

July 1949--Favored a closed season on quail in the face of disappearing fencerows.

September 1949--"Preservation of habitat is more important than artificial propagation."

December 1949--"Let's go full-speed ahead to save the native prairie chicken."

January 1950--Campaigned for more funds for wildlife research and for conservation education.

Harry was no bar-stool conservationist. Professor Harold E.

"Bud" Jordahl, former Chairman of the Wisconsin Natural Resources Board, can recall Harry at work in the field. Bud was a game biologist in northern Wisconsin at the time, charged with playing host to Harry's Wisconsin Conservation Congress Wildlife Habitat Committee.

"I thought they'd want to retire to the nearest tavern while I explained our deer problems with charts and slides," Bud says. "Not Harry Nohr. He led us over hills and into swamps at an all-day pace that left me puffing. Only late in the evening did we stop for refreshments."

Harry was not only a statewide leader; for a number of years he headed up the Mineral Point and the Iowa County Conservation Clubs. There are trout in southern Wisconsin waters today because Harry and his fellows helped bring back fishable populations. There are grouse in southern Wisconsin coulees because Harry and his fellows campaigned to "get the cows out of the woodlots." There is a Governor Dodge State Park because Harry and his fellows took up the cudgel, along with Ed Mundy of the Dodgeville Chronicle.

It was his love of the outdoors and his keen knowledge of trees that led Harry to his craft as a maker of exquisite wooden bowls. He spent hours and days afield looking for just the right burls to shape into those famous paper-thin bowls, and every finished product had in it the glint of the morning sun, the smell of autumn leaves, the faint sound of a babbling brook, and the touch of a friendly hand. Harry was a perfectionist at whatever he tried.

It was only natural that a man of Harry Nohr's vigor and foresight would intrigue another man of vigor and foresight, Gordon MacQuarrie. Gordon was the premier outdoor editor of the Milwaukee Journal and a frequent contributor to Field & Stream. His stories often dealt with the doings of the Old Duck Hunters Association, Inc. (The "Inc." stood for "Incorrigible".) The ODHA was a fun-loving organization, and Harry Nohr was a fun-loving man. It was only a matter of time until he signed on. The Association boasted a membership of two; MacQuarrie, the member, and Harry, the president, known affectionately as "Hizzoner." Harry was actually the second president. The first was Al Peck, MacQuarrie's father-in-law, from Superior. MacQuarrie disbanded the Association for a time after Al died, but the gavel sounded again when he met Harry Nohr during a Wisconsin Conservation Congress meeting in Madison. The rest is literary history, and some of it can be read in a book called Tales of the Old Duck Hunters and Other Drivel--"Red" MacQuarrie at his best.

"Red" MacQuarrie died before Harry did. In tribute, Harry formed the Gordon MacQuarrie Foundation for Conservation Journalism. The Foundation annually recognizes outstanding Wisconsin environmental communicators and graduate students in conservation journalism. Harry's constant theme was the need for "better communications to get the findings of research biologists to hunters, fishers, and other users of the outdoors to assure understanding and better environmental management."

I once wrote a Sunday newspaper column for 15 years. A newspaper

columnist can get by on a modicum of writing talent and even less
reporting skill, but he or she can't make it for long without a
Source. For those 15 years I had a superb Source, Walter Scott.

Walter was the Special Assistant to the Director of the Wisconsin
Conservation Department (later to the Secretary of the Wisconsin
Department of Natural Resources), and he had been with the department
a long time, so his knowledge of past and present events and personnel
was intimate. But it was more than that--Walter was a human pack
rat. He saved every piece of paper he ever got his hands on, and
filed it in his office or his garage. There was no card catalogue,
but Walter knew where everything was, nonetheless. No matter what
striking or obscure WCD statement or action I needed background on,
Walter could fill me in.

But Walter wasn't simply up on WCD; he was involved in some way
or another with just about every voluntary association or inter-
agency committee on the Wisconsin conservation front. And he
personally was an accomplished naturalist. So I scarcely even wrote
two columns in a row without checking something out with W.A.S.

Walter was actually a prolific writer in his own right, although
most of his manuscripts appeared under the byline of whomever he was
ghostwriting for. Vintage Scott is the annual Christmas card
newsletter from Hickory Hill, the miniaboretum he and his wife,
Trudi, have lovingly created on Madison's far west side.

Walter Scott probably personally represented the Conservation
Department to more people in the state for a longer time than any
other single individual. Directors and assistant directors came and
went between 1946 and 1976, but Walter was always there--intensely
loyal to his chiefs yet working in quiet ways to give his department
character and conscience. He epitomizes the dedicated middle-
management person that can make bureaucracy responsible and responsive.

And when Walter "retired," did he just sit in a rocking chair?
Not on your life. He just went on collecting conservation chores
and sherds. So even though I stopped writing a weekly outdoor
column to switch to books, I could still use Walter as the Source.
If ever a person were irreplaceable, I'd nominate Walter Scott.

Just about everybody knows of Sigurd Olson, the poet laureate of
Minnesota's "singing wilderness." But, in her own way, Sig's Ely
neighbor Florence Peterson did as much or more to make possible the
magnificient Boundary Waters Canoe Area.

Beginning in the 1920s, Florence and her husband, Pete, created
a famous fishing camp on the south shore of Hoist Bay on Basswood
Lake. Getting to it was a major undertaking. You left your car at
a Winton dock, took a launch up Fall Lake, transferred to an old bus
to negotiate the Four-Mile Portage, and then motor-boated down the
bay to the camp, being careful to avoid the rusting remains of old
logging machinery. One such trip is graphically reported in Aldo
Leopold's Round River. At its peak in the thirties and forties,
Peterson's camp had a lodge and cabins accommodating 50 guests at a
time. In the general area were about 45 other resorts and some 100
individual cabins. Today the canoeist paddling Basswood Lake cannot

now discern any visible evidence of permanent human activity. But the loons know things have changed; they have returned to Hoist Bay. So you can turn back the clock.

It was Florence and Pete who took the lead in turning back the clock in the BWCA. When the federal government took the first steps in 1948 to begin to restore the boundary waters in the Superior National Forest to what is now congressionally-classified wilderness, there was a great outcry in Ely. No Basswood resort owner was eager to sell his property, and the townspeople feared an end to the tourism on which the economy of the area was partly based. But Florence and Pete saw the vision of a tourism industry based not on outboard engines and dining rooms but on canoe paddles and campfires. They were the first to sell out to the Forest Service, in 1955. Although the camp was immediately torn down, the Petersons were allowed to keep their private cabin for 15 years. Pete's interred nearby.

Thanks to my wife's warm friendship with Florence, we had the privilege of sharing her cabin in the final summer of '70. It was a sad occasion, in a way. The forest halls echoed with the shouts of long-ago pike fishermen and their happy families. But the wild loon laughter from the bay testified to something special in the Peterson spirit--an abiding love of the land.

Florence is special in another way. She is a throwback to a pioneer woman. Despite her 60-odd years, she is forever ricing by the hour, casting for northerns, sitting in a drafty duck blind, swimming in the buff in icy waters, cross-country skiing, cooking marvelous stews, toting heavy packs--all in spite of a hip injury that would have pub most people on the shelf. One very windy day we paddled the length of the bay and back--and it was my back that gave out.

For sentimental reasons Sheryl and I once went back and tented on the site of Florence's last cabin--or what we decided was the site. Nature had already moved in swiftly to reclaim her own. Many people can leave a house, or a farm, or an office building to posterity. Florence Peterson left a lakeshore as she found it.

My four-year-old granddaughter Chrissie in California is one of the new breed of conservationists. Visiting there recently, I excused myself from the kitchen to go to the bathroom. Chrissie followed. "Remember, Grampa," she said, "We can flush the toilet only once a day because there's a water shortage, you know, because it didn't snow in the mountains enough last winter." Now when a four-year-old can expound, if not understand, a profound environmental proposition like that, it means the ecological conscience has a chance.

All of these people are representative of an old-new environmental movement, and purveyors of an old-new environmental education.

To help explain what has happened, and what may happen, in regard to that old-new environmental movement, let me cite a bit of ecological history:

When the very first settlers came to Wisconsin in the early 1800s, they found much of the land covered with "oak openings," or savanna--a striking combination of scattered, mature trees amid prairie patches, the whole array appearing, in the eyes of one early observer, "like so many old orchards."

The trees were principally bur oaks, their characteristic thick bark protecting them uniquely from the fires that raged over the prairies each year. When the fires were stopped by the settlers, a rapid change took place in the oak openings: they became filled with dense stands of oak saplings. But surprisingly, the new oaks were not burs; they were largely blacks. Frequently a pure stand of black oak would spring up amid widely spaced bur oaks even though there might not be any mature blacks for miles around. Some early observers attributed this black oak irruption to a mass seeding of the openings by flocks of passenger pigeons. Each bird was presumed to have carried a single black oak acorn across the prairies to the bur oak grove and dropped it, in concert with his fellows. We now understand that no such charming an explanation is necessary. The black oaks had been there all the time, growing as brush or grubs among the prairie grasses, suppressed by annual fires. When the fires stopped, the black oak developed swiftly into tall, mature trees, gradually shading out many of the open-grown bur oak veterans. Today a genuine prairie grove with an intact ground layer is the rarest plant community in Wisconsin, yet there are more oak forests than there were in 1800.

Since the 1900s the American conservation landscape had resembled a savanna. Here and there on a broad prairie of indifference you could identify scattered bur oak individuals, organizations, and agencies, their tough hides protecting them from annual fires of covert carelessness and overt retribution. Then in the 1960s, with breathtaking scope and velocity, the scene changed. The oak openings of conservation became thick with saplings. And these saplings were a different species, springing from submerged roots, displaying a distinctive foliage. This much we can see. What lies ahead is problematic.

What will our prairie grove look like 20 years from now? Will the black oaks of the new environmentalism be the dominant species, the old burs rotting and fracturing in the shade? It could happen. After all, some veteran resource management agencies and organizations are not particularly ecological in their orientations. On the contrary, they tend to espouse unilateral programs and cultivate special-interest clientele. On the other hand, our prairie grove of the year 2000 may be punctuated only by the old bur oaks. It could happen. The new environmentalism could turn out to be only a passing fad, like hula-hoops. Hopefully there can be a third broad possibility-- a wedding of old and new. In many cases today, what was once a natural prairie grove is dominated neither by bur oaks or blacks but by thrifty white oaks. These white oaks exhibit some resistance to fire as well as a tolerance of shade. Perhaps we will likewise see emerge a lay ecologist with all the lore and savvy of the old-line conservationist and all the heightened idealism and sense of mission of the new environmentalist--a conservation movement old enough to have traditions and young enough to transcend them.

What characterizes the "new conservation"?
There are indeed important distinctions between the "old conservation" and the "new environmentalism." In terms of its scope, environmentalism attempts to be multifaceted. Whereas yesterday we tended to treat soil conservation, water conservation, wildlife conservation, urban engineering, and so on, as separate pursuits, today we try to understand, relate to, and adapt to the ecosystem unity of all humankind-environment relationships. In terms of its focus, then, while environmentalism is humanity-centered, while our primary concern has shifted from the survival of remnant redwoods and raptors to the survival of the human species itself, yet the shift has been accompanied by a new-found recognition that any concern for human welfare must encompass a concern for the total environment of which humankind is a part, not apart. In terms of its locus, while the old conservation conjured up images of open country, environmentalism incorporates the pressing problems of the city. In terms of its political alliances, conservation was linked to such orthodox causes as depression pump-priming, national defense, and outdoor recreation; the new environmentalism, on the other hand, owes allegiance to neo-Malthusian population control. It is in its basic cultural orientation, however, that the new environmentalism differs most strikingly from its antecedent, conservation. The latter stood clearly for economic development, for the infinite goodness of "progress." Gifford Pinchot himself said so. Environmentalism, on the other hand, reflects a growing suspicion that bigness is not necessarily better, slower may be faster, and less can be more. While we are concerned about quantities of natural resources, we are also concerned about the quality of the human experience.

Who is "the new conservationist"?
First there is the old conservationist who has acquired an awareness of the global nature of what once seemed a parochial problem, an understanding of some new points of entre toward constructive action, and a vastly heightened sense of urgency. He is the erstwhile county Conservation League member who has shifted his emphasis from prairie chickens to air pollution. He is the Sierra Clubber who has added "human survival" to his agenda. He is the Park Service specialist who is trying to take his parks to the people instead of vice versa. Witness the words of the National Wildlife Federation: "Conservation is no longer just the story of vanishing wildlife and vanishing wilderness areas. There is a new urgency in the word today. Suddenly, as we stop and look at our total environment, it has taken on the meaning of human survival."
The second distinct type of new conservationist is a "she." But she is not the proverbial "little old lady in tennis shoes" who has graced the ranks of the bird watchers. She is the sharp young housewife whose automated kitchen has rendered her under-employed,

and who, in looking around for new worlds to conquer, has discovered the environment and its problems. Through such local fire brigades as a Capital Community Citizens and such national organizations as the League of Women Voters she is lying down in front of bulldozers, accosting legislators in their lairs, baiting conservation bureaus, plumping for bond issues, and in general raising polite hell in the best traditions of American populism. She may even propagandize her Rotarian husband!

Perhaps the truest type of new conservationist is the committed college student who made his or her presence felt through such activities as a national campus environmental teach-in, in 1970. They are saying to their elders, in effect: "It is you and your system that have brought about the environmental mess which is making much of the world unlivable. Now, before it is too late, let us have a say about the planet that we are to inherit." They represent everything from art to zoology. They come from Boswash and Grover's Corners. They have long and short hair, full pocketbooks and lean. Their folk heroes may be George Wallace or Bertrand Russell. They may know everything or nothing about the hydrologic cycle. Yet they have certain attributes in common: a neo-transcendental feeling for the human-land community, a revulsion for the excesses of a technological society, a suspicion of the Establishment, a sense of so little time, and a consuming desire to act, now. No group is more concerned, or more disgusted, about the growing destruction of the American environment than the young. First, they haven't been around long enough to become accomplices in the pollution violence, assuming they might want to. Second, the young are more concerned about saving the environment because they will be the worst casualties if it is not saved. Although many student environmental activists have used little more than the scream method, others have dug in for a long siege by finding out about the economics, the technology, and the politics of environmental problems. The young eco-activist, in sum, is the same disenchanted American who came over in steerage, who pushed into the West. He is the same American who took off with a song for Bull Run, Belleau Woods, and Buna. Now the environment is their only frontier left, and the eco-war the only one they want to fight.

What triggered the mass irruption of the new environmentalist?

It isn't true, of course, that environmentalism "burst upon the scene," so to speak, in the 1960s. The antecedents of environmentalism as a concept were many, going back at least to George Perkins Marsh's <u>Man and Nature</u> in 1864. As a political force, environmentalism inherited the infrastructure of a number of strong conservation organizations, some of which had been operative since the early 1900's. Yet, just as there were qualitative differences between the old conservation and the new environmentalism, so did public awareness, interest, and even support take a quantum leap at the turn of the decade, epitomized by the passage of the National Environmental Policy Act in 1969.

Even from the perspective of history we are still not sure what inspired the rise of the earlier conservation movement at the turn of the century. Did it take its impulse largely from a technocratic gospel of efficiency, or from a populist revolt against wasteful monopolies, or from an evangelical concern for nature's vast, pulsing harmony. Probably from all three. Wisconsin Professor John Gaus once identified the critical elements in the "ecology" of any institution or movement as "people, place, physical technology, social technology, wishes and ideas, catastrophe, and personality." A brief review of these factors at work in and around 1970 may help us understand the emergence of environmentalism.

American people--all of us--had been on a decade-long emotional trip that had left us both frustrated and pent up: multiple assassinations, civil rights confrontations, Vietnam, cost of living, crime in the streets, campus sit-ins--as F. Scott Fitzgerald once described a somewhat similar era, "all gods were dead, all wars fought, all faiths in man shaken." We were ready for a cause we could believe in. It was natural that the new conservation would supply it. Ever since we first dropped anchor off Plymouth Rock, we have turned periodically to natural systems for inspiration and challenge.

Yesterday's environmental degradation was usually over the hill and far away--in somebody else's dust bowl, somebody else's canyon, somebody else's Boundary Waters Canoe Area, somebody else's forest. But the place of environmental degradation in the 1960s was where most people live--in the foul air, fetid water, and clogged arteries of the city. Millions could smell, taste, hear, and see the problem now.

The physical technology of the sixties had vaulted us to the moon, and thus had given us renewed confidence in our capacities, but from our new vantage point in the cosmos we looked back and were struck as never before by the fragile, finite character of Spaceship Earth. By invading one new frontier we rediscovered another, settling a state of harmony between humankind and nature.

Continuing along the Gaus outline, developments in the social technology of the sixties played a signal role in the rise of environmentalism. The voice of the mass media had become increasingly dominated by a relatively small coterie of paperback publishers, magazine editors, and TV commentators. When these communication gatekeepers almost simultaneously seized on the pesticide-population-pollution syndrome as the big story, the message was inescapable. Beginning with Rachel Carson's Silent Spring in 1962, on down through Arthur Godfrey's "Portable Electric Medicine Show" in 1972, the mass media brought ecological awareness into America's living rooms. The 1969 National Environmental Policy Act energized press coverage of environmental impacts. Wisconsin newspaper reporters and editors testify that by "officializing" environmental issues, NEPA and its WEPA spin-off have given the press new hooks on which to hang environmental coverage.

In the wishes and ideas, all the great ecological philosophers had always said that true conservation would require a profound change in American values. Few people listened. But in the sixties the youth of the country began to understand, if only because it matched a wave of antimaterialism sweeping their ranks. Perhaps nothing so accounts for the current popularity of environmentalism as this marriage of orthodox ecological ethics and the innate iconoclasm of the young, coupled with their commitment to the tactics of confrontation.

There was no single, Pearl Harbor-type <u>catastrophe</u> responsible for the rise of environmentalism, but there were multiple mini-castrophes: death-dealing smog in the east, oil spills in the west, water pollution in the north, lung disease in the south--there was no place to hide any more.

No single <u>personality</u> dominates the field of environmentalism as TR and FDR dominated the first two waves of conservation. Rather, the new conservation is characterized by the diversity of its exponents and troopers. It is, in itself, a complex ecosystem, and this speaks well for its stability and longevity. Perhaps one day a Bill Mauldin will capture in cartoons the personality of this new-style World War III, and it will not be a Patton, but the peace-time equivalent of G.I. Joe.

Out of the changing people, places, technology, aspirations, fears, and personages of America at the turn of the decade came a new spirit, the spirit of an embryo ecological conscience. From the sentiments and scenes of the 1960s the broad realization has grown that humankind itself is a part of the environment, that our welfare is at stake, and that it hinges upon the welfare of all other things, animate and inanimate. For thousands of years people had gone forth to multiply and subdue the earth as a chosen species; now that premise has come under examination. There has emerged a more ecocentric view of life, a recognition that we must ameliorate our impacts on the environment by knowing before we act what they are likely to be. Today, environmentalism seeks a rather fundamental reordering of thought and action away from growth, control and mastery over nature, and progress traditionally defined, and toward an ecologic ethic and different definition of "quality of life" than that which has incurred such environmental cost.

Whatever their family or genus, no environmentalist today is so naive as to believe modern humankind will necessarily achieve complete harmony with the natural world any more than we will surely achieve world justice or liberty for all people. In these higher aspirations, as Aldo Leopold wrote, "the important thing is to strive." The capacity to live without befouling and denuding the environment--this was Leopold's test of whether we are civilized. Environmental education can be one of the means of developing a culture that will meet that test.

Barring reading, writing, and arithmetic, few subjects are being taught today in so many diverse ways and places, by such a mixture of agencies, groups, institutions, and people, as that complex of cognitive content and affective process known, precisely or not, as environmental education. To paraphrase Aldo Leopold, it is, by common consent, a good thing to engage in environmental education. But wherein lies the goodness, and what can be done to encourage its pursuit? On these questions there is confusion of counsel, and only the most uncritical minds are free from doubt. The latest definitive book on the subject concludes there is "no clear, single answer" to "what makes education environmental".

If one is pressed for a succinct definition of environmental education, the latest attempt may be as good as any--UNECSO's "Belgrade Charter": "Environmental education is a life-long, interdisciplinary approach to the development of a world population that is aware of, and concerned about, the environment and its associated problems, and which has the knowledge, skills, attitudes, motivations, and commitment to work individually and collectively toward solutions of current problems and the prevention of new ones."

Whatever definition of environmental education you employ, all will invariably have certain common denominators. First, there is a hard core of ecological content. Second, a recognition of worldwide problems of crisis proportions. Third, a component of conscience, of a value system. And fourth, a commitment to private and public action. The whole is focused on a comprehensive rather than a compartmentalized approach to change in people-land relations, be they open-country or urban.

Environmental education has come gradually to first flower. It is a plant of many roots, many stalks, many branches, and many fruits, some of the latter relatively unpalatable. From its antecedents, several of them dating back a century, environmental education has drawn a number of its characteristics. One of the oldest rootstocks is nature study, a sort of transcendental search to understand our natural environs. Ecology represents a more sophisticated study of the interrelations of organisms and their environments. Conservation education adds the concept of a concern for the wise use of natural resources over time. In a recent form, conservation education becomes energy education. Outdoor education contributes a hands-on approach to experiences that can cut across the curriculum. Citizenship education seeks to generate an appreciation of the American endowment and a commitment to social action. Consumer education focuses on the shortcomings and excesses of our economic system. Population education attacks the twin shibboleths of limitless growth and conspicuous consumption. Resource management education represents the professionalization of certain distinct people-land relationships: soil conservation, water management, game management, park management, urban and regional planning, landscape design, architecture, metropolitan management, environmental engineering, environmental health, environmental law, and so on through the departmentalization of universities. Philosophy and religion, on occasion, address the esthetic and ethical dimensions of Leopold's community of life that "includes the soil, waters, fauna, and flora as well as people."

A small illustration drawn from Wisconsin country may sharpen the distinctions among environmental education and its predecessors:

We purchase a back 40 in the country. In the process of acquiring the wherewithall to do so, we have used natural resources-- gas, light, heat, food, shelter--in earning money providing people with certain goods and services. With the proceeds we opt to stake out our own private preserve rather than cruise the continent or carouse. This is consumer education in operation.

On our 40 we fence the cows out of the rocky hillside woodlot, with government aid we dam up the pasture gully that would otherwise continue to silt downstream cornlands, and we also plant pines in appropriate locations. This is conservation education applied.

On the pond that forms in our valley, one morning there are two small wild waterfowl. One has a white crescent in front of the eye and a chalky-blue patch on the fore edge of the wing; the voice, a peep. The other is brown-mottled, with the same blue wing-patch, the voice a soft quack. They are blue-winged teal. We watch them cruise and feed and bob their heads in unison. They are paired. This is nature study in action.

The next morning our bluewings are joined by another pair, which attempts peacefully to occupy a corner of the pond, but the "owner" drake is having none of the intrusion. He attacks with a great flurry of bill and wing. Why? He is exercising his territorial instinct that tells him there is only room on the little pond for one pair of teal--only so much nesting space, so much food, so much resting area. This carrying capacity concept we know to be a tenet of ecology.

On our 40 acres we install No Trespassing signs every 50 yards around the perimeter. We are exercising our own territoriality, escaping from intolerable "social distance" in the city. This is outdoorism.

Whose territory will last the longest, ours or the teal's? Will we contaminate our pond with assorted run-off until it is no longer fit habitat for a bluewing, or will the population-pollution-pesticide syndrome ultimately catch up with us humans ourselves. This is the challenge posed by environmental education.

It is environmental education that tries to put it all together. Environmental educators of many stripes seek a rigorous understanding of the integrity, stability, and beauty of the community of life, a hearty awareness that a thing is right only when it tends to preserve that community, and a tough rejection of the argument that an action is impossible if it does not yield quick profits, or that an action is necessarily to be condoned because it seems to pay. That philosophy, as Leopold said, "is dead in human relations, and its funeral in land relations is long overdue." To make this "ecological conscience" operational constitutes the intellectual revolution, the "subversive science," that applied ecology seeks to foment. A basic message of enviromental education is interdependence--that everything is connected to everything else. That is the principal intuition of the twentieth century. The practical problem lies in how to recognize and effect sound, fair trade-offs among energy, economy, and environment.

It is ecology that is at the heart of environmentalism and environmental education.

The word "ecology" has been lying in the dictionary for some 100 years, but it has been only recently that the term has begun to flit about in everybody's vocabulary like a bat emerging suddenly from a cave into bright sunlight.

Just exactly what does the word mean? What *is* ecology? What does it *do*? What can *we* do with it? Is it one of those complex things that only a scientist can really understand and employ, or is it something within the ken of the average person?

Well, there are all sorts of approaches to ecology, because ecology is a very rich word; that is, we can put it to many uses. Like the celebrated committee of blind men examining an elephant, we can come up with all sorts of answers to our questions about ecology.

From one point of view, we can define ecology scientifically as "the study of the interrelations of organisms and their environments." This is the classic way the term is used in college catalogs, to distinguish ecology from other basic divisions of biology like physiology, embryology, and so on.

Viewed a little more broadly, ecology is not simply the study of something; it *is* that thing. In other words, the word refers in a grander sense to the makeup and operations of the living world, to the structure and function of nature, including humankind.

Or we can use the term to refer to a property of a piece of nature, like a lake or a covey of quail. By this we mean the whole complex of living conditions of a body of water or a group of birds. So we can speak of "the ecology" of a park, or of a walleyed pike, or so on. It used to be that we applied this ecology concept only to living organisms in "nature." In more recent years we use the term in connection with any structure or organization. So we can speak of the ecology of a suburb, or of a labor union, or of the environmental movement itself--meaning, still, the relationship among an "organism" and its environment.

And thus we come to the more philosophical meaning of ecology. In its broadest sense it is a way of looking at things--a viewpoint that sees not the things themselves so much as their connections with other things. So it is a concern with processes--with the myriad of mechanisms that make up the web of life of whatever it is we are looking at. In other words, in an ecological look at an oak woodlot, for example, we concentrate on the spaces between the trees, spaces that are actually filled with all sorts of mechanical and chemical operations, or processes. What is more, in this eyeball shift from thing to process, we recognize that the human observer is an integral part of the picture. So ecology really becomes a way of looking at "things" from the inside out, rather than from the outside in.

Who, then, is an ecologist? Well, obviously, a modern ecologist can be a scientist, although not all scientists are ecologists by any means, not even all those who carry "ecology cards." Some "ecological" pundits get so concerned with bits and pieces of nature that they literally do not see the forest for the trees. Other professors of ecology, on the other hand, are today's leading representatives of ecological thinking. But so are some politicians and some English professors--those who see that everything is connected to everything else.

Prehistoric man was a superb ecologist. He could not run fast enough to escape his enemies; if caught, his teeth and claws were small protection. So he had to become a student of his relationship to the veldt. Peering from his hiding place in the bushes around a clearing or from the opening of his cave, his science was the practical kind. His laboratory was the place he lived; the success of his observations could be measured by the fact that he made it through the night--or didn't.

So, today, an ecologist can be simply anybody who appreciates our two-way-street relations with our environment and with all of life everywhere: the hunter who knows that you look for whitetails not on a prairie but along the edge of a forest, the fisher who understands why DDT sprayed on a carrot patch can affect the eating quality of lake trout caught miles away, the teenagers who see the connection between their automobile engines and air pollution.

We give this sense of interlocking community the term ecological awareness--an awareness that the community to which each of us belongs includes soil, waters, plants, animals, and people. Then, if we have an ecological conscience as well as ecological awareness, we know that an action is right only if it tends to protect the health of our human-land community; that is, its integrity, stability, and beauty--and we act accordingly, regardless of what may be momentarily convenient or profitable. So what we used to call conservation becomes applied ecology--the ethics that should govern the relations between humans and the living or built landscape, the "resistance movement" that challenges anybody's right to pollute or over-populate the environment.

In a nutshell, then, while there are a number of approaches to the use of the term ecology, when we "take all the feathers off of it," as the saying goes, ecology is a way of looking at our world that says to us: "I am a part of my environment, and my environment is a part of me."

Ecology is in everybody's bailiwick. Much modern science all too often seems to be a no-laypersons' land of abstruse concepts and unwieldy laboratory equipment, of arcane processes and complex formulas, of particles too small to be seen, and power too great to be controlled. Not so, ecology. Ecology is where we live--in backyards, on boulevards, in parks and apartments, in fields and factories, in swamps and suburbs, on mountain and in metropolis. And everybody can think ecologically. It enriches our pleasures and perceptions alike. It can stir us to respect and love.

Will we make it? Is an emerging environmental ethic a fad or a fixture?

I think American environmentalism has a promising future because it is a movement indigenous to America. You know, we have had poor luck in this country with imports, at least in the field of wildlife management. We have tried desperately to bring over Scotch grouse, Turkish quail, Hungarian partridge, Bavarian deer, on down through a list of 126 species that we have tried to stock, and we have had success really only with one, the ring-necked pheasant (and it may be an interesting turn or fate that he came from China). So because environmentalism, on the other hand, is a very "native" movement, I believe it has a high survival factor in this country.

Let me explain why I think environmentalism is very American. In the first place, the environmental problem lends itself in part to technological solutions--gross scientific and engineering approaches. Well, we Americans are simply very good at big, massive engineering problems. Look what has happened just in the lifetime of adult Americans. For better or worse, we have lassoed the mountains and deserts of the West with sinews of concrete and steel. We have inundated simultaneously the forces of Fascism on two continents with tons of tanks and howitzers and war planes. We have in turn revitalized whole continents with massive shipments of technological know-how. And more recently we have gone to the moon, from hindsight almost as easily as a Sunday drive. We are superb at accepting big technological challenges and licking them. I think we are going to respond in exactly this same way to the environmental problem. It's a natural for American know-how.

Second, there is an ethical, or moral, dimension to the environmental movement which is also very American. This country was born as a moral movement. We made the conquest of Trans-Appalachia a moral movement. Its real leader was not Daniel Boone but John Wesley. Our great-grandfathers were taken up by an intense moral movement in the 1830s and 1840s--the abolition movement. We tend to forget the great clout that movement had as we carried it through to a very bloody resolution. At the turn of the century the prohibition movement swept this country and again we carried it to a resolution; short-term, yes, but nonetheless a moral resolution. We didn't really start getting out of the Depression until we changed it from an economic problem to a moral movement. That was FDR's signal contribution. When he got up on that dark day in Washington and said, "We have nothing to fear but fear itself," he changed the whole gestalt, if you please, of the country. We made World War II a moral movement as well. Mr. Eisenhower didn't call his after-action report <u>Campaign in Europe</u>, he called it <u>Crusade in Europe</u>. We made the Marshall Plan not just an economic device but a moral movement. More rently we have experienced the profoundly moral civil-rights and anti-Vietnam movement. So, in the sense that environmentalism requires changes in standards, requires value judgments, requires, as Mr. Leopold says, the emergence of an ecological conscience, it is a moral or ethical movement; and to me this, too, suggests that it has high survival value.

Fundamentally, it seems to me that what environmentalism has to contribute and can contribute at a minimum is that it will get us to restore freedom of choice--freedom of choice in the marketplace, freedom of choice at the ballot box, freedom of choice in the home, and in our places of work. One of our basic problems as individuals right now is that even if we want to be 100 percent environmental we don't have all of the options. For example, the whole transportation system of my city of Madison is designed to encourage and support the individual automobile. I really do not have a viable choice among driving a car, riding a bicycle, mass transit, and/or walking. Somehow or other government, business, and education have to restore that kind of freedom of choice on down through a whole range of options. Environmental interpreters particularly will have to point out continually that there are no easy solutions, there are only choices and many of them are very tough. And then, if we give ourselves and our fellow Americans decent choices, and if we don't make the sound ones, OK. That will simply mean that we weren't the species that was supposed to survive anyway, and a more adaptable or a smarter one will emerge.

In other words, if environmentalism as a movement turns out after all to be a passing fancy, I don't think it will be a reflection on the movement, I think it will be a reflection on us. It will simply mean that we have not demanded of ourselves the same high quality that we are demanding of the environment. I am personally betting that we are going to make it, because I think the human animal is very smart.

Letters from a Lobbyist

Ordinarily, I suppose, Sammy Squirrel and his mate, Sylvia, would have lived out their lives quietly in their woodlot haven near Blue Mounds, Wisconsin. But Sammy got elected by his fish and wildlife chums as "legislative representative" for the Southern Wisconsin Alliance of Fur, Fin, and Feathers (SWAFFF). So Sammy went to Madison to become a unique sort of lobbyist. Every now and then he would write to Sylvia back home, recounting his impressions and adventures in the world of <u>Homo sapiens</u>. With Sammy's special permission, I'm reproducing some of those letters here. Through Sammy's eyes we get a comical yet thoughtful view of the oneness of humans, our environment, and our wildlife comrades on the only earth we have.

Well, here I am, Sylvia, in Madison as the lobbyist for SWAFFF--the Southern Wisconsin Alliance of Fur, Fin, and Feathers. Some of the other lobbyists are having trouble finding a good room, but I'm all set in handsome quarters in an old bur oak right on the capitol grounds. What's more, I'm finding plenty of nuts in Madison.

How are things back in our Blue Mounds woodlot? I'll keep you posted regularly on things down here during the next couple of years, and I'll appreciate an occasional letter from you and our fellow wildlifers.

The legislature hasn't convened yet, but I'm going to pay a visit to the attorney general tomorrow to protest some strange goings-on. What has happened already is this:

The conservation boys propose to print and sell special stamps that must be affixed to the licenses of trout fishermen.

Now this strikes me as very unfair. As a matter of fact, I think this plan is a direct violation of the federal Civil Rights Act of 1964, which specifically prohibits discrimination on the basis of race, creed, or color.

Just because we squirrels do not have green backs like a trout shouldn't mean that we can't have a stamp issued in our honor, do you think?

As far as that goes, I suspect this conservation proposal is downright subversive. Otherwise why would they cater to German brown trout while ignoring us 100 percent American squirrels?

I'm going to ask the attorney general to investigate this whole business right away. If the conservation boys need money, the least they can do is issue stamps for all of us SWAFFF folks. There could be a grouse stamp, a rabbit stamp, a perch stamp, a pike stamp, and so on.

For that matter, why stop there? I'm going to propose a mosquito stamp for campers, a hidden-stump stamp for motor-boaters, a poison-ivy stamp for hikers, and a rose-breasted grosbeak stamp for bird-watchers.

Think of the revenue my plan would produce! Anybody who stepped outdoors would have to have a bookful of stamps, and stamp collectors who never go outdoors would be after the stamps, too, especially if the printer made a little mistake on a sheet or two.

Maybe I could even work out an arrangement with a supermarket so that a sportsperson could exchange a trout stamp for a package of frozen halibut.

If I keep getting ideas like this, Sylvia, there's no telling how high I can go here in Madison.

I got a letter the other day from one of our Fur, Fin, and Feathers members--a mallard--asking me if I could help put a stop to his water problems. It seems that between draining and polluting he doesn't have much to swim in any more. So I started making the rounds of the Madison bureaus. Believe me, that's an experience.

Somebody told me the Wisconsin Department of Natural Resources was in charge of ducks, so I went there first. They were very nice but they said ducks, being migratory, are federal birds, and referred me to a U.S. warden. He was very nice, too, but he said the drainage was under the Soil Conservation Service and the pollution was under the Environmental Protection Agency.

The SCS boys agreed they give farmers technical advice on how to dig ditches, but that the ditches themselves are under the Agricultural Stabilization and Conservation Program. The ASCP people referred me to a farmer. He wasn't home.

I tried the EPA next. They sent me to the state Water Pollution Committee, which referred me to the state Hygiene Laboratory. They said I would need a water sample to be analyzed.

I went back to the conservation boys. "Let's talk about water levels," I said. Depends on what water and what levels, they explained. There's the Great Lakes Compact Commission, the Commission on Interstate Cooperation, the Portage Levee Commission, and the Water Regulatory Board, not to mention the federal Corps of Engineers, and the state Public Service Commission.

That's if you're talking about surface water. If you're talking about ground water, there's the state Department of Agriculture, the U.S. Geological Survey, and the PSC again.

"Maybe we'd better talk about land management," I said. That depends, they told me, on whether it is county land, state land, federal land, or private land. Unless a highway is involved, and then you talk to the Department of Transportation.

I wanted to know if anybody is doing any planning and coordinating. Well, it seems some state planning is under the Department of Administration, which consults an Advisory Committee on State Resource Planning; and some is under the Natural Resources Department, which consults a Forestry Advisory Committee, a Program Coordination Committee, and the Conservation Congress.

I also got referred to the University of Wisconsin, which conducts research on water. One of the professors out there said they might be able to set up a migratory waterfowl water committee, provided they could get the College of Agricultural and Life Sciences and the College of Letters and Science to agree on a chairman.

In the meantime the professor said I should talk to the Mississippi Flyway Council, the Wildlife Management Institute, the Bureau of Outdoor Recreation, the Fish and Wildlife Service, and the Bureau of Reclamation. It turns out they're in Washington.

I did find one state bureau that seemed interested in our problem--the Board for the Preservation of Scientific Areas and Rare Species. The only trouble is, they don't have any money. So I wound up appealing to the State Commission for the Relief of Innocent Persons. It turns out they handle humans only.

I have a temporary change of address. Instead of residing in Capitol Park, I'm currently behind bars. It's a long story.

As you know, I've been lobbying in Madison as the representative of the Southern Wisconsin Alliance of Fur, Fin, and Feathers. The other day I attended a hearing on the Department of Natural Resources pheasant management program.

It seems there's a big debate on whether or not to stock pheasants, where, and when. Before going to the hearing I made the mistake of reading a department research report, and I kept quoting from it. I wasn't very popular.

For instance, one legislator testified that pheasant stocking never pays. I said that "with various improvements this program should continue to be an important game-management tool under certain conditions."

One hunter said the pheasant-stocking program should be greatly expanded. I said that "Wisconsin's pheasant-stocking program is not the ultimate answer to quality hunting and is strictly a put-and-take program." Another hunter protested about pheasant shooters paying for a special stamp. I pointed out that "the cost of a bird stocked is at least $6.03."

Somebody said what is needed is more swamps and marshes set aside as preserves. I said that "the best pheasant range is two-thirds cultivated land and one-third cover."

A state senator claimed that what should be stocked are brood hens instead of young cocks. I quoted a statement that "because few hens survive, there is no long-term effect on the pheasant population."

About this time, the committee chairman asked just who I was, anyway, and what my credentials were. I told him. He asked me if I had complied with the lobby law. I said, "What law?"

Then he asked what I was being paid, and I said, "Nuts." That did it. I was rushed out of the room and over to the City-County Building. Some judge there found me guilty of language unbecoming to the capitol, and sentenced me to 10 days in a Vilas Park pen.

I don't understand these humans at all. When some general says "Nuts," they erect a statue to him in Bastogne, but when I say it they think it's a federal offense. What I really think upset them, though, was my quoting all that official literature.

Oh, well, I'll be out of here in a couple more days and then back at the capitol, where I certainly won't cite any more Department of Natural Resources bulletins.

As a lobbyist for the Southern Wisconsin Alliance of Fur, Fin, and

Feathers (SWAFFF), I've got to try to keep on my toes about all sorts of government acts and agencies from town board zoning practices to UNESCO wildlife conservation programs. And believe you me, all this is no small job these days. As a matter of fact, alphabet agencies just about have me swamped.

Let's take one simple problem as an example. Let's say the county of Dane proposes to develop a new outdoor recreation area, and it wants some state and federal assistance. Is there any? You bet there is--enough to cover the whole park knee-deep in red tape.

Under a couple of different acts, the URA of the HHFA can provide grants for open-space acquisition. The HHFA, by the way, is in HUD.

Under the LWC act, the BOR also makes money available for open spaces. The BOR is in the DI.

If wayside and scenic overlooks are involved, the HBA is in the picture. This comes under the BPR of the DC.

If the area in question has fish and wildlife value, two programs can provide funds--DJ and PR under the FWS of the DI.

The LAA helps government bodies acquire land for recreation. The LAA is administered under the ACP by the ASCS in cooperation with the SCS--all in the DA.

I could go on. To do the park development work, you might involve the JC run by the OEO, the NYC run by the DL, the WEP run by the HEW, or the APWP run by the DC.

It's not inconceivable that the ARD would be interested; that's a DC venture separate from the RADP in the DA.

You begin to get the federal picture? I haven't even talked about the potential roles of the BLM, the NPS, the BR, Public Law 566, the ERS, the CES, the FS, the REA, the CE, the FSA, the PHS, and the SBA, not to mention the new maze of laws and bureaus involved in water management and pollution abatement.

In state programs we have a cigarette tax providing for outdoor recreation areas. These funds are allocated by the legislature according to guidelines propounded by an inter-agency committee representing the DNR, the SSWCC, the DRD, the SDPI, the DPW, the HD, the SBH, the DA, and the governor's office.

At the county level there are committees on just about everything except outdoor recreation. Town boards can block any plan, anyway.

<u>Reporter</u> magazine sums up the whole problem in these words:

"Probably no series of legislative enactments in U.S. history has created more complex administrative problems than those passed in recent years. They have three things in common:

"Their implementation cuts across existing departmental and agency lines within the federal government; they demand almost heroic responses from local governments in order to succeed; they require a combination of technical and administrative skills that are critically scarce.

"The critical shortage (in conservation) today is not money, but people to carry out the programs."

How about coming down here and giving us a hand, Sylvia? I think the League of Women Voters could use you. They're getting in the act, too.

I wandered past some show windows here in Madison the other day, and what do you know? Once upon a time they used to name new cars after men; now they name them after wildlife. What Detroit is now selling is not so much a car as a personality. I imagine this presents quite a psychic hurdle for our human friends. The male car buyer, for example, is forced to ask himself whether his outlook is more aptly expressed by beast or by fish or by bird.

If he decides he is a fish type, he must then wrestle with the question of whether he is most nearly in harmony with the Barracuda, the Stingray, or the Marlin. If the Marlin seems to express him best, he has more problems, for he must then decide if he will order it with a "four-on-the-floor super sports transmission for the husband with the adventurous wife."

Is his wife adventurous? This would seem to me like a dangerous question to ask a man. It may start him making discreet inquiries in the neighborhood and lead to nasty family scenes.

But suppose the buyer decides that his personality is bestial rather than marine. He must then undergo elaborate analysis to determine if he is more in tune with the swift Impala, the fierce Wildcat, or the wide-track Tiger.

On the other hand, he may feel more affinity for a Skylark or a Thunderbird. Incidentally, did you ever see a Thunderbird in our woodlot?

One species is a sort of hybrid called the Dart, which is neither exactly fish nor fowl but something in which you can "fire up that snarl under the hood" and "head out from the herd," plus "run barefoot through the wall-to-wall carpets."

If the choice were strictly among wildlife species, it might not be too difficult to pick a new car, but Detroit doesn't let humans off that easily. There are also some brand names that describe hunters we have known; for instance, the Rebel, the Marauder, the Rogue, the Fury, and the Caprice.

What a simple old country boy does when confronted with these alternatives, I don't know. It's obviously becoming harder and harder to buy a new car without psychiatric help. By offering a greater variety of personalities each year, Detroit is forcing our human friends to decide who they really are, when most of them probably would prefer to forget.

One thing makes me mad, Sylvia, and that is that nobody has yet named a car after us squirrels. Why do you suppose that is? I've always thought we had a sort of charm about us, not to mention strength of character. I guess the trouble is that humans use the term squirrelly to describe somebody who's not all there. Maybe Detroit is reserving that title for itself.

You aren't going to believe this, but a lot of old friends of ours here in Madison are fugitives from the law. The name that shows up on the police blotter is <u>Populus deltoides</u>, but you know them better as cottonwood trees.

Until recently, the cottonwoods were honored members of the Madison community. Now they are criminals, the city council in its wisdom having declared cottonwoods to be enemies of the people.

It seems that cottonwoods insist on doing what comes naturally to cottonwoods; namely, disseminating their seeds in cottony masses over the landscape. In the view of some persons, this apparently constitutes a serious threat to law, order, and lawns. Hence the cottonwood has been condemned, since it can't be expected to learn birth control.

This city has dispatched its assassination squads into every ward; their orders: to saw, chop, or poison to death every cottonwood. In the meantime, other squads of city employees are inoculating elm trees to keep them alive. The trees are confused, not to mention us squirrels and some citizens.

A lot of us have a special affinity for the cottonwood. It certainly doesn't look like a crook. Its massive branches spread evenly upwards to form a graceful, open top. Its leaves flutter and rustle in the faintest air current, like the echoes of never-quite-forgotten shouts.

Now that the cottonwood has been placed on the city attorney's list of subversive agents, it will be only logical if the cottonwood's cousins fall heir to guilt by association. Next spring we can confidently expect that quaking aspen, large-toothed aspen, Lombardy poplar, white poplar, silver poplar, and balm of Gilead poplar will join the cottonwood on the list of Madison trees to be exterminated.

For that matter, the city council may not stop with the _Populus_ family. There's a lot of nuisance vegetation around, if you want to look at it that way.

In the spring, spent honeysuckle, spirea, and forsythia blossoms litter lawns. In the summer, grass insists on encroaching over the edges of sidewalks. In the fall, maple leaves create traffic hazards on city streets. In the winter, we squirrels dig holes searching for acorns that wouldn't be there if they outlawed oak trees. All year round, evergreens disturb the peace with their perpetual sighing in the wind.

According to my tree guide, the name _Populus_ was given to the cottonwood family because "the music of their fluttering leaves resembles the murmurings of an assemblage of people." Between the murmurings of the city council and the murmuring of the cottonwood trees, some of us will take the cottonwoods.

In between attending legislative sessions and hearings, Sylvia, I pass a good deal of time watching television. Television is a box with a glass front through which you can watch portrayed all sorts of human doings. By watching TV I have learned a lot of interesting things about people.

For example, I used to think there were many different kinds or types of people, but that isn't so; at least, not on TV.

There seem to be only two kinds of American women. One spends all her waking hours at the sink, enamored of cleansers and making hysterical exclamations about very small matters. The other is gloriously young, beautiful, and wildly flirtatious, and continually swings her long, shining hair back and forth.

Both kinds of women are constantly baking--or heating up--the richest possible cakes and cookies, yet they have figures like those of young girls. The pastries, it seems, are all done for the children. Heaped plates are put before them, and they gobble them up without so much as a thank you.

There are only two kinds of American men. One is a young, handsome bachelor who, unfortunately, is afflicted with dandruff. But he pours a secret elixir on his scalp and goes on to countless conquests.

The other is a husband who comes home very tired from a hard day at the office, and his wife (in the kitchen, naturally) greets him and says not to forget the PTA (whatever that is) meeting that night. He is annoyed and snaps at her, but then he takes a pill, and everything is all right.

I feel right at home watching television, because a lot of our wildlife friends and neighbors can be TV stars:

A dove who flies into a kitchen window, excites all the neighbors, and then turns into a detergent.

A bear who turns a beer can into a swimming hole.

A duck who moves a whole houseful of furniture to Arizona.

A collie dog who helps put out forest fires every week.

A porpoise who cavorts in and out of all sorts of situations.

A kitten whose paws are as soft as a baby's diapers, provided the diapers are washed with a certain soap powder.

A lion who announces movies.

An elephant and a donkey who preside at political rallies.

A badger who is a football team mascot.

All of these bird and animal performers are the proteges, they tell me, of people who occupy cubicles in a huge glass slab in New York, where they crouch over typewriters trying to formulate new ways to make 60 million other people buy new products.

Some day, maybe, one of those ad copywriters will get the idea that a squirrel is a natural-born salesperson, and then you and I will be on television, Sylvia. I can hardly wait.

I may be in trouble, Sylvia. I got one of those forms from the census bureau the other day, and had to supply what they call demographic data. The way I filled the thing out may subject me to a full field investigation by the FBI.

For example, right off the bat they asked me what color I was. I hedged by saying "western fox," which is technically correct, but now I'm wondering if they'll realize that means I sport a red flag for a tail. If they do, I may be pilloried by some internal security committee. Of course they wanted to know if I was married. What can I say? According to Trippensee's standard text on wildlife, "squirrels are promiscuous in their breeding habits." So that's what I wrote. That will shake them up. Next they wanted to know how big a house I live in. That stumped me. As you know, our den is about two feet by one foot, but during the course of a day we range over two to three acres, and during a season we cruise up to 40 acres. I put down "30 rooms." That ought to stump them.

"Where do you live?" they asked. I said, "In a rural agricultural district on a farm woodlot bordered by cropland." I probably should have added that we need cover lanes connecting with neighboring woodlots and fields. After all, if people need highways, we ought to be able to say we need fencerow travel routes. Then they wanted to know my principal diet. I told them, "mast." I bet they have to look that one up. You can't find anything called mast in the A&P. "What do you think of the international situation?" they wanted to know. I told them I was much more worried about hawks than about doves, and about domestic shooters with 12-gauge shotguns than about overseas insurgents with Russian rockets. I'm not sure they'll be able to feed that answer into the computer.

"Do you have any thoughts about law and order?" the form asked. Here I quoted Trippensee again: "If a squirrel must be handled manually for longer than a brief moment, it is advisable to anesthetize it first; squirrels are vicious, and their bite is painful." They'll probably think that means I voted for George Wallace. The census boys wound up by pumping me about welfare programs. Here I referred them to our old friend Durward Allen, who once wrote about squirrel management:

"Food and belly-fat, living space, tree dens and protection, healthy squirrels and many litters--that, it seems, is the formula."

I can't find anything about such things in the platform of either party.

All over town on Fall days human beings are engaged in one of the most curious ceremonies I have ever seen. They are raking leaves off their lawns and consigning them to municipal dump trucks.

This is a strange ceremony for several reasons, it seems to me. First, the people who so fastidiously manicure their own lawns apparently never give a thought to the fact that their leaves become the trash that scars somebody else's environment somewhere else. Second, the people who remove natural fertilizer in the form of leaves in the Fall are the same people who dose their lawns with artificial fertilizer in the Spring.

Years ago, they tell me, people either let their leaves accumulate, or they burned them in the backyard garden--the bonfire making a splendid autumn pyre, the pungent smoke penetrating youngsters' nostrils so as to last for years, the ashes restoring nutrients to the soil. But not today. The suburbanite who lets leaves go untended is socially ostracized. It's even against the law to burn them. To assist in raking, hauling, and maintaining status, a whole industry has grown up--mulcher attachments for power mowers, wide bamboo rakes from Japan, big plastic bags from Monsanto, and of course the fancy dump trucks and street sweepers, some with vacuum-cleaner attachments.

Thus in another minor yet meaningful way does humankind interrupt the ecological cycle. Instead of husbanding tree humus it's carried off to pollute somebody's watercourse. We can only be happy, Sylvia, that nobody rakes our country woodlot. It may look a bit untidy, but it's healthier than any Madison yard.

Today is something called Easter Sunday here in Madison. Easter is a rather curious festival. At least it is difficult for a squirrel to understand.

At first glance, you might think Easter was some sort of farm produce fair. For weeks, store counters have been full of eggs-- eggs of all sizes, colors, and materials. Store windows have been full of little chicks and ducklings, and baby domestic rabbits.

A chief rabbit, otherwise known as the Easter Bunny, is supposed to have visited every house in town last night and hidden assorted eggs in assorted places for youngsters to search for this morning. I thought maybe this was another example of the way the government disposes of surplus agricultural commodities, but the custom turns out to be much older than the farm problem. In fact, it can be traced back to pagan rites at the dawn of time.

From another view, you might think Easter was a fashion parade. This morning all sorts of humans could be seen on the streets, many of them wearing weird hats of many hues. Interestingly enough, unlike the case with our bird friends, it is not the male of the human species who takes on fancy plummage in the Spring; it is the female. She displays herself much in the manner of a cock pheasant, and the drab males cluster around her. I suppose some biological function is served by this performance.

As I have discovered upon further research, however, that the true Easter has nothing to do with rabbits or regalia. It is a religious holiday. In fact, it is at the very center of the Christian faith, commemorating as it does the Resurrection from the tomb of one called Jesus, and the promise of immortality to those who believe in His name.

This faith is not held by all humans, and even some Christians can be classed as doubters, because it seems to be popular in some circles these days to speculate that "God is dead."

I can understand how such an idea might find currency among city folk. After all, there is little about the urban landscape to suggest that there is an order to the universe, and that Spring's rebirth follows immutably the hibernation of Winter. City life suggests just the opposite--that the disorder of traffic jams is a fundamental law, and that when something dies it is dead as a doornail and nobody cares.

Somebody familiar with our woodlot, on the other hand, would have a hard time _not_ believing in a natural order and an eternal life. Our oak tree loses its leaves each Fall, but it has never failed to revive each April. It will certainly decay and topple over some day, but only to shelter and fertilize a crop of seedlings.

I don't know whether such an observation makes me a cultist or a saint, and fortunately we squirrels don't have to worry about such labels.

Spring is the time of the year when a strange malady affects many of our human friends. The symptoms are varied, but they usually consist of things like glassy eyes, sweaty palms, and a twitchy forearm. Victims putter around in basements or sit staring out of office windows. Doctors call the disease "fishing fever." There is no known shot that you can take to ward off this fever, but fortunately there is a sure cure. You get a pole, a hank of line, and a hook, which you dangle in a stream or lake. Within moments the fever calms down. The only problem is, it comes back again, and you have to repeat the cure. You can see hundreds of humans taking the cure along or on any body of water.

Fishing fever is catching. It is spread by word of mouth over backyard fences or around poker tables. Some carriers of the fever are particularly virulent. They are the writers who spin what are called fish stories in magazines and newspapers. Some nurses do not believe in allowing the victim to take the cure. They are the families who draw up lists of yard work and housecleaning chores in an attempt to bleed the fever away. There is no evidence that this approach will abate fishing fever, but it will break up families.

America being the kind of society it is, manufacturers have learned how to capitalize on fishing fever. They turn out all manner of antifever aids, which are displayed flamboyantly in sporting goods store windows and on the sprawling counters of discount houses. These aids are known as fishing tackle. They consist of a bewildering array of rods, reels, monofilament lines, lures, tackle boxes, vests, boots, and the boats to haul them.

No doctor has ever proved that you need all this special dope to fight fishing fever, but that doesn't seem to make any difference. Victims fill their closets and garages with patent medicines nonetheless. On all this tackle they pay a special tax that is used to buy and develop public fishing waters. It's a very strange case of humans financing the fever that attacks them. To cater to people with fishing fever there has grown up an industry called the resort business. They tell me it is one of the biggest businesses in the state.

Maybe we should open up a resort along the creek that runs through our woodlot, Sylvia.

The reason you haven't heard from me for some time is that I've been on a vacation. A vacation, Sylvia, is a peculiar institution that humans engage in, most frequently during the summer months. According to the dictionary, a vacation is a "surcease from labor." The truth is though, Sylvia, that nobody works so hard as the average American on vacation.

Take, for example, the typical family tour to northern Wisconsin. There is, first of all, the "prior preparation" stage, in which you collect by dint of laborious correspondence the data on where to go and what to see, culminating in a moment of decision that is probably responsible for more divorces than any other single domestic confrontation. Once the objective is distilled over the fires of family debate, you collect by dint of excruciating commandeering a stockpile of exotic gear that always adds up to one more boxful than you can cram comfortably into your station wagon. So at the last minute you leave behind a duffle bag that turns out to have contained a crucial camp item like toilet paper. At your appointed "rendezvous with relaxation," as it says in the tourist literature, you devote so many hours to the sheer logistics of maintaining minimal creature comforts that you have less time to lie in a hammock than if you had stayed in your own backyard. And it will take at least a whole day out of your schedule just to pack up for the return trip, at which time you will again wind up with one carton too many. So you leave behind a priceless shank of driftwood or a genuine Chippewa warbonnet. You do not, however, fail to bring back 27 rolls of film, from which you make slides to edify neighbors and friends. The only trouble is, they will have vacation slides of their own. Thus a winter evening in suburbia is spent in the sheer agony of watching an out-of-focus sun set over Lake Minnewhozite.

Why all the grim determination to make a major expedition out of even the most minor vacation? It's what they call the Puritan ethic, Sylvia, under which hard work is Godlike and idleness is of the devil. Hence you turn your time off into toil in order to get to heaven dead tired. All in all, Sylvia, I doubt I will ever participate in another human-type summer vacation. It's much more satisfying just to sit curled up in the crotch of our woodlot oak, getting to heaven at last by going all along.

To us members of the Southern Wisconsin Association of Fur, Fin, and Feathers, Sylvia, it may be a little hard to realize that outdoor living has become sort of a Holy Grail for our human friends. We take pretty much for granted the privilege of sitting on a woodlot log, or playing tag in a treetop. Not so <u>Homo sapiens</u>. After eons devoted to escaping from the veldt, he is now bent on a headlong return to nature, or what is left of nature. I joined this twentieth-century crusade this past summer, and discovered some interesting things about Outdoor Recreation, AD 1980s.

First, there is developing a peculiar Outdoor Recreation philosophy--a strange combination of Yankee grit and oriental mysticism. The muscular strain traces back through the fadism of physical education cultists and the Puritanism of the pioneers to the Spartanism of the Greeks. The mental strain stems from Eastern and Occidental Indian postures as interpeted by the Thoreaus and Muirs who have seen in nature a vision of humankind in tune with the cosmos.

Second, to implement this philosophy, Outdoor Recreation now represents a growing matrix of government bureaucracy and private enterprise that may well come to rival the military-industrial complex. The federal, state, and local agencies devoted to husbanding outdoor resources are exceeded only by various forms of commerce devoted to exploiting those resources--all in the name of Outdoor Recreation.

Third, in every Outdoor Recreation area today we see the cataclysmic confrontation of a rampant population and a rampant technology versus a fragile, finite resource base. People have spent enough money to get to the stars, but not enough to handle their sewage. They have learned how to destroy a Vietnamese jungle but not how to protect a Vermont mountain. They treat every stretch of countryside as if they had a spare in every pocket. So human Outdoor Recreation today is sort of a dream castle anchored on quicksand. Will our human friends get their priorities straight in time? It will take an earthbound Apollo program of the first magnitude.

I toured the sporting goods stores here the other day, and I tell you, when hunting season is open, you're going to have some very fancy lead thrown your way. Science, you see, has come to shooting.

For example, for years gun designers have been trying their best to take the "kick" out of shotgun shooting. It now appears they have succeeded. A new recoil reduction system--utilizing hydraulics and powerful springs--measurably reduces shoulder impact from firing to a gentle, almost sociable, nudge.

By effecting a 78 percent reduction in recoil--or about half the kick of a 20-gauge shotgun--this new device will be a boon particularly to oldsters suffering from ailing joints, as well as to young hunters. According to the manufacturer, "the veteran shooter might also find the new system to be the difference between consistent hits and misses."

In other words, Sylvia, you'll have to dodge a little faster this fall. You'll get some help from another new development--an illuminated tracer load that visually pinpoints the center of a shot charge in flight.

The heart of the new tracer load is a specially designed capsule containing a pyrotechnic element that ignites when the shotshell is discharged. The tracer element is visible to the shooter all the way to the target. According to the label on the box, the shooter is thus provided with a true indication of the trajectory of the shot charge. Instantly one can see why one hit or missed and adjust the next shot accordingly. What it doesn't say on the box, Sylvia, is that you'll be able to see that shot charge, too, and duck all the quicker.

Humans have been making firearms of distinction and aiming them at us squirrels for a hundred years now, it says in the papers. It was in 1866 that Oliver Winchester made the first firearm bearing that famous name--a lever-action piece. The Indians called it Yellow Boy because of its brass receiver, and it was held in great respect due to the efficiency of its 17 shots.

Winchester commemorated its hundredth anniversary by issuing a modern centennial descendant of that first lever action. Having the appearance of its famous history-making ancestors, the new lever action has an octagon barrel, a shiny gold-plated receiver, and a crescent-shaped solid-brass butt plate. The walnut stock and forearm have the straight classic lines of the old Model 1866. The sights are the same buckhorn style that frontiersmen used to draw down on buffalo.

Fortunately, Sylvia, you won't have to worry about this fancy new weapon, because it is being made only in 30-30 caliber. At least I haven't heard yet of anybody using a 30-30 on squirrels. You never can tell, though. This is a day when people are trying to get a bigger bang for a buck.

I know you must think us squirrels live a tough life, trying to raise families in holes in trees, and dodging owls and shot. But, really, things aren't so bad for us. At least we don't have to get a permit to harvest nuts, nobody tells us how many we can take, and we don't need a passbook in order to store them. In contrast, listen, if you will, to the sad fate of Wisconsin duck hunters this year. Their daily bag is reduced to three birds a day. This bag cannot include more than one canvasback or redhead, one mallard, two wood ducks, two black ducks, or one hooded merganser. To go hunting they of course need a state license, a state stamp, and a federal stamp. On top of the state license and stamp and federal stamp, Canada goose hunters need a special permit. Around Horicon Marsh this will entitle them to one bird a year. In the rest of the state they can take four if they can find them.

It's all because duck populations are way down, and goose populations are too concentrated at Horicon. The regulations are very necessary, in other words, but they make a pretty regimented business out of what was once the epitome of free America. And it's not only hunters who are regimented these days. They held a "democratic" convention in Chicago one year, and the policemen outnumbered the delegates.

To understand all this, Sylvia, you have to realize that human beings are really just numbers, or rather lots of numbers. There are social security numbers, draft card numbers, credit card numbers, bank account numbers, and so on. Even students registering at the University of Wisconsin are assigned numbers. You can forget your name and carry on, but if you misplace a number, you're sunk. Of course humans have one privilege we squirrels don't have. They can shoot us, but we can't shoot back. To be sure, they need a permit to do it. Oddly enough, they don't need a permit to shoot other people. All told, I'm not sure I'd trade places.

There's one business I wish I owned, Sylvia, and that's the business of writing speeches for chamber of commerce secretaries. A chamber of commerce is sort of a flock or covey of businessmen and industrialists, and every chamber has a secretary, or leader, who makes a lot of speeches defending the chamber from all manner of threats. The nice thing about being in the business of ghost-writing for a chamber of commerce would be that you'd never really have to change the speech. Oh, you'd have to modify the introduction to fit the particular circumstance, but the main body of the speech you could warm over again and again.

For example, here in Madison a member of the city council has recently introduced an ordinance aimed at doing away with non-returnable bottles, cans, and cartons. The humans who live in Madison are about to be inundated in their own waste, and Councilwoman Ashman is trying to do something about it by getting rid of the throwaway containers that make up a big part of Madison's garbage. Well, they held a public hearing on her proposal the other day, and you-know-who trotted out "the speech." It goes something like this: You can't pass this or do that because it will (1) force businesses out of business, (2) make items unobtainable, (3) increase prices, (4) discourage economic development, and (5) hurt people on fixed incomes.

I think this speech was first written in 1902 to oppose workmen's compensation, and it has been used against social security and against war and against peace and so on ever since. In other words, every time anybody comes up with an idea, you can count on "the speech" to knock it down. On second thought, though, there is one part of "the speech" that does change. If the proposal is for a local ordinance, "the speech" says that the problem is a national problem and can only be tackled at the federal level. But if the proposal is for a federal law, "the speech" says that the problem can only be handled at the local level.

After the hearing on her ordinance, Councilwoman Ashman said "the attitude of the businessmen at the meeting makes me pessimistic." In other words, she is not sure the new drive for environmental quality and conservation can carry the day against "the speech." I'm not so sure she's right, Sylvia. Once upon a time they said humans would never have fair employment practices and all sorts of other things that are "bad for business." But human society has made strides, anyway. I'm more inclined to think it's "the speech" that is just about over the hill. At least so long as there are courageous women around like Alicia Ashman.

Mark Saturday, October 2, on your calendar with a big red skull and crossbones, because that's the date the squirrel season opens in southern Wisconsin west of Highway 78. You might tell our grouse friends they become fair game the same morning.

I'll be safe here in Madison, because they don't permit the discharge of firearms in the city, but your Iowa County woodlot is apt to be a pretty dangerous spot.

If it's any satisfaction to you, no human being can go hunting until he or she has paid $5 or so for a license. They don't have to take any test, just pay their money. That's not really very much dough these days, and yet average hunters expect a whole lot for their bucks.

For one thing, they expect to be able to go hunting as many days out of the season as they can get away. Second, they expect to tramp unmolested over any hill and dale, no matter who owns the land. Third, they expect to be able to bring something home to eat. And fourth, they expect to be able to tell off the Department of Natural Resources when anything goes wrong. All that for about $5 a year.

In contrast, the very same individual thinks nothing of paying at least $3 each and every time he or she plays one round of golf, and expects to wait in turn at a crowded first tee. Yet he or she doesn't expect to break par, and doesn't write a letter to a legislator if the greens are rough.

It all makes you wonder just who invented the human laws of economics. The economic approach to nonresidents of Wisconsin is particularly peculiar. Let's take the nonresident fisher, for example.

First of all, Wisconsin humans spend more than 900,000 tax dollars a year to lure nonresident fishers into the state, not counting the millions of commercial dollars spent for the same purpose.

Then this nonresident fisher is charged only $5 for a fishing license, unless he or she is under 16, in which case they fish for free. If a husband and wife guarantee to stay only 15 days, the two of them pay a mere $6.

Now let's say this nonresident is not a fisher but a university student, who proposes to stay a whole year in the state, spending money like a sailor. You'd think Wisconsin humans would welcome them with open arms. Not so. In the first place, they have to be extra-intelligent before they're allowed to come. In the second place, they're charged more than $2,000 for nine months of study at Madison, and another $1,000 or so if they spend the summer here.

Human agricultural economics are crazy, too. The farmer who owns a woodlot can get his taxes reduced by one government bureau if he fences cows out of the woodlot, and can get money from another government agency to help turn a marsh into a cow pasture. One government bureau will help pay for fertilizer to grow more alfalfa, and another will pay for not growing corn.

Say, how'd I get off on this subject, anyway? All I wanted to tell you was to be alert on October 2. On second thought, maybe it's about time we squirrels started shooting back.

CBS (that's a TV network) put on a show the other night that was the most violent, sexist, racist, not to mention innane performance I've ever seen. It was called "The Wizard of Oz," a wizard being sort of a magician and Oz being a technicolor woodlot. The Wizard was OK. He was an old male stumblebum. But nothing else was true to modern scripting requirements.

In the first place, the show opened on a Kansas farm. Whoever heard of Kansas? It should have been set in the Imperial Valley of California. The farm had contented hired hands, not unhappy illegal Mexican migratory workers. And Dorothy--she's the main character-- had a dog of uncertain lineage instead of a purebred like Lassie.

Dorothy is zapped by a tornado, collects no federal disaster area aid, and winds up in this land called Oz. She doesn't even file an environmental impact statement when she makes a crash landing. She is immediately met by a good female witch, who would have been much more properly portrayed by a San Francisco gay, and then Dorothy is subjected to a welcoming ceremony by midgets celebrating as if they didn't know they were handicapped persons.

To find her way back to Kansas, Dorothy is told to follow a yellow brick road. There is no suggestion that a brick road may be an uneconomical employment of scarce natural resources, or that hitchhiking can be hazardous to a young girl's health. What is more, in her precipitous arrival Dorothy has wasted a witch, but there is no police investigation. She departs in total equanimity, accompanied by her mongrel.

Now the plot really gets complicated. Along the road Dorothy encounters in turn a male scarecrow without a brain, a tin man without a heart, and a cowardly lion. Obviously, at least one of these characters should have been a black female; but which one? Can a black female lack brains, or a heart, or courage? Maybe it's just as well they were all portrayed as white, Anglo-Saxon, Protestant males. But surely the villainess--the Wicked Witch of the West-- could also then have been a WASPM, yet she wasn't. She was a female of dusky color and aboriginal religion.

You see how it goes? The U.S. Supreme court may have decreed desegregation and affirmative action, but CBS apparently hasn't caught on.

In their travels, Dorothy, the scarecrow, the tin person, and the lion walk through a big field of poppies and are seen to become very drowsy--a clear suggestion that they have been smoking pot excessively. As a climax to the tale, Dorothy wastes another witch, and once again there is no inquest. In fact, she is cheered as a queen by a tribe of winged monkeys. Imagine letting <u>our</u> children watch something like that!

Well, at any rate Dorothy finally gets back to her Kansas farm, thanks to two CIA agents disguised as magic slippers. And then everybody, we suppose, lives happily ever after. All in all, Sylvia, I've never seen a TV movie so out-of-touch with modern political and social realities. And they call us "squirrelly"!

You may think there isn't much doing down here at Madison when the legislature is not in session, but actually this is a very busy time of the year, thanks to committee meetings and conferences all over the place.

Aldo Leopold once complained that conservation consists mostly of "letterhead pieties and convention oratory." He may have been right. At least I find myself attending one heck of a lot of hearings, all of them supposedly having something to do with conservation, many of them producing little more than printed proceedings.

You even need a scorecard to keep track of the players in this business, because there are all sorts of groups and causes and people, all of them devoted, they say, to the "wise use" of our natural resources.

Some of these people are "resource-oriented." That is, with them the husbanding of natural amenities comes first. Other advocates are "people-oriented," and talk about the greatest good for the greatest number. Still others are "moneyoriented," and say that what's good for business is good for the country.

At one end of the spectrum, for example, are the hard-line environmentalists, who tend to emphasize protection and preservation of fish and wildlife. At the opposite end of the scale are the exponents of resource development, who tend to look for maximum returns from tourism. In the middle are people like the outdoor recreationists and the regional planners, who are concerned with esthetic appreciation, ecological design, and things like that.

I guess all together everybody in the conservation movement is really on the side of the angels, but it gets pretty confusing to a squirrel who's just trying to save his woodlot from a crosscut saw.

All of these people do a lot of talking, but not always much communicating. New ideas and programs do really come into being here, but only a computer on very friendly terms with all the layers of decision-making in Madison could tell you exactly how ideas become actions. There's even much talk about talk itself.

A conference chairman the other day, for instance, opened the meeting by quoting the crusty farm leader of the 1930s, George Peek. Peek once said that "the common characteristic of all up-lifters is an unquenchable thirst for conversation; they are all chain talkers." Whereupon the chairman gave a talk.

Still, as the Bible says, in the beginning was the word. The problem is to make sure that the ending around here is not also the word. Sometimes that seems a clear and present danger.

It used to be that when you called somebody an animal, you were somehow separating him from the human race. Writers who talked about "nature red in tooth and claw" were not including people. Now, after observing things here in Madison and on TV, I'm beginning to wonder.

This <u>Homo sapiens</u> is a pretty violent species. Racial warfare is a constant threat, crime is increasing, and the city is at least as dangerous a place as our woodlot. I've watched Chicago police clubbing hippies and yippies, and I've read about other riots, murders, and a random assortment of rapes in the streets. It's all not much different than what takes place in the so-called wild.

Maybe this isn't so strange after all. You can make a case for the view that humans are the only carnivorous apes, and that they wouldn't be here as humans today if they weren't violent. It's a pretty good bet that at some fateful moment in history a long-extinct ape uncle turned back to the bush to starve on a dwindling supply of berries, while ape grandparents took to the savanna with murderous intent and a taste for meat.

People are still the only species that casually kill their own kind, and lately they have become fascinated enough by the habit to keep IBM records of the incidents. Americans don't have a corner on violence, although you might think so by listening to some politicians. German massacres of Jews, the strife that accompanied Indian partition, the destructiveness of the last days of French Algeria, mass executions in Russia and Indonesia, civil wars in Africa, fighting in Iran--it seems pretty clear that the knack of violence is widespread.

From all of this, Sylvia, you might get the idea that human beings are not different than our fellow fur, fin, and feathered friends. But I have to admit there is an opposite side to the coin. Humans have a concern for each other that goes beyond mere words. It is expressed today, for instance, in a massive spontaneous effort called the ecumenical movement among the churches. There is a growing concern in business, in government, and in the private conscience for the unemployed, for the uneducated, for the ethnic minorities, for women, for the old, the deprived, the brutalized, the homeless, and the disenchanted.

We have to remember these traits when we assess <u>Homo sapiens</u>. That species has always been inclined to think the worst of itself-- immature, uncivilized, materialistic, violent. I think it would do well to put aside its obsession with its faults, look at itself realistically, count its blessings, and get on with solving its problems.

After all, that's what we wild animals do.

Yours truly,

SAMMY

Badger Almanac

Some ecological news doesn't make the papers. There are times, at almost any season of the year, when we make news by creeping out of our close and crowded houses into the night or noon, shucking the accoutrements of custom, and partaking of what Emerson called "the medicinal enchantments" of nature.

These halcyon experiences may be looked for with a little more assurance in that pure Autumn weather we call Indian Summer. There is one particular day in October when the countryside reaches its perfection, when the air and the land are in perfect tune. The day before, the oaks and maples were not quite at their umbre prime. The day after, a rain driving out of a dull sky will have stripped the leaves. But this particular day, immeasurably long, ineffably quiet, embraces broad hills and warm wide fields in a tempered light, casting an ancient spell on any who have chanced to be abroad in the magic moment.

But headline days can occur anytime in outdoor Wisconsin. The fall of snow in still Winter air, preserving to each flake its perfect form, and embroidering in crystal the twigs and trails that ordinarily lead the anonymous life of the woods. A Summer sun sinking slowly lakeward to touch with gold the precipice of a mapled bluff. The odorous south wind of Spring, waving with shadowy gust a field of soft young rye, and carrying with it the mysterious piping of migrating pintails.

Newspaper headlines typically are made in faraway places with strange-sounding names, but we can experience the inspiring, healing news of nature without leaving home. In every landscape the punctuation point is the meeting of sky and land, and this is to be seen from Sauk Prairie as well as from the top of Mount McKinley. The stars at night glitter above the homeliest hillock in Vernon County with all the incadescence they shed on the Campagna. The clouds and colors of morning transfigure even backyard box elders.

Nature is seldom caught in disarray; beauty can break out anywhere. The only real difference in landscapes is in the eye of the viewer. It is good, then, in our present days, to look for action where the action always is, in those odd moments of ordinary existence when reality and romance meet in outdoor vistas within our daily grasp down Wisconsin sideroads.

And, as we share Mr. Emerson's enchantments in nature, we can grasp, too, his vision of our oneness with "the unity of nature-- the unity in variety--which meets us everywhere": "All the parts incessantly work into each other's hands....The wind sows the seed; the sun evaporates the sea; the wind blows the vapor to the field; the ice, on the other side of the planet, condenses rain; the rain feeds the plant; the plant feeds the animal; and thus the endless circulations of the divine charity flourish man."

Signs of Spring

March is the month when the out-of-doors begins to come to life again, hesitantly yet surely. Flowers, birds, and humans shuck off their winter lethargy according to an ancient and immutable schedule. Before any wild blooms brave the still-frosty air of March, daffodils begin to spangle dun city lawns. To poets, the adventurous daffodil has been an inspiration of long standing.

Bryant called the daffodil "our doorside queen" as it pushed up "to spot with sunshine the early green." De Vere dubbed the daffodil the "love-star of the unbeloved March." Shakespeare wrote of "daffodils that come before the swallow dares, and take the winds of March with beauty." Perhaps the most famous tribute to the daffodil is that of Wordsworth, describing "a host of golden daffodils beside the lake, beneath the trees, fluttering and dancing in the breeze." But it doesn't take a poet to appreciate a March daffodil. We all respond with lifted hearts to this innocent yellow harbinger of spring.

The birds come back in March, too, waterfowl in the vanguard. Geese from Louisiana bayous bring new life to Dodge County cornfields and sloughs. Pintail and blue-winged teal stop over on their tour from South America to Canada. Whatever the geological or biological reasons for this annual spring migration, we know that the trigger is, if you'll pardon the expression, sex. Light stimulates development of the breeding glands of birds. As the season turns from Winter to Spring, the hours of daylight increase, and with it the sex drive. Finally, as breeding condition reaches full force, the birds strike out for nesting grounds in the north. The phenomenon can be produced by exposing captive birds to increased hours of artificial light. Fortunately, love life is triggered for different species at different weeks. Some migrants press northward in the footsteps of receding snows, while others sop up sunlight until late Spring. The result is that the big migratory push is spread over several months, to the benefit of flyway traffic.

But the surest March sign of Spring's impending return is furnished by humans. Youngsters begin to rebel against trooping off to school in coats, preferring to shiver in sweaters. On the campus, student leaders begin to plan perennial spring uprisings like panty raids or sit-ins. Matrons are lured into shops to emerge wearing the unlikeliest of bonnets. The man of the house stomps around the backyard wielding a rake or an eight-iron.

True, in any March there is still to be experienced the last dregs of Winter. A brief blizzard may blot out daffodils and defy geese for a day. The basketball season comes to a blazing climax in the state tournament. And you may have to keep your topcoat in the closet indefinitely. Yet the change is undeniably in the March atmosphere. As you drive home from work one evening, you are aware the sun is higher. When you get up one morning to fetch the paper off the front porch, you get a whiff of a languid south breeze. And then you know you have made it through another Winter.

I was out looking for Spring one March weekend, walking along the railroad track that separates Rock Lake from the marsh. At first I didn't find much in the way of signs. A bull cardinal calling. A faint hint of softness in the air. That's about all. It is that in-between time when the heart says the season ought to be turning, but the outdoors offers little to prove it. The marsh was still frozen, the muskrats still asleep in their houses. Only a few scattered, bounding tracks showed where some venturesome rabbit ran the gauntlet of foraging owls to frisk about on the ice.

A duck blind juts up like an unwanted brown wart on a finger of bog-land. From the railroad bridge, in the bright, blue days of October, it was just barely discernible behind a screen of waving cattails. It belonged. Now, under the dull sky of March, its haphazard boards rear in disarray abouve the matted sedge. I hiked over for a visit.

By kicking around under ragged planks and rusty chicken wire, I uncovered the old box that must have served as a seat and the discarded thermos that probably cracked under too sudden a change in temperature. Here and there lay bright red shell casings. I picked one up. It still bore the haunting smell of nitro.

A shadow of wings drifted across the ice. Instinctively I crouched down among the rattling stalks. But it was only a crow, winging his solitary way over the frozen marshland.

Back at the bridge, I gave up my search for Spring. And then I heard it. At first it was only a distant, quavering echo; then the chant began to swell, and I knew it for the distinctive clamor of Canadas. Finally I spotted the great birds themselves--geese from Baton Rouge--whipsawing in a ragged line high above the lake basin, heading north toward Horicon, with Spring trailing in their wake.

This great passage is one of the surest signs of approaching Spring, but although we can smash atoms and use the smithereens to cruise under the north pole, the old riddle of bird migration still baffles us. Some theorists wonder if birds migrating north are following routes dictated to them by ancient ice caps. They postulate that the ice sheets of the glacial ages drove all life before them, and that birds moved north or south as the glaciers receded and advanced. Others say that the northland may have been the ancestral home of all birds, and that they seek out old home ranges each Spring. Still other ornithologists postulate the ancestral home was in the south, but became so crowded that birds pioneered to the north.

So much for some of the "whys." The "hows" of Spring migration--especially homing ability--are even tougher to explain. How can a hen mallard possibly find the same Nebraska farm for seven straight nesting seasons? How can blue geese leave Louisiana's Sabine County and fly unerringly to the mud flats of Baffin Island nearly 3000 miles away? There's evidence that birds may travel by landmarks, or by the positions of the sun and stars. But there must be more to it than that. How do some sea birds find their way through dense coastal fogs to offshore rookeries on small islands? The earth's magnetic field may have something to do with it, or forces produced by the earth's rotation. And how much is learned from older birds, and how much is instinctive? Geese seem to learn their lofty trails from experienced leaders, but juvenile ducks can find their way on their own.

Nobody really understands bird migration, but all people know that when geese fly north, Winter is almost over. For most of us, that is enough.

While calendar-makers recognize March 20 as the first day of Spring, wild creatures tend to disagree. In Wisconsin at least, you won't find a lot stirring this time of year. Besides Mr. Skunk, the only animals up and about will be woodchucks, chipmunks, prairie moles, leopard frogs, and earthworms. Only a few bird migrants are back with us by March: marsh hawks, bluebirds, meadowlarks, red-winged blackbirds, bronzed grackles, robins, kildeer, waterfowl, mourning doves, woodcocks, and fox sparrows.

One of the first sure signs of returning Spring you will find right on your urban street. Before many denizens of the country brave the chilly winds of March, city-bred forsythia bushes break into flower, flinging golden arcs of bloom against gray lawns. On mucky country meadows, you will then find that wild floral pioneer, the skunk cabbage. He pushes up his gnomelike hood with his bronze-and-purple spathe even in these uncertain days of wayward warmth. The ugly duckling of the wild-flower world, the skunk cabbage is nonetheless a welcome sign that Spring is surely on the way.

By mid-April, if you are browsing through a woodlot, you will find at your feet the delicate radiance of the hepatica, rising alone upon its hairy stem, one of the earliest blossoms on the waking earth. Wild anemones are another sign of Spring. Though they may seem too delicate, they manage to cling to their white, pink, or rose petals all through the winds of April.

Perhaps the most diagnostic sign of Spring's return is the arrival of the upland plover.

"Whe-e-e-e-e-o-o-o-o."

More like the wail of the Spring wind itself than like a bird's call, a long, weird whistle will come rolling down out of the April sky. High above the prairies a brown comet will gyrate, now mounting, now gliding, to the pitch of its plaintive cry. The upland plover, he of the errie voice, is back--signaling once again in his own distinctive way the return of Spring. You can practically set your watch on the basis of the arrival of the upland plover. For the past 13 years in Jefferson County, Wisconsin, this bird hasn't varied more than three days from his April 16 average, even though he comes all the way from the pampas of South America.

Not all signs of Spring are as predictable as the arrival of the plover. As everybody knows, bird migrations and plant bloomings vary with weather conditions from year to year. Some years the onset of Spring will be as much as three weeks early or late. Year in and year out, however, you can be pretty sure that Spring will come in April, signaling the start of another outdoorsperson's year--the beginning of another opportunity to seek out those adventures in outdoor recreation that are everybody's for the finding down the sideroads of Wisconsin.

I suppose it was only a question of time before science overtook an old-fashioned symbol of Spring. I guess it was bound to happen sooner or later. But some of us are still not sure we like the new streamlined way of making maple sugar.

Time was when maple sugaring was as much a Spring ceremony in the life of a small boy as the state high school basketball tournament or Easter. It all began in March. With a little auger you bored a hole in the tree trunk. The hole would begin to weep immediately and you would tentatively taste the sap as if it were communion wine. Into the hole you would push a twig of elderberry out of which you had poked the pith to form a pipestem. Below the pipe you would hang a tin bucket to catch the dripping sap. Each morning and each evening you would make the rounds of your buckets, pouring the precious sap into a pail to be carried home to the kitchen.

They don't do it that way anymore. They have a network of long plastic tubes which transports the sap from tree to tank untouched by human hands or Spring spirit.

Once you had collected enough sap to fill a washtub, you came to the central point of the maple syrup ceremony. You put the tubful of sap on the back of the kitchen range and you boiled and boiled and boiled. Gradually the sweet aroma filled the whole house. If you were making syrup you took the tub off the stove before the liquid crystalized. If you were making candy, you boiled some more. Knowing when to quit was an art.

They don't do it that way anymore, either. A radical method of making maple syrup that eliminates most of the boiling operation has been developed by chemists as a spin-off from research aimed at recovery of potable drinking water from sea water. Called the "reverse osmosis" system, the new method involves pushing maple syrup through a semipermeable membrane under high pressure. In other words, you get rid of the water in the sap by straining it out instead of by boiling if off in the form of steam. The new method is faster, cheaper, and surer, but the aroma has been taken out of the process, and with it a delightful symbol of Spring.

The outdoor year in Wisconsin really begins in April, not in January. The outdoorsperson doesn't pay much attention to man-made calendars. We go by natural signs. It is in April that the sap surely starts to rise in maple trees and human spirits. By April 1 we usually have some sure sounds and sights of Spring's return in Wisconsin.

Heartening as are sounds and sights, it is the smell of Spring, I think, that really gives a lift to Winter-weary folk.

It isn't easy to put a typewriter finger on the ingredients of Spring's perfume. I suppose you would have to say you start with the aroma of wet earth, distilled by the warmth of the higher-riding sun and wafted across a windy world into office windows and school yards to produce a delightful dalliance. Certainly there is mixed with this basic fragrance a hint of dripping snow-water and a breath of cloud floating in the blue lake of April's sky. To these add the mild scent of tender grasses on the sides of gentle hills, the fragile bouquet of hepaticas hidden in an arboretum woods, the tang of last year's sodden leaves.

Then there is the musk of the moss just beginning to stir under frost-heaved rocks, the scent from muskrat houses on the shores of new-melted ponds, the woodsy aroma of old fence posts and piers warmed almost to life again in the balmy air. The sweet smell of Spring partakes, too, of sap rising in bare-limbed maples, and of the swelling buds of forsythia sprays outlined bright against drab drifts of lingering snow.

Someday, perhaps, in this age of science, we may be able to buy a bottle of "Spring" at our favorite perfume counter, but it won't be until the chemists discover how to synthesize that most important ingredient of all--a whiff of optimism from human hearts.

When you live on an RFD route, Spring comes slipping through the door in your big mailbox. The free catalogs arrive, addressed to "Rural Boxholder"--messages of hope in a world still burdened with some snow flurries, somber skies, and dormant earth.

Sporting goods catalogs are not so numerous as they used to be. Some of us were weaned on grand publications from Dowagiac, Michigan; Denver, Colorado; Toledo, Ohio; Kansas City, Missouri; and West Bend, Indiana. These Creek Chub, Cook, Pflueger, Gateway, and Shakespeare books have disappeared, and with them an early hint of lake and stream delights. The Weber Lifelike Fly Company of Stevens Point, Wisconsin, still puts out a catalog, but it is a pale image of its former self, once replete with gorgeous full-color plates of Royal Coachman, Parmachene Belle, Grizzly Tip, and Dunn's Mist.

Carrying on in the great tradition of outdoor literature, however, are the L.L. Bean Catalog from Freeport, Maine, and Eddie Bauer's Catalog, from Seattle, Washington. The flavor of these catalogs is enough to stir the soul of the most jaundiced sportsperson. It is not only that they picture a complete line of everything woodsy, from cabin cribbage boards to scotch grain moccasins. Mr. Bean and Mr. Bauer talk to us personally, if not always grammatically, extolling the virtues of their various wares, and inserting little tips on how best to cast for walleyes or how not to portage a canoe.

Some of us in our wanderings have visited the warehouses from whence come these marvelous catalogs. It is, frankly, a letdown. Mr. Bean and Mr. Bauer are in Florida, and the sales girls on duty don't know a tackle box from a tortilla. But, come April, the authentic Bean and Bauer messages show up in our mailboxes again, and we are once more intrigued by a "soft sell" that no Madison Avenue merchant has ever duplicated.

If sporting goods catalogs are paler than they once were, not so with seed catalogs. Spring comes early in a riot of cataloged color that puts nature in the shade. In summer bloom, the Queen Bess rose will never quite match the flaming orange of its cataloged portrait. The hybrid sweet corn will never be as golden nor its kernels as full. Nature simply cannot match the printer's petunia.

Turn the pages of these seed catalogs and you can almost smell the warm breezes of Summer, the ripe earth, the gentle showers, lilacs abloom, and the sweet scent of new-mown lawns around the corner of May. Here are everything from asters to zinnias in a chromatic effusion which beggars description. And the names of the flowers! They are right out of Peyton Place, hinting of glamor, excitement, and intrigue: Jamboree, Gladiator, Christian Dior, Buccaneer, South Seas, Pink Parfait, Apricot Nectar, Show Girl, Golden Rain. The bountiful harvest of picture fruits and vegetables is almost good enough to nibble, paper and all.

Someday, in an age of ever more super supermarkets, perchance nobody will shop by mail any more, and the catalogs that harbinger Spring today will be found only in historical libraries. It will not be progress.

If there is any Sunday when you will find the outdoorsperson in church, it is Easter Sunday. Some will say this is just because the hunting season is long gone and the fishing season is yet to come. In other words, because the outdoorsperson has nothing else to do but go to church on Easter. Such a charge is the rankest kind of calumny. The truth is the nature-lovers of the world were celebrating a sort of Easter long before the churches patented the day. As a matter of fact, it was B.C. outdoorsmen who invented many of our Easter customs.

The Easter bunny, for example, traces back to the huntsmen of ancient Egypt, who venerated the hare as a symbol of reliability and fertility. Persian sportsmen long, long ago had a custom of coloring and eating eggs during a Spring festival dedicated to the return of the birds. The very name of Easter is a barbaric term borrowed from the Teutonic tribes of central Europe, who commemorated the death of Winter and the waxing of the sun with elaborate pagan rites. Even the date of Easter has an out-of-doors flavor, it being the first Sunday after the first full moon after the vernal equinox. Prior to the Civil War, Easter was not observed in most of the Protestant churches of America, because of a Puritan reaction against Catholic ritual. It was the Transcendentalists, with their affinity for nature, who kept the spirit of a Spring festival alive in New England. In the light of this ancient and honorable connection between nature worship and the central Christian celebration, it is little wonder that outdoorspersons feel comfortable in church on Easter Sunday.

But observant outdoorspersons are the first to realize it is easy to carry too far the simile of Easter and Spring's rebirth. There is, after all, something entirely automatic about the return of the birds and the thrusting up of green grasses. But there was nothing automatic about the profound event that is commemorated by the true Easter. The Easter story is something more than nature lore. It is recorded in John that "the stone had been taken away from the tomb." That is the great Easter message. It is a message you cannot hear in the voice of a warbler or read in the bloom of a rose. The messages of nature are mortal. For intimations of immortality we must seek another source.

You don't have to go out of town to find Spring flora and fauna. I once identified some interesting species of bird life right in my suburban neighborhood.

For example, right in our house we had an Early Morning Warbler, distinguished by its habit of rising with the sun and awakening its parents with a call that sounded exactly like "Cookie, Cookie, Cookie," repeated at regular intervals, growing louder each time.

Then we had that common species, the Eagle-Eyed Collector, easily identified by its habit of cluttering its nest will all manner of fascinating but useless objects, like sprigs of faded wild cherry blossoms, shreds of glass, odd-shaped rocks, hanks of string, Canadian pennies, and bubble-gum wrappers. The call of this bird sounded like "Hey, Dad."

The Eagle-Eyed Collector is closely related to the After-Dinner Bit Saver, another common bird. The name of this species is derived from its passion for scraping a tablespoonful of this and a smidgeon of that into small jars and placing them in the refrigerator for a period of several weeks, at which time they are thrown into the garbage. Sometimes there is an intermediate stage in this process, known as a casserole dish. The call of the Bit Saver is unusually distinct and penetrating. It sounds like "Money, Money, Money."

We also had in our house a Dead-Ended Phone Hogger. This species inhabits a world of its own, eschewing the company of all birds except fellow Phone Hoggers. It has no call which can be described in the English language. Its most distinctive habit is one of perching motionless (except for the mouth) on the sharp edge of a chair, vainly attempting to push a telephone receiver into one ear and out the other. This species has practically lost the ability to fly--except when the phone rings.

While it did not inhabit our house permanently, I frequently saw that other species of bird life common to suburban neighborhoods, the Coffee Bird. In fact, we had a number of Coffee Birds on our street. These birds are rarely seen singly. They prefer to flock together, particularly about ten o'clock in the morning. Like the magpie, the Coffee Bird has a long repertoire of calls. It is also remarkable in the fact that its morning plumage is dull and disarranged, while its evening plumage is colorful and chic.

My street also had several Lyre Birds. This bird likes to appear on the scene out of nowhere when you are working in the yard or in the basement. Its Summer call starts out like "Let's go fishing," followed by a long trill accompanied by gestures. In the Fall this call changes to "Let's go hunting."

One of the Lyre Birds on our street was said to have written a book about the out-of-doors.

It is only with the greatest reluctance that Nature gives up her claim to city subdivisions. For 11 months of the year, people seem to gain steady ascendancy, but each May the forces of nature stage a rear-guard action which temporarily wins back some ground. Lakelets in low places, meadowlarks on telephone poles, dandelions on manicured lawns--these are some of nature's ways of saying, "I was here first."

Out on the far west side of Madison, for example, where the platters have laid out a new housing development, nature has just reclaimed a marsh plump in the middle of what is supposed to be an avenue. Here each evening hie mallards, spoonbills, teal, and baldpate to feed in the shadow of giant earth-moving equipment. By June their pothole will be a boulevard, but in the meantime the ducks are having a last fling.

Wherever nature once had standing water, she is quick in May to move back in, despite the presence of human "improvements." Suburbanites with damp basements in Kenosha County are paying the penalty that comes from tampering with nature's drainage system. So are the gardeners who try to grow early peas in what was once a Horicon slough. According to the city assessor, our property values go up as nature retreats. Some of us are not so sure. We exchange pastures for lawns and lose larks. We lay out streets and lose dogwoods.

In the long run, perchance, Nature may win back some of the footage she so reluctantly gives up to the real estate experts. In some places it will take her eons, in other spots not so long. There is, for instance, another subdivision of Madison known as Lost City. This was to be the dream suburb of another era, but its development was snuffed out at full stride by the Depression, and Nature moved back to reclaim her own. Today a Lost City boulevard is as exciting as a woodland trail. Little turtles sun themselves on the smooth, hard surfaces that once held the dreams of people. Frogs croak a strange, prophetic rhythm from the sloughs that once were yards. Along the sagging streets is a decayed symmetry in a living marsh--straight lines softened by a kindly and haphazard nature, pavements nourishing life with the beginnings of topsoil, cracks in the walks possessed by root structures.

For some, Lost City represents blight. For others like me, it is a city of solace, untouched by ranch houses and parking meters.

The outdoor maternity wards of Wisconsin spring to life in May. When it comes to replenishing their kind, the workings of wild things occur in endless variety, yet with marvelous planning.

Consider, for example, the case with most birds. Fertilized eggs are laid at daily intervals, yet they all hatch at about the same time. The reason is temperature. In the egg-laying process the female is away from the nest for extended periods, and with the variable nest temperatures, the growth of the embryo is halted. But when the last egg is laid the clutch is held at a uniform temperature by the setting bird. Then, and only then, does embryonic growth begin--for the first egg laid as well as the last. And a good thing it is. Without such control over beginning incubation, hens of large-brooded species, such as pheasants, grouse, and ducks, would have real problems. The first-born would be two weeks older than the last, and trying to tend the fleet-of-foot while incubating others yet in the egg would bring neurosis to the mother and high mortality to the young.

Mammals, too, can "blow the whistle" on prenatal development. Minks, weasels, and certain other species will mate at various times of the year, yet the young are born during a given period in the Spring when the weather is warm and food is more readily available. In these instances, fertilization occurs with mating, but development is suspended, then resumed at a time to give birth during a favorable season. Bears make easy work of having young. Birth occurs during the mother bear's hibernation period. The little cubs fend for themselves until mama bear wakes up a month or so later. You might think porcupines would have a sticky time of delivering babies, but nature has developed a way out. Young porkies come packaged in puncture-proof bags which the mother tears open on delivery. Exposed to the air, the soft, moist spines harden in a matter of minutes. Then the animated pincushions are prepared to face the world with confidence.

Unusual--and significant, too--is the way many kinds of wildlife regulate their production of young to fit conditions in the environment. Given plenty of food and cover, rabbits, for example, will have more and larger litters than they will under adverse circumstances. Increased production and a determination to swell numbers to fit the capacity of land to support them has been noted in deer, muskrats, quail, and other species. Sex in the wild is a determined force, and sparsity stimulates it to full reckoning.

For many a moon now I have kept a field journal in which I record the highlights of outdoor excursions. That annual period known as "Spring vacation" has always provided an abundance of entries. It is a pleasant experience to leaf back through dog-eared diary pages and recall Spring-vacation sights and sounds of other years.

My very first journal entry, for example, says that on April 9, 1938, "I spent the day on the Faville Grove Game Area (near Lake Mills) with Irv (Buss) planting 375 young Norway pines." I can still remember the hermit thrush that kept us company all afternoon.

The same day "we drove down to the prairie to get a count on the upland plover that had arrived back on the 13th." Later that week "we sloshed through the tamaracks to Farmer's Island, lush with the first Spring flora." According to my journal we found spring cress, hepatica, May apples, rue anemone, wind flowers, pitcher plants, bloodroot, spring beauty, Dutchman's-breeches, and dogtooth violet.

A year later, on April 19, 1939, my field book tells me "I hiked in to Bean's Lake (in Jefferson County) where a pair of lesser scaup drakes, performing for a lone female near the west shore, saw me through the trees and flushed noisily."

Saturday, April 20, 1940, "Art Hawkins and I spent the day at

the Leopold shack on the Wisconsin River near Baraboo. High points--
a pair of mallards feeding in the 'front-yard' marsh, a big hen
woodcock flushing from an inky-black pothole, grouse droppings
three inches deep under a grape tangle, two deer bounding across
the road, Estella's pet squirrel, and Mrs. Leopold's stew."

So goes my journal in those ancient years when Spring vacation
was worthy of the name.

What did I enter another year? It looks like this:

"Apr. 6: Basement is leaking. Had to slop on two coats of thoroseal."

"Apr. 7: Downspouts are frozen shut. Overflow from eaves is washing out our rock wall. Opened up the spouts with an ice spud and boiling water."

"Apr. 8: Offered to take the girls on a hike, but they preferred to go to a movie."

"Apr. 9: Family says basement is so full of clutter they can't keep the house clean. Spent the day throwing away valuable documents, antique lamp shades, broken coffee pots, jelly jars, 27 remnants of paint, and a 48-star flag."

"Apr. 10: Uncovered the tulip and daffodil beds. Found a heap of dog bones."

"Apr. 11: Beautiful day for a hike. Spent the morning grocery shopping and the afternoon raking and fertilizing the lawn."

"Apr. 12: Another beautiful day for a hike. Had to work in the office in the morning. Spent the afternoon writing a newspaper article about the joys of Springtime."

"Apr. 13: Took off down a Wisconsin sideroad!"

May is that magic time of the year when people and nature can be
most in tune. The inhospitable winds of Winter are but memories.
Yet to come is the almost obscene flourish of Summer vegetation.
In May our bodies and minds can strike a balance with the out-of-
doors.

But to do so we must have open space--that priceless vista
where trees and plains meet an untrammeled sky. This need for a
view, for the long look, may be a peculiarly American requirement.
Europeans do not seem to have cultivated it. They have gone in
more for temples and formal gardens. But not Americans. The
craving for the long look brought us here in the first place, and
sent thousands of Lewises and Clarks beyond one range after another,
until finally we stood, like Balboa, silent upon a peak in Darien.
My great-grandfather Jones came from New Jersey to Wisconsin in the
early 1800s, looking for the long look. He stayed only briefly,
and then went searching still across the wide Missouri and beyond,
like so many others of his era. He and his kind won the West while
they were looking, and set aside some parks and preserves so we
could look, too.

Recently George Gallup discovered just how precious open space
is. Polling Americans about conservation, he found that although
the bulk of his interviewees lived in cities, they didn't really
like to; nine out of ten said more land should be set aside; and

most of them said they would pay extra taxes for it.

To really look beyond the ranges, of course, you have to get on a high peak on the Kenai, where your eyes can encompass a whole world that still knows not humans. But you can get a little taste of long-looking on a May evening even in the city by plunging off the beaten tracks to a place like a park and soaking yourself like a muskrat in the spell of woodland Spring. Old, open-grown bur oaks will be weaving their ancient lacework against the horizon, at your feet will be the fragile flora of a remnant savanna, and hidden lagoons will be loud with frog voices.

We stood the other night, listening for the "peenting" of woodcock, as a pair of teal threaded their way through the dusk and the willows to land with so soft a splash in waters that have known their kind since Pierre Radisson first came long-looking to the valley of the Mississippi. It was only for an instant. Inevitably we had to consign ourselves again to the cacaphony of a bulging beltline highway. But for a magic May moment we took the long look and preserved it on an island of the mind.

Summer Solstice

June is the month of brides, bugs, and outdoor buffs. It is the month when the most important things don't get into the newspapers.

For those who have always lived in the city, the coming of June may mean no more than the smell of hot asphalt, but to country people June and the heavy odor of elder blossom are as one. A month ago the feathery leaves and young green canes of the elder shot up from the muck of the thickets along country roads; today the elder stand full blown, a queenly flower, with its hundreds of tiny blossoms displayed in a broad parasol cluster.

A generation ago, in Prohibition days, there was a widespread surreptitious interest in the big, dark juicy berries of the elder. Kids, too, had a practical use for the bush. We made whistles. It was easy to push out the pith and then, by making a neat, crescent opening and blocking one end we had a pipe that Pan might envy. Today we buy our wine and toy horns at a shopping center; but there still is something in the odor of elder, and the sound of honey bees buzzing in it, that brings to mind inevitably the long hot midday of a childhood June.

In June there also come to flower certain blooms about which the botany manuals say, "Escaped from old gardens." One is Bouncing Bet. Brought over from the Old World long ago for the delight of Colonial ladies, Bouncing Bet has now become a little gamin in a gay pink dress, living out her days like a gypsy along the roadsides.

Another immigrant is the Japanese honeysuckle. With its pale, gold flowers and its stealthy, conquering growth, it has been called "the yellow peril." It multiplies with a rapidity no native plant seems to equal. But it has at least a propensity for covering unsightly places, like tin-can dumps. Amid the same rubble there often spreads, too, the misty blue of chicory. Like most weeds, it is an Old World plant, and was brought here as a garden crop; but it escaped and turned vagabond.

Wild cousins of the garden pink are on display in June: the wild pink, its petals nearly crimson in shade, arranged like a five-pointed star; the bladder campion with puffy calyx striped purple-brown; the starry campion of elegantly fringed petals; and the night-flowering catchfly, with its large, white blossoms that close at dawn.

These are the days when the insects inherit the earth. All day and all night their humming chorus prevails, of voices so threadlike that only their mighty numbers make them audible. The insects alone of all the heterogenous dwellers of our world inhabit with equal triumph the air, earth, and water. With the coming of the warm days, lazily buzzing, the flies carve incredible geometric arcs through the heavy air. At night the moths dance giddily in the light; mosquitoes sing high, thin malice; and baffled June bugs bump clumsily against cabin porch screens.

As William Wordsworth once wrote, I can't quite paint what then I was. Suffice it to say that in the twenties in a Mineral Point parsonage, as the six-year-old son of a preacher and a protective mother, I was penned in the back yard by a six-foot chicken-wire fence, lest a heathen world somehow contaminate me. Then on one grand June day that shall forever live in glory, I was rescued bodily from my penitentiary--by none other than Mrs. Vine, the President of the First Congregational Church Ladies' Aid Society. Mrs. Vine pulled up in a big black Reo and announced I was to go fishing with her and her little boy Bobbie. Such is the hierarchy of a congregation that my mother had absolutely no recourse but to bundle me off.

That is over 50 years ago now, but I can still hear the side curtains flapping as we went out the Belmont road, down Schaaf's Hill, turned into a pasture lane, and parked on the banks of a branch of the Pecatonica.

The setting was so picturesque as to seem in retrospect almost pat--a meandering river, a low dam, a deep fishing hole at its base with fluffs of foam riding the eddies, and the foundation of an old mill forming a convenient ledge on which to sit in the Spring sun. I would like to report the water was crystal-clear. It was not; it was coffee-colored. The steep slopes of Iowa County had been mined as cornfields for 50 years. Nobody had heard of contour plowing or grassed waterways, much less of retiring the hills to beef pasture. Now that Iowa County is Aberdeen Angus country the Pecatonica is a lot cleaner than it was in 1924. But to two little boys then it was clear enough, and the suckers and redhorse it harbored were as worthy as bass or pike.

Mrs. Vine unstrapped the tackle from the sides of the Reo and took the bait bucket from the running-board rack--a 1924 touring car being inadvertently yet superbly designed as what much later came to be called a recreational vehicle. Bobbie and I were each equipped with a cane pole, a hank of line, a cork bobber, a sinker, and a hook. The worms we had to thread on ourselves. I have loved night crawlers ever since, and the sounds and smells of a stream. Whether we caught any fish or not I honestly can't recall. It was enough to be free. Mrs. Vine had introduced me to that priceless scepter of sure escape, the fishing rod. I never wield one today without thinking of Mrs. Vine, a Reo, and a June river long ago.

When I was a boy, July 4 was celebrated outdoor-style in a rather simple way. At the crack of dawn we would shoot off firecrackers in our back yard. Then we would head for a prairie grove at Waldwick or Latto for a potluck community picnic, featuring a stirring address by Fighting Bob LaFollette and an equally long invocation by my father. After which we would sneak off to the nearest sucker stream with a cane pole and a bobber.

    All that is considerably changed. Outdoor Recreation Model 1980 comes in a bewildering array of shapes and colors, many of them manufactured in Japan or at least in Detroit. At one end of the spectrum is the big boat race, as staged recently in Madison, Wisconsin. It is a little hard for some of us to understand how 50,000 people can get their kicks out of watching a dozen hydroplanes make mincemeat of Monona, but suffice it to say they do. At the other end of the spectrum the same weekend was the small cadre of folks who followed biologist Jim Zimmerman around the Arboretum's restored prairie, drinking in the wonders of lady's slipper, Indian paintbrush, and spiderwort. The boat buffs probably don't understand the wild-flower fanciers.

    In between are the mushrooming numbers of recreationists who hie to such places as Governor Dodge State Park, where the Department of Natural Resources is turning what used to be a secluded hollow into a center of mass diversion; or to arty spots along Highway 23 between Dodgeville and Spring Green, where music and theater fans enjoy all sorts of performances, wander through curio shops, or try to sit in Frank Lloyd Wright-designed chairs. Still other folk just go fishin' on the Fourth, although the equipment they take along these days would be completely beyond the capabilities of that Reo touring car.

    All of these forms of modern Fourth-of-July recreation have one thing in common; they are the fruits of a technological age. No longer can we expect to serve the wants of our fellow citizens with baked beans on a buckboard under a bur oak. We have to plan, and build, and develop, and charge fees. Nature, in short, needs help. The many forms of modern Fourth-of-July recreation have another thing in common: they are essentially competitive. The powerboat jockey on Lake Wingra can effectively ruin the day for a Sunday afternoon hiker on its shores. And the lady's slipper preservationists can preempt woods that might otherwise harbor campers.

    All of which suggests that the spirit of '76 will have to be reactivated. We have to be very concerned about the rights of many minorities. The consumers of outdoor recreation are not a single majority "public." They constitute a congeries of minority "publics." To protect in some way the rights of each of these publics, we can't apply the classic slogan, "greatest good for the greatest number." That leads us down the path of a grey concensus satisfying nobody. We have to learn how to determine and meet many divergent demands and fit them into a pattern of zoning that will develop outdoor resources without needless destruction and protect them without penalizing proper use.

Summer is the time of year when wild things are replenishing their kind the natural way, quite independent of state commissions or federal subsidies. Squirrels and rabbits already have produced a first installment on the year's capital stock. Some bushytails will shuck out a second brood, and cottontails will have several more litters before the end of Summer. Pheasants, grouse, some quail, and waterfowl are herding early broods of chicks. Those that fail in their first attempts will try again--and again.

One week I came upon a teal nest, and the mother bird performed the ancient ritual of fouling the clutch as she flushed. It was her instinctive way of making the eggs unacceptable to the marauder. Another day I rescued a tiny grouse chick from being stranded in a woodlot depression. The hen partridge alternately flew at my face or fluttered away with a simulated broken wing. It was her way of protecting her brood.

This effort of wild things to perpetuate their kind is a study

in determination that humans can well envy. From one point of view, it's a wonder we aren't up to our eyeballs in animals of all types. But while nature is lavish on the production line, she is also highly indifferent to the well-being of her charges. For example, among ground-nesting birds you'd think a 50 percent loss of nests would be nothing short of a catastrophe. Yet the fact is that such a loss is common among most birds, and occasionally nest destruction may run as high as 75 per cent. The causes vary from time to time and place to place. Mostly it's a combination of things like the weather, predators, and farm practices. Whatever the causes, the fact is that more nests fail than succeed. That's where persistence pays off.

All of our game birds will and do renest. Their efforts continue until either they are rewarded with a hatch or are closed out by the lateness of the season. That's why it is a common occurrence to see a covey of bumblebee quail or half-grown ringnecks in the hunting season. In either case, don't credit the mama bird with having raised two broods. It doesn't happen. The most and least you can say is that she gave it the college try and finally brought off one brood.

This determination to produce a crop through repeated nesting efforts might suggest that Fall populations should be about the same each year. But here's the joker: renesting involves progressively smaller clutches. So even though all of the breeders may eventually bring off a brood, the end result is not the same as when good conditions permit a high rate of success on the initial try.

In the interest of building bigger game crops, it's reassuring to know that nature, fertile and persevering, is on the side of numbers. Where conditions can be changed for the betterment of a species, the potential for rapid increase is always present. Some things, obviously, are out of reach. The weather, for example, we can only talk about. But there are many means of preserving and protecting nesting cover that farmers can practice on their own land, and that the state can follow on the growing number of Wisconsin acres under public control. Modern-day game management simply aims for those readjustments of the landscape that will permit a great realization of nature's built-in capacity for increase.

Everybody thought he was dead. He certainly had not been seen for a long time. Not since he was reported walking along the Mississippi River a few miles south of Hannibal, Missouri; or swinging a big 40-ounce bat in Yankee Stadium; or taking on a platoon of Boche single-handed in Belleau Woods. Everybody knew what he looked like because his picture was in almost everybody's cedar chest. If it wasn't there, it was certainly bound in the archives of the Library of Congress, or simply engraved on the minds of millions.

He was the Great American Hero: Old Hickory. Buffalo Bill. Huckleberry Fin. The Sultan of Swat. The Railsplitter. The Son of the Wild Jackass. Sergeant York. He was that picaresque lone operator, larger than life, who set himself against the tide and rode into the sunset, trailing clouds of glory.

Walt Whitman once pronounced his eulogy: "As now taught, accepted, and carried out, are not the processes of culture rapidly creating...a man (who) loses himself in countless masses of adjustments, to be so shaped with reference to this, that, and the other, that the simply good and healthy and brave parts of him are reduced and clipped away?"

There is, indeed, little in our era hospitable to the Great American Lone Ranger. Most of our public figures come prepackaged in Brooks Brothers suits. They are adept at the politics of concensus. They muster about as much charisma as a Kewpie doll. Even the stardom of the astronauts is vitiated by the teamwork behind their feats. More than anything else, the idea of "the team" seems to have made the American Hero obsolete. There are scientific research teams, offensive and defensive teams, fund-raising teams, diplomatic teams, sales teams, team teachers. For a time, outdoorspersons resisted the team approach, posing rather as reincarnations of Daniel Boone. Then came the doctrine of togetherness. When that modern Don Quixote, the late Bobby Kennedy, braved the gorges of the Colorado, Ethel and ten little Kennedys went along.

But the Great American Loner isn't really dead. You can still find him on a golf course in July. And that may account for the rather sudden and sensational rise of the Arnold Palmers as folk heroes. Arnold is not just another number on a well-oiled football machine. He is out there all alone, with nothing between him and disaster but his trusty putter. He is not an amorphous, anonymous scientist in an off-limits laboratory. He is a grimacing, glowing human being in the full glare of the TV cameras. The course he is attacking is in every sense a replica of the American frontier. There are forests, swamps, and deserts, great prairies, lagoons, and quiet meadows. He drives off from a tee as if he were embarking from Fort Dodge, and he strides down the fairway with no sign of fear for the savage traps lurking along the overland trail to California gold. In his wake is Arnie's Army, the hundreds of thousands of acolytes who each summer weekend pack their shooting irons, saddle their carts, and fare forth to do battle with 6,000 yards of wilderness. It's a pretty antiseptic wilderness. But it's about all we've got left. It is the last stamping ground of the lone American hero.

There is a special spirit in the outdoor air of early August. It is almost as if nature were aware of people's habits. Like hundreds of thousands of humans, she tends to take a vacation this time of year. You can see and feel her pause perceptibly. Past is July's green avalanche of maturing vegetation. Yet to come is September's fire dance. Now is a quiet interlude.

August dawns are moist, and fog fingers hover in the river valleys and the coulees. Lawns and pastures are spangled with cobwebs. By noon, however, the sun will have burned through and the landscape lies hot and seared. Wherever you go, a Summer drought will be leaving its scorching mark on upland pastures.

Lowlands that in Spring stood four-fifths under water will seem half-deserts now.

The temperature will be torrid by noon, and great thunderheads will mount in the afternoon sky. Only an occasional vagrant wind will wave the woods and sweep with shadowy gust a field of corn, inhabited by a lengendary Indian Goddess, her limbs swathed in the nodding leaves. Goldenrod is yellowing brightly along the roadsides. Sweet corn is plentiful. (Incidentally, a cob of corn ought to be pulled, husked, and put in the pot, like a brook trout, while it is still flapping.)

Bass, pike, and muskies are in retirement, lolling in lake and river depths, coming out to feed only at dawn or dusk. Trout lie wary and unresponsive in the gin-clear water of their streams. The strident voice of a young crow serves only to accentuate the silence of inactivity. Big bumblebees drone by. Around a sudden bend in a country road you come upon a flock of partridge pullets dusting themselves in the sparse gravel. They take off in a flight not yet purposeful.

A lowing herd winds slowly up the lane. A distant canning-factory whistle summons the evening shift to work, the lights begin to twinkle from the barns, the long day wanes, the pale moon climbs, crickets call 'round with many voices.

Yes, in August you are almost tempted to think that nature has struck a balance, that some power has indeed commanded the seasonal moon to stand still. Yes, this is the time of the late-summer doldrums, of the dog days. The midday sun sears the land in a brassy haze. The woods, fields, and marshes are silent. Leaves wilt and droop in the listless air. At no other time, save in the sub-zero days of northern Winter, does the outdoor world seem so still. The appearance is deceiving. Hidden by the lush Summer vegetation, the land throbs with life. Wildlife populations are at their annual peak, ranks swollen by young ones hatched or born in earlier months.

There's little hint of this abundance at midday. But venture afield at dawn and you enter a different world. The air pulses with bird song. Roadsides and woods edges are alive with cottontails, in a stepladder of sizes; with tidy, bright-eyed families of quail; with cautious does and stilt-legged fawns. Here and there a hen pheasant or grouse doggedly incubates a late clutch of eggs, her earlier efforts thwarted by weather or nest-robbers. If she succeeds, hunters in the fall will call her later-hatched brood "squealers." The waterfowl marshes are strangely quiet, even in early morning. Gone is the riot of sound and color of the Spring courtship displays. The brilliant plumage of the drakes has disappeared, replaced--in a molt unique among all birds--with drab, henlike feathers. Most of the drakes themselves have vanished from the marshes, banding together on more open waters before this molt deprives them of all flight feathers.

While the drakes seek the safety of open water, the hens, also molting and flightless, remain close to cover with their broods. For some of them, the peace will be disturbed by crews of waterfowl biologists, taking advantage of the molting period to round up,

count, and band the earthbound birds.
   By midmorning across the landscape the flow of life ebbs into the shade for a long siesta through the heat of the day, to venture forth again with the lengthening shadows of late afternoon. Stuffing themselves on the abundance of late Summer, the wild youngsters-- all unconsciously--are racing against time. All too soon the days will be much shorter; the hint of frost will be in the air. Young wings must be strong, and new feathers full, to carry those who will migrate beyond the reach of Winter. The youngsters who remain, the earthbound mammals and the nonmigrant birds, must develop strong bodies, well fortified with reserves of fat. People throng the beaches, huddle in air-conditioned rooms, and cluster around fans. But in the dog days of August, the hidden hordes make ready for the harvest dance of Fall.

Autumn Odes

For everything, says the Book, there is a season. For many of us the season is Fall. On the face of it, there may appear to be something pathological in our love for the season of dying. On the other hand, Autumn comes and goes with such a flourish in Wisconsin that we can scarcely be faulted for our devotion to a blaze of glory. For us Fall people, autumn is our Camelot, our shining hour.
   There is, first of all, the sheer avalanche of color. The crimson of the maples, the evanescent gold of the hickories, the frosty purple of the asters, the candle yellow of the poplars, the scarlet of the sumac, the lavender of the oaks--all set against stark white birch trunks and soft green pine boughs. You can hardly encompass the riot of nature's brawl.
   Then there are the activities of Fall: the upland grouse hunt, with a russet bird rocketing away through the rasping trees; the marshland pheasant hunt, where an immigrant Chinaman matches with his own burnished breast and silvered wings the colors of his adopted home; the pothole duck hunt, where a long line of mallards sends down from great heights that susurrant sound of wings and chatter of conversation that raises hackles on the neck of the waterfowler; the arboretum hike, where the haze from burning leaves across the lake infilters a prairie grove to become ghost smoke from Indian campfires; the living room evenings, with good red apples and nuts; football--in Camp Randall, where the crowd roars as eleven men in cardinal trot out onto what is now perpetually green turf, or on TV, where the Green Bay Packers sponsor seances in myriads of homes; or that last golf match, when your ball rolls an extra 30 yards on the baked fairways of Indian Summer, and the greens lie strangely quiet in the still air.
   You don't even have to engage in vigorous diversions to get a lift from Autumn. A ride through the purpled hills will do it, or simply sticking your nose out the front door on that first frosty morning. Trout fishers and gardeners may vote for Spring, swimmers

for Summer, and skiers for Winter. But as for me, give me Fall, in Wisconsin, where the year ages with abandon, and I know that life can reach its zenith after 40.

If you are abroad early enough on the morning of September 1, you feel her presence once again. There is only the merest hint of her, you understand; a rasping in the poplars as she rustles her crimson cape for the first time each year, a subtle fragrance in the dawn air as of poppy fumes and apple oozings, a gust of cool wind like a gentle hand on earth's fevered brow. But the hint is enough to set hearts astir to the first foot-beats of approaching Autumn.

True, Summer has at least a month still to run. It can yet be a time of torrid weather, when great thunderheads mount in the west toward close of day, while the land yields up from its pores what moisture the usurious sun has not already squeezed out. The lovely Queen Anne's lace will open to the sky like a handkerchief. It makes even vacant lots and waste ground beautiful. (Where appearance is concerned, the Umbellifer family are the poor relations of the plant people, but there is something as royal in the bearings of Queen Anne's lace as in its very name. Yet an idol can have feet of clay, and though Queen Anne's lace may be an apparent monarch above, underneath the sod it is nothing but the garden carrot run wild.)

Bees hum in the ivy on the wall; the early apples turn their reddened faces to the sun. Hollyhocks and zinnias bloom; dahlias, asters, and mums are yet to come. Yet for all the somnolent warmth of September, there is--in the early morning hours or even at midday in the lee of the woods--that hint of Fall.

You may hear it in the metallic liquid "kon-queree-ee" of red-winged blackbirds, or in the restless twittering of swallows. You may see it in the sumac already turning cardinal against the hills. You may feel it in a sudden whisk of wind out of the west, carrying with it--you imagine--a touch of brisk Canadian air, a fragile fragrance of fringed gentians, a whispering of wild rice, and even, if you listen hard enough, a haunting call of migrating Canadas.

The first breath of Autumn renders outdoorspersons as unstable as milkweed seeds. We start peering into sporting-goods windows as clerks switch fishing rods for shotguns. We turn off the main roads to run our dogs through thickets where immature quail burst out like meadowlarks. We pause in our bass casting to trace a family of teal as they dart over the lake.

It's well to savor this pre-Autumn period, because Autumn itself can be deceptively short. After a line storm in September, there is frequently a period of two to four weeks when brooding mellowness does bless the countryside. Crops mature, and upland woodlots are a painted fairyland. Then comes a turn. Perhaps there is a three-day driving rain that strips the leaves. Perhaps it is a killing frost that blights grasses and reeds. On a late October evening you stop a moment to savor the weather. There is a cold, raw edge to the rising wind. You catch a harshness in the swish of tree limbs by the house corner. Early Fall has come and gone.

Autumn was made for hunters, or vice versa.
    It is not simply that the game season is open in the Fall. There is something about the scenery itself that gets under a hunter's skin. You won't hear them talk much about it, because to rave about the painted countryside is to display an effeteness unbecoming to a rugged outdoorsperson. But if you follow hunters through their Autumn ramblings you will see them pause more than once simply to gaze at purpled hills or whiff the fragrance of a fringed gentian. And if you ever ask them to recount a past exploit, you will invariably catch them including some of the stage setting as well as the action.
    It is the rare pheasant hunter, for example, who cannot recall that first ringneck. In the mind's eyes one can quickly conjure up a vision of that rooster bursting out of a corn shock, his bronzed wings and burnished breast blending into the scarlet and gold of a nearby hedgerow. When duck hunters stir up a log on memory's fire, they may picture the green and gray and blue and yellow blur of a drake mallard springing straight up from a swamp pothole to fade into the green and gray and blue and yellow of tamarack, goldenrod, and sky. The grouse hunter, too, partakes of the very essence of Autumn, as one wades through russet woods and thickets in search of a russet bird that rockets away with the abandon of the departing year.
    As the yellow poplar candles gutter out, as the tamaracks turn from green to brown, as the maples shed their leaves and the oaks take on a sombre cast, as the skies of October change to the leaden shroud of November, as Autumn breezes take on the harsh breath of Winter, hunters change, too. They switch from the drab coat of the bird shooter to the scarlet mackinaw of the deer hunter, as if to fill the void of color.
    Most painters picture Heaven as a place of perpetual Summer. Every hunter hopes it's Indian Summer, at least.

"Where do you find nuts?" I asked my youngest daughter one day.
    "Well, they're usually near the candy, but sometimes they're next to the bread," she replied promptly.
    You can't really fault an answer like that. But it does suggest how antiseptic life has become in an age of supermarkets, in contrast to the bucolic "olden days." Time was when if you wanted nuts you had to go out in the country well in advance and pick them. In fact, nut-hunting was one of late Fall's highlights, along with apple-picking, church bazaars, and rabbit hunting. Those were the days, of course, when a harvest moon wasn't just something in a song.
    Rare was the youngster of yesteryear who couldn't tell a butternut from a walnut at 100 paces, didn't know unerringly the difference between a pignut and a hickory, or who didn't have a

cluster of prime hazelnuts spotted by mid-September. Then on an appointed day in November the whole family fared forth for the harvest. Walnuts were a particular prize. Across the hills you carried your gunnysacks and "knocking" sticks. In a favorite draw stood the laden trees. First you scoured the ground for downed fruit, and then you rattled the spreading branches.

Back home the fruit was spread out on the barn floor to dry. In a couple of weeks or so you husked--stamping and twisting the walnuts under your boots until they came free of their tough brown coverings. If your gloves had holes in them, your fingers acquired a brown stain that resisted every brand of soap.

Now you had to wait again for the husked nuts to dry. To have some for Thanksgiving you sped up the process by keeping a tray in the warming oven of the kitchen range. Finally came the night when you assaulted a pan of nuts with crackers and picks. To wind up with a fruit-jar of meats you had to start with a big pile of nuts.

It was all part of the fun of late Fall. So was apple-picking. In the good old days you had your choice of some thirty varieties-- like Russets and Baldwins and Wealthies and Wolf Rivers and Greenings. Now the homogenization of American life has cut commercially available varieties down to four--all of them brighter than red and absolutely free of defects. (It is inconceivable that our children would have to learn how to eat around an apple-worm.)

In between nut-hunting and apple-picking you went to church suppers. Every city congregation and every country parish had one, seemingly competing to see who could load the plank tables with the biggest array of turkey, ham, oysters, jello, pumpkin pie, mince pie, and devil's food cake. In one corner was the inevitable "fish pond" for the kids and in another was a counter of fancywork. As I remember it, the price of a meal was 25 cents for adults and 10 cents for children--with no sales tax. They don't make that kind any more.

The family of more than one Wisconsin sportsperson will be emulating our Pilgrim forefathers this Thanksgiving by sitting down to a dinner of wildfowl. The choice is even wider today than it was at Plymouth Rock. And there are about as many ways to prepare wildfowl as there are hunters.

To hang or not to hang is Question No. 1. It all depends on whether or not you like your game birds with a "high" flavor. If you like as little gamey flavor as possible, you don't hang your birds at all. If you like a medium-high taste, you hang your birds in a cool, dry spot for a day or two. If you like a really high flavor, you let them hang indefinitely. Some hunters hang their birds by the feet. Others prefer to hang their birds by the heads. Each side can expound some very plausible arguments to back its case.

Do you dress immediately, or leave the feathers on until ready to use? Here again there is divided opinion, but everybody agrees you ought to draw your birds as soon as possible, particularly if they have been gut-shot. Do you wash the cavity with water or do

you merely swab it out with a vinegar-dampened rag? You can get
into an argument on this point, too.
   Do you pluck out the feathers, leaving the skin intact, or do
you simplify the whole procedure by skinning wildfowl as you would
a squirrel or rabbit? Both methods have their supporters. If
you're a plucker, dip your upland birds in hot--not boiling--water
before you start. With waterfowl, dry-pluck and then dip in
melted paraffin. When you peel off the hardened paraffin, the
pinfeathers--most of them at least--come off with it. Do you soak
coarse birds in salt water? Some do and some don't. Some cooks go
in for elaborate stuffings. Others are satisfied with an apple, a
carrot, an onion, and a celery stalk. Some cooks favor a high,
fast oven. Others are sold on a low, slow oven. Your best bet is
to experiment until you find the system that matches your palate.
   Whatever your method, when you pull up your chair to a Thanksgiving dinner of wildfowl, you're practicing a great American
tradition. Before you pitch in, why not round out that tradition
with a Thanksgiving prayer for Wisconsin's outdoor blessings:
   For flocks of waterfowl high in the blue vault of March,
winging northward in flying wedges and wavering lines, the leaders
calling the tired stragglers on, their wild chant ringing across
the breadth of the lake basin to stir jaded human hearts.
   For a Summer sun sinking below the willows and touching with
gold the precipice across the lake.
   For the secret ministry of Winter frost that hangs up on the
eaves trough a row of silent icicles quietly shining to a quiet
moon.
   For vesper sparrows that jingle their silver change on the
broad counter of a trout-stream meadow.
   For the charging, churning black bass that broke your leader--
and your heart.
   For the northern mallards pirouetting down over your blocks
out of a gusty November sky.
   For the fat young spike buck drifting like a rusty cloud
through a thicket.
   For that hardy alien, the ring-necked pheasant, who has made
your land his own.
   For the walleyes that gang up below the river dams.
   For a gnarled Iowa County hillside, where the Sabbath hunter
has a phoebe for a choir master and an orchard for a sanctuary.
   For a Coon Valley canyon, steep, tortuous, full of shapes
damned and beautiful.
   For a Fond du Lac marsh, alive with minstrel mosquitoes, and
ringing with the tinkling bells of swan language.
   For a Vilas County forest, where the snort of a rutting buck
echoes for half a mile down the fir halls.
   For myriad Wisconsin lakes, glinting in the sunlight.
   Yes, and for all the Wisconsin men and women who make it their
life work to help keep fish in streams and birds in skies.

Winter Winds

Outdoor fans have a special affinity for the Christmas season. This is the time of the year when everywhere there are revived the ancient rituals of nature worshipers, and when the trappings of the countryside are transported to every living room.

The yule log, the candle, the colored light--they date back to pagan bonfires built to give the Winter sun more strength. The date of Christmas itself was set to coincide with the Winter solstice and the age-old celebrations surrounding that natural event. The Christmas ham or turkey that today come from chrome meat markets were once the contributions of huntsmen who scoured feudal forests. St. Nicholas, who originally rode a white horse, has been transmuted into a character who drives a team of woodland deer, although in recent years people with no feeling for sentiment have pictured him riding in a helicopter.

Sportspersons used to use Christmas as an excuse to tramp out and cut down a tree. Now Christmas trees are big business. To satisfy the modern demand for bringing the out-of-doors to town at Christmastime, Wisconsin producers alone put nearly four million evergreens on the market each season.

While the lights and the greenery of Christmas stir something primordial in the breast, outdoor fans have a tough time facing the holiday jam at a shopping center. They are very apt to duck out to a stretch of countryside, where they can really savor the Christmas spirit, particularly at night.

You stop your car along a sideroad at the crest of a ridge, out of sight and sound of neon and TV. You step out and pause long enough for your eyes to adjust to the blackness. The cold air hones your senses to the sharpness of a skinning blade. Stars that in Summer glow fitfully at great distance now seem to glisten just beyond shotgun range. A myriad of snow crystals pick up moonbeams to make a lustrous link between sky and land. Ice-laden aspens crack like rifle shots. Distant oak and pine are dark with the mysteries of the evening.

It is now the sportsperson recalls the real kinship of countryside and Christmas. It was to a cluster of outdoorsmen on an open hill that the greatest story ever told was first announced. The Christmas angel did not make his historic revelation to the crowds in a Jerusalem store or even to the congregation in a Bethlehem church. The angel chose instead to appear out in the country, on a starry night, to a handful of attentive shepherds and doubtless also to an audience of hunting dogs, rabbits, and quail.

In Wisconsin a New Year's Day hike has an appeal all its own: bright berries against soft evergreens, hardy Winter birds, animal tracks, the squeak of pacs on complaining snow.

Perhaps you will find a stand of mature pines where the forest floor is a thick carpet of needles and only a few errant rays of sunshine filter through interlaced boughs. In the cathedrallike atmosphere even the turmoil of trucks on an adjoining highway can take on an organlike quality. Or perhaps you will tramp toward an oak opening, its frost-tipped branches performing a rugged etching against the azure sky.

(There is a growing interest in trees in southern Wisconsin as the result of Dutch elm disease, and this revived interest can contribute greatly toward tree planting and care programs. The Wisconsin climate favors 25 or 30 species of trees native to the state. The most popular tree for urban planting has, of course, been the elm. The sugar maple, second in popularity and our official state tree, is not really adaptable to some soil conditions. Horticulturists recommend such native trees as hackberry, oak, ash, linden, locust, and ironwood where replacement for an elm is sought. Trees not native to Wisconsin but which grow well are the sycamore, ginkgo, and redbud.)

When some people go hiking, they prefer to strike out cross country, the more remote the country the better. I prefer a well-worn path in familiar surroundings. Your feet will follow it naturally and your thoughts will do the wandering. That, to me, is the real tour of discovery--to keep to the beaten trail, to look at customary sights--and to bring home a new idea.

The most striking view on a Winter walk can be the view at your very feet--the stories told in snow.

Here, perhaps, is where a ringneck has strutted and strained to reach some nightshade berries growing high up on a fieldstone-and-bramble arbor. Over there, down a fire lane, a big buck has bounded through in five-yard leaps. At the edge of the field is a delicate brushwork of wings on snow, where a marauding owl has made a pass at a careless cottontail, who then has taken off in long, frantic bounds into the shelter of an old woodchuck hole. In the lee of the woods is the aimless trail of Br'er Possum, that southern carpetbagger who has so successfully invaded the north. Here, too, a squirrel has been foraging for the acorns he so carefully stowed away in October. And all around are the faint tracings of the little people of the fields--mice, shrews, moles, and snow birds.

It is a fascinating book, this novel in the snow--a book given only to outdoor hikers to read. In the city its pages are much too smudged to be legible. When the countryside snow itself grows cluttered with repetitions and erasures, along comes another storm to lay down a clean, white parchment. Just so can a January hike clear our cluttered minds and present us with a clean, white page on which to draft the story of another year.

There are all sorts of things a sportsperson should be doing in Winter, like stowing gear, studying maps, tying flies, cleaning equipment, and stuff like that there.

The first thing I do after the hunting season closes is to think about retrieving my duck boat and my decoys from our hidden cache at Blank Lake. I and my partners think about this chore for some time, because it takes a good deal of planning to pull off an expedition like this. By February we have agreed that a Sunday is the proper day to go. But somehow a Sunday in February always finds us in church, even though during the season we are conspicous by our absence there. If things go according to form this year, we will manage to get that boat by July 4, and we never will find the decoys. One year we didn't even find the boat.

Another thing I do this time of year is to take down my gun and my outboard motor. By this I mean I take them down to a sporting goods dealer who knows how to put them back together again. Then there are hip boots and hunting coats to stow away. I store this sort of gear right where I left it lying last month, because then I can find it easily next season, and moths never find it because it's not in a moth-balled closet.

Mostly in the Winter, like all avid sportspersons, I watch the weather. Although in the Fall I long for the dark skies, high winds, and dropping temperatures that send mallards down the flyways, in February I wince at the first sign of a snow cloud. Should the driveway become covered with drifts, I develop a severe ache in the very same back that toted a dozen decoys deep into Horicon Marsh, and a very bad vein pops out in the same leg that covered half of Iowa County.

To escape any chores that might sap my strength for next season, I go to the basement and get out my magic lamp. My magic lamp is an expended shotgun shell. I load it in my gun, rub the stock vigorously, and wish. It takes only a little wishing, and a little more imagination, before my basement is filled with canvasback and grouse and ringnecks.

John Tucker was the milkman of my boyhood days. He had a small dairy farm on the outskirts of town where he and his Jerseys produced Mineral Point's milk and butter. In Summer John made his daily rounds with a one-horse cart, in Winter with a two-horse bobsleigh. The rear of the sleigh had slats. If you linked a long rope to your Flexible Flier sled and tied a big knot at the end of the rope, you could slide the rope between two slats and get a free tow all over town behind John's sleigh. It was known as hooking on.

You practically had to have a Flexible Flier, by the way. No other make of sled permitted you to perform the necessary turns in the wake of John's sleigh. If your parents were well-to-do you had a Flexible Flier No. 3, a truly impressive piece of equipment. If you were a preacher's kid you were reduced to a Junior Racer, but it worked.

John's route was such that he performed a perfect three-mile-or-so circle from our front door to our back alley, so you could hook on at Maiden Street, glide at ease over hill and valley, and wind up right back at home without once trudging. Thus I first viewed the terrain of a small Wisconsin town from belly-down on sled.

I have never really understood why I was permitted to accompany John Tucker and his other hookers at all. Perhaps it was because he was a church deacon, with explicit instructions never to permit me to de-hook. Perhaps it was because snow-laden streets suggested a certain antiseptic environment. More likely it was because my brother was quarantined with the measles, and my mother judged me to be safer out in the cold world, whatever its dangers. At any rate, I could hook on, on Saturdays.

Hooking on, I discovered, demanded a certain amount of dexterity. Unless you dragged your feet at the right time, you could slide under the sleigh when John reined to a stop. Unless you maneuvered around occasional piles of steaming horse manure, your mackinaw could acquire a distinctive aroma. And unless you steered your sled with vigor when the sleigh turned a corner, you could whip out into the path of on-coming teams.

But such hazards only served to heighten the appeal of hooking on. The squeak of sleigh runners on cold snow, the jangle of sleigh bells, the labored breathing of John's horses as we climbed a steep grade, the squeals of us hookers as we glided down the next hill, John Tucker's shout of "Milkman!" as he deposited his bottles on each customer's porch--of such sounds is fond memory made. If I remain today a fan of small towns, it may well be because my introduction was paced to the intimate clop-clop of Percherons, and colored by views of houses and sheds "white-roofed with Carrara."

If the national press--and my family--are any indication, Winter is now a time when city folk perform mass treks to the out-of-doors in a manner to rival Summer tourism. The new-found lure is the ski slope. "Ski bunnies" and "ski bums" are making newspaper and magazine copy around the country, and the bug bit the junior denizens in our house, to the end that the snow conditions at Telemark rivaled the Middle East situation as topics of conversation around our dinner table.

For parents about to be engulfed by the ski fad, I offer this friendly warning: make no little plans--or budgets. As practiced by today's teenagers, skiing is no simple sport. It is very much a far cry from the plain Winter diversions of yesterday.

My generation can remember when all that was required for Winter recreation was that mackinaw and a sled. Some of us even engaged in a form of skiing in those dear, dead days. The skis consisted of barrel staves to which we riveted crude leather straps. It was even an easy matter to create a "ski jump" by piling up a cliff of snow at the bottom of the slope in Cochran's Woods (The woods, incidentally, were in the middle of town.)

That time is past, and all its rudimentary joys. Today skiing is a combination of style show, assembly line, carnival, and expedition. The minimum equipment required will stagger your imagination--and your pocketbook. There are, first, the skis themselves. They must have mortised metal edges, and be fitted for length and camber with microscopic preciseness. Then there are the bindings, which are at least as complicated as the suspension system of a Mack truck. Safety straps, carrying straps, and six types of wax are essential trappings, as are ski poles, which come in an array of materials, colors, lengths, and forms. But the

hardware is only the beginning. You must have ski boots. The
bindings won't work without them. The boots in turn must have boot
trees. You must also have ski pants and a ski jacket of prescribed
texture, a headband or cap of distinctive flair, special mittens,
several weights of ski sweaters, and goggles. The only thing that
will seem familiar to old-timers is the long underwear that is
enjoying a glorious revival. (This year's colors are red and white
candy-stripe, no less.)

  To transport all this gear you will either have to buy a
special cartop carrier, trade in for a big station wagon, or knock
out the rear window of your sedan.

  Now that you are so elaborately equipped, you might think you
could at least go out and ski on the nearest hill. Are you kidding?
Modern skiing is practiced only where there is tailor-made snow,
plus rope tows, T-bars, and chair lifts. No self-respecting skier
would wait for a natural snowfall, or climb to the top of a slope.

  (There may be something symbolic in the fact that while today's
generation is anxious to glide down a hill with great speed and
elan, it is unwilling to get to the top without mechanical assistance.
It is doubtless also significant that this observation was made one
day by my teenage daughter. At her age it would have been beyond
me to examine the philosophical implications of "hitching on"
behind John Tucker's horses.)

  At the bottom of today's ski slope there must also be a chalet
where varieties of fellowship, food, and first aid are dispensed.
As a matter of act, you can be a full-fledged member of the "ski
crowd" without ever leaving the chalet.

  As you can see, modern skiing is all good, clean, vigorous,
expensive, elaborate outdoor recreation in the best traditions of
"The Great Society." If you want to develop your own ski resort
you can even qualify for a federal loan. Or if you prefer to
demonstrate your eligibility for an antipoverty handout, just send
your kids out on the street with nothing but a sled.

The city youngster who associates skating with a flooded playground
or even with a park lagoon is missing one of the great delights of
the out-of-doors--exploring the glasslike surface of a lake which
has been frozen to perfection. It takes a fairly rare concatenation
of natural events to turn a lake into a first-class skating rink.
Only every ten years or so do you get the recipe: nights of
penetrating cold and utter calm, and absolutely no snow. Given
these conditions you can wind up with an expanse of flawless ice
half a foot thick.

  It was so with Rock Lake at Lake Mills one day in January, so
I took our girls out to our marsh shack for an introduction to real
skating.

  First we got a fire going in the boathouse. There is little
so satisfying as a fire in a pot-bellied "Round Oak" stove. Heat
has nothing to do with it. An oil or gas furnace is ever so much
more efficient, but the click of the thermostat does not convey the
same message as does the popping of a red-hot stovepipe or the soft

singing of burning oak.

Thawed out and bundled up, we then whisked over the ice for half a mile in any direction, with only a few baby pressure ridges to mar our passage. We watched ice boaters and skate-sailers. We twirled in utter freedom. We inspected the doings of winter anglers. One was angling for pike with a live perch for bait. He had caught a mess of small perch with grubs that he had retrieved from the center of an old tamarack log split asunder with an ax. Such a man has a real right to fish. We looked into his pail of perch, and it was as if he had somehow mastered the secret of capturing Summer and storing it up for Winter use. We marveled at the pickerel he pulled out to lie flapping on the ice. A June pike has no special charm, but a January pike takes on a dazzling beauty. He is not just green like the pines, nor gray like stones, nor blue like the sky; he exhibits rarer colors under the low-lying Winter sun, as if he were a precious pearl that glints under only certain light conditions.

We looked down through the fishing holes into the quiet parlor of the pike, pervaded by a softened light as through a church window. The sandy bottom stretched away like a bright summer beach. Long strands of pickerel weed undulated as if to the strains of some music forever denied to human ears. Little green-eared sunfish swam up sedately, and then twinkled off to all sides as they perceived our eyes upon them. You may be able always to have as slick a skating surface within the circumscribed limits of a city rink as you occasionally find on a lake, but you enjoy only half a world. There is no window to that perennial waveless serenity that reigns beneath the ice as in an amber twilight sky. In Thoreau's words, "on a lake in Winter heaven is under your feet as well as over your head."

It is what you can't see or hear that really marks the turn of a season. In the Wisconsin woods and fields, wildlife populations know when Winter is just about over, and they act accordingly, even though snow may still cover the ground.

Way up north, Old Man Bobcat goes a'courting in February. Over most of the land, fox vixens are rigging their dens for kits about to be born. Nearby, cottontails will be doing the same thing. In woodlot leaf-nests and forest den-trees, many litters of young squirrels already have been born. Small, blind, hairless, and helpless at first, they'll grow fast. They have to. If it's a good year, there'll be a second crop to make room for in August. Hibernating in her Vilas County den, Mother Black Bear beat them all. Her youngsters arrived in January, weighing in to this world at less than a pound apiece.

About the earliest of the early birds is the great horned owl. The first of the horned owl's two eggs appear in February. This means the big bird gets at least a month's head start on hawks and other owls, so she gets her pick of the nest sites. Lesser birds of prey have to be satisfied with second best when they start shopping for real estate, and this isn't the end of their trouble.

About the time they're nesting themselves, the horned owl chicks have hatched and are yelling for a square meal. Their parents don't mind in the least plucking old or young redtails, Cooper's hawks, or screech owls off a nest and bringing them home to the kids. And talk about eating crow[In Michigan, wild-lifers studying birds of prey ranked the horned owl as a major limitor of crow productivity. In fact, they rate the big hooter as a regulating force over the whole predatory bird community during the breeding season, due mainly to the early start the big owls get in nesting.

The surest sign of approaching Spring, however, may not involve a species of wildlife at all. It is likely to be a Winter-jaded outdoor fan, poking under leaves in vain search for an early hepatica, or vaulting out of bed in the middle of the night when an ear catches the call of migrating Canadas.

Give an angler like me a February thaw and I begin to dream.

In my mind's eye I row out in the stillness of the mists of the morning when the lake is like polished onyx. I row slowly and silently in the hush of the birth of the day, feathering the oars with a twist of the wrists. I think how miraculous it is that the boat moves even when I hold the oars poised in midair. What an angler thinks about is not to be understood by other people. I conjure up the lily pads, the sedge, the coves, the points of land, the snags, the little recesses, and I think, "If I were a fish, I would be right there."

Particularly I picture a little lane between the pads that leads to a sort of hidey-hole against a deep-cut bank. Suddenly I know that there is a fish there and a good one, just because I know it. I grease my line and put a touch of graphite on it so it will slide slickly through the guides. I open the bend of the hook so that it will work just a trifle better than the manufacturer made it, and I hone the point until it is needle-sharp. Perfection is a matter of trifles and the February fisher is a perfectionist. I false-cast with my fly rod, and then I place the bass bug with its twitching rubber legs exactly where I want it, way back in the hidey-hole, six inches from the bank. I let it lie still. Then I twitch the fly line, bringing the bug forward a notch, and then let it rest again.

"Hit it! Hit it! Hit it!", I plead.

Nothing happens. I snip off the bass bug and tie on a split-tailed streamer. The lure is a thing of feathers and it does not look like a frog until I drop it back into the hidey-hole and give it action. I watch it opening and closing a couple of inches under the water. The black bass sees it, too. He charges out through the little lane in the lily pads and strikes.

With that symphony of coordinated response that only an angler can muster, I set the hook, desperately pull in slack, grab an oar with one hand and give it a pull, switch the rod, elevate it, and give a heave to the other oar. It is good luck that the bass is heading for open water. He might have tied up the leader in the lily pad stems.

"Give me room, lots of room, to play him," I pray. "He is a big one."

The bass comes to the top, half out, and shakes his open mouth and rattles his gills. He is too big to jump all the way out, like a smaller bass.

"Oh, what a bass!" I think. I am a happy man and it is a beautiful morning, even if it is all happening only in a February daydream.

It is quite possible that modern humankind was never intended to inhabit an environment like a mid-Winter day in Wisconsin, with the chill factor hovering around the 45-below mark. The only way we can make it is to hole up in the jungle hideaways we have re-created in our homes, warmed to a temperature of 68 degrees above by ancient sunlight stored in fossils. To make sure these suburban caves are not only physically but psychologically to our ancestral tastes, we decorate them with the ferns, flowers, and grasses of forest, savanna, and veldt, and we invite bird and animal pets to share the long winter nights with us.

Hairless, and without the traits to hibernate, it is not clear that we could make it through February even in our humidified retreats were it not for our divine ability to anticipate the future and draw inner strength from the visions we thus can conjure up. Myths about the groundhog to the contrary, humankind is the only species that can look ahead, and this may be the single most significant factor in accounting for our temporary ascendancy. We know for sure, for example, that when Winter comes, Spring is not far behind.

February is that time of the year when snow and bitter cold hold sway outside, when there is not a football game to be seen on TV, and you wonder of a Sunday afternoon, "How will I ever make it?" Then comes that grand reprieve--the annual February thaw. The sun rises with returning warmth one precious morning. By noon gushing rivulets fill every gutter. You go for a sideroad drive. You see things stirring.

Somebody on a tall ladder is striking the ice from the over-loaded eaves of a house. In the woods you see the flash of a lifted axe before you hear the sound of it. A vast flock of starlings cries in a bare elm top. There are hens scratching and cackling in sunny barn doorways. Cattle, long mewed up in dusky stables, yawn complacently in the open yards or scratch their rumpled hides upon convenient posts.

You get out and take a long tramp through waking woodlots and fields. The air is sparkling with welcome warmth. The lingering snow is like a map, with tracings of rabbit runs, the footprints of mice and pheasants, here and there a galloping fox, and often the proof that a squirrel has ventured out. You find many little holes dug through the snow to the leaves and the berries and the roots beneath. The tag alder, shaken by the wind, scatters from its small brown cones a shower of seeds upon the snow--manna for wild, shy birds and shrews. You walk through an old orchard, looking narrowly at every tree for swelling buds. You look hopefully in woodlot duff where you know are hepaticas. With a longing you cannot describe you follow the flight of crows high across barren fields. You see a flock of juncos among the bushes, flitting about with a kind of lively, fearless excitement, and you know why it was that St. Francis could so love the larks of Assisi that he could petition the emperor for their protection.

There is nothing sensational about a hike in a February thaw, but then the chief part of every life consists of small things anyway. It is strange how competently, even grandly, some people can ride out the great storms of sorrow and tragedy, only to be wrecked upon the little reefs that litter the calm waters of their daily lives. Fortunate is the person who can draw from a February walk the assurance that even as nations go wrong, in Wisconsin country the unobserved world goes onward with its daily affairs: Winter wears to its end, Spring comes on, life turns ineffably upon the poles of its ancient routine.

Back home, buoyed up by February sunshine, you take your shovel and turn a clod of soil, breaking the glebe up with the flat of the blade and spreading it thin on the sidewalk. Out of the mass some white grubs stir; numb beetles on their backs stretch stiff legs; and a chill earthworm squirms his coral length. The split half of a crocus bulb lies there too, slipping out of its old brown coat and showing clear, young white beneath, with just a tip of sprouting green.

In the sprouting green of leaves of grass, Walt Whitman read the message of Wisconsin country: "American democracy, in its myriad personalities, in factories, workshops, stores, offices-- through the dense streets and houses of cities, and all their manifold sophisticated life--must...be fibered, vitalized by regular contact with outdoor light and air **and** growths, **farm scenes**, animals, fields, trees, birds, sun-warmth, and free skies."

Wisconsin Country

The Fourth of July is a symbolic day on which to discover the meaning of Wisconsin country.

July Fourth will find most Wisconsin folks celebrating Independence Day out-of doors. It is fitting that this should be so. From the moment we dropped anchor in the shelter of Plymouth Rock, we have been children of wide open spaces. There was at hand the forest in all its primeval arrogance; beyond, great prairies, and mountains running to unknown oceans, a geography written on by few, a history unmade, an inland empire to shape and fill. Trappers penetrated the wilderness, lead miners followed them to make a frontier, lumberjacks cleared the forests, farmers poured in after them, railways hacked their way across the savanna. This is our heritage.

Little wonder that modern Wisconsinites possess an almost mystic yearning to get into the out-of-doors, and that they do so with particular fervor on July Fourth. Be we a Thoreau or a lathe operator, when we look for meaning in life we seek it not in ancient ruins or in canyons of a city but in a forest, by a lake, or at the edge of a river. The out-of-doors is our inspiration, an opportunity to recapture, if only on a picnic in a park, a sense of that magic potion of wide skies and free minds that is America.

You will find it good to get out into your state in July. You read and hear so much nowadays about how things have gone sour, and you start believing it, until you get out and see for yourself that they haven't, and that it is pretty much the same friendly, bold, naive, surging land it has always been. It is still an open land, full of space. It is still a country of striking beauty: standing on a bank of the Mississippi and watching that green giant snake its way to Louisiana; coming upon a hidden lake in the bucolic hills of the Kettle Moraine; experiencing the Main Street of a small town in all its charm; or driving into the shoulder country of northwestern Wisconsin's eroded mountains, each rise opening new vistas, until you can stop the car and get out and just stand in awe of the might of Lake Superior glistening in the sunset.

Perhaps what you will be struck with most in July, however, along with the beauty and the energy of the countryside, is a very simple fact: the normalness of the people you meet. We get so wrapped up in the country's problems that we tend to overlook normalcy nowadays. We accentuate the kooks. Actually we Wisconsin people are pretty much what we always have been. We wake up each day, sniff the morning, and wonder what's in store; we dress, eat, work, think, argue, read, hunt and fish, drive our cars, worry about the bills, take pride in our children, try to outdo our parents, cut our fields, mend our fences--and finally sleep again with hope in our hearts for tomorrow.

That's what a Fourth-of-July really is all about--rediscovering a Wisconsin country of beauty and excitement, of raw possibilities, of hard work and ingenuity, of dreams, of opportunity, of patriotism and pride.

You may find the meaning of Wisconsin country in its natural beauty.

Wisconsin's natural beauty is neither spectacular nor challenging by national park standards, but it is everywhere, it is comfortable, and it is America in microcosm. There is not a country window in Wisconsin but what is a charmed, magic casement opening on rocks and rills, woods and templed hills, fruited plains, and foaming seas. No matter that none are listed among the world's wonders; they are real, they are here, and they are within our mind's grasp.

For example, the frontispiece of the scene from our cabin den is a magnificent American elm, not yet struck down by beetles. Its circumference testifies it was sown a century ago. In its marvelous pendant branches is the swaying cradle of Baltimore orioles. Lord Baltimore and his mate are busy performing aerial acrobatics as they seek insects to replenish the ravenous maws of their four fledglings. Any parent feels kin to their ceaseless activity.

At the base of our elm runs J. Jones Road. There's something to be said, of course, for a cabin accessible only by foot, but give me a sideroad site. A sideroad has its own natural beauty as it snakes along the nap of the earth, and it offers periodic reminder that nobody can really make it alone in this world; we can count on at least two vehicles to come past each day. One is the U.S. mailman, who brings us the weekly mimeographed Barneveld <u>News</u>. (I see where Tom Hodgson will be collecting Town of Brigham taxes in the Fire Station this Saturday.) The postman's friendly wave is a signal that all is well along the Potomac. The other vehicle is the morning milk truck, going up to Ernie and Albert Peterson's place to pick up a bit of America's dairyland that will find its way, perchance, to a cheese counter in Sydney, where my Aussie daughter will pick it out. That we are on a mail-and-milk route means our sideroad is plowed in winter. Between a personal shovel and a patrolman I'll take a patrolman every time, particularly one that takes a samaritan swipe at our driveway. There's nothing like a snowplow blade to double your pleasure in Wisconsin country.

Beyond J. Jones Road we can see the west end of our pond, sparkling under the massage of a brisk breeze. The wind has come from Missoula, Montana, across fecund fields of Iowa corn. From our window we cannot see the east end of the pond. Perhaps it runs on and on to nameless oceans. A muskrat is foraging on the north shore, and an occasional crappie dimples the surface, causing a kingfisher to dive down to investigate.

Beyond the pond lies an old pasture, now studded with invading sumac and poplar. A redtail is cruising the field. He is not an endangered golden eagle soaring about a Wyoming wilderness, but our hawk adds his own wild grace to our cabin view.

Beyond the field the ground pitches sharply upward to form a rugged ridge. We cannot see the crest from our windowseat. We know it to be 800 feet in elevation but from our perspective it could be an 8,000-foot crag in Colorado. Birch mingle with oak and hickory on the sharp slope. At their feet is a seasonal parade of wildflowers. The ridge harbors grouse and deer. This evening a graceful doe may lead her fractious fawn down to the pond, and we can certainly count on a cock grouse to drum the announcement that he has prior claim to an acre or two, despite what our abstract of title may say.

Tonight our casement will open on a sea of stars, and that sight may indeed become an eighth wonder of the world. For millions of smog-ridden Americans, a star-studded sky is already a thing of the past. To see a clear moon they must watch television. And that is another meaning of Wisconsin country--that her natural beauty is not immutable. Eternal vigilance is the price of spacious skies.

You may have, like me, a particular affinity for the beautiful hills of southwestern Wisconsin. While the rest of the Great Lakes states were being racked in the grip of the great glacier that swept down over the North American continent at the close of the last ice age, the so-called driftless area of southwest Wisconsin, some 200 miles long and half as many wide, escaped the avalanche of snow and boulders. Alone out of all the northern states, this region remained unglaciated, probably because a giant mountain range warded off the monstrous onslaught. So southwest Wisconsin's terrain bears no recent battle scars. No lakes were dredged out, no valleys filled in, no streams plugged. Here in a stretch of hills and coulees is a museum piece, discounting the weathering since, of what American looked like before the last great glacier pock-marked her face.

Sandstone castles and mural escarpments punctuate the skyline. Springs gush forth from the great maws of grotesque crags. Steep hillsides defy grazing cattle and cruising hunters. Hidden valleys provide food and cover for birds. You find a deep satisfaction in knowing you are tramping a region geologically unduplicated on the continent.

Most of the area was once sea bottom. Because the hills escaped the glacier's whittling, the rock records of that strange marine age are still preserved, and are plainly visible wherever the layers of surface soil have been washed away. The creek banks are virtual historical libraries. Showing in bold outline are the skeletons of fish with odd armored heads, the only vertebrates of their time; snail and clam shells; fossil seaweed; and the delicate scrollwork of carboniferous ferns--a veritable textbook of paleontology, inscribed eons ago.

On the mesas of southwest Wisconsin a lush growth of bluegrass flourishes in the limy, sea-distilled soil and supports an equally lush growth of beef cattle. But back in the hills the farming comes hard. Slopes too steep for corn and cows have been allowed to revert to oak-hickory woods, interspersed with grape tangles, sprawling cedar, and old drumming logs. Cash crops and farmsteads are lean here, but the ruffed grouse finds a way to piece together an existence denied him in more progressive surroundings. This great native American game bird seems to feel particularly at home in southwest Wisconsin as he jumps with a roar out of an ancient conifer or wheels silently over the crest of a razorback hill to drop out of sight into an eroded canyon.

To cruise these preglacial hills and to know that everything around and underneath has been from prehistoric times as unaltered as the stars overhead--this gives ballast to minds adrift on change. You can catch, if you will, in the haze of these mellowing hills, a glimpse of eternity.

But southwestern Wisconsin does not have a monopoly on Wisconsin beauty. I know, for example, of one small northern lake within 25 miles of a county seat which retains a sense of wilderness because you can't get to it except by a half-hour cross-country hike. Its only accommodations are a charm known to me and to ospreys.

I like to pay an annual pilgrimage to my lake each August-- over a railroad bridge, along a tamarack swamp, and through the hazel thickets. The painted tortoises drop from the willow stumps in the slough along the tracks. A vireo sings incessantly. Poison sumac shows its green berries, all unconscious of guilt. A breeze displays the white sides of the maple leaves to give the woods a fresh and flowing look. From his loafing ground in a tangle of cedar a buck deer bounds away. Red squirrels forage on the ironwood ridge.

As I near the lake, a pair of widgeons see me through the trees and flush noisily. A flock of startled teal jump out, and the sky is soon full of wheeling waterfowl. Swiftly, gracefully they circle the blue pothole, now outlined dark against the sky, now flashing white against the hemlocks. When I hunker down in the cattails, they come to rest again, their soft conversation saying, "All clear."

"All clear" for natural beauty is not automatic. John Muir was a Wisconsin farm boy who educated himself at night after working 16 hours in the fields. At the age of 22 he went to the University of Wisconsin, where he was recognized as a genius at mechanical inventions. But an accident temporarily handicapped him, and Muir became, by his own admission, "a tramp," exploring America's scenic wonders--the pure air of the upper Sierra, the majestic sequoias, the mighty glaciers of Alaska.

Carefully recording what he saw, Muir gradually began to write and lecture, awakening his fellow citizens to the preservation of natural wonders. The Sierra Club he founded in 1894 was to play a crucial role in the creation of our system of national parks and wilderness areas. A dozen Wisconsin scenic areas bear his name today.

In 1952 a David in the guise of a young Green Bay attorney took on the twin Goliaths of power companies and the Wisconsin Public Service Commission--to try to halt construction of a dam on the scenic Namekagon River, 80 miles of wilderness turbulence that stirs through Wisconsin's northwest woods.

Virgil Muench pled his case before the State Supreme Court:

The Constitution declares the state's navigable waters to be "common highways and forever free," he argued. Such waters are to be "held in trust by the state for public purposes."

In a landmark decision, the Court agreed: "The right of the citizens of the state to enjoy our navigable waters for recreational purposes, including the enjoyment of scenic beauty, is a legal right that is entitled to all the protection which is given financial rights."

You may find the meaning of Wisconsin in her varied wildlife, and in the people pledged to its protection.

Louis (Curly) Radke, Horicon sportsman, was speaking to the state convention of the infant Izaac Walton League in 1925.

First he painted a picture of the Horicon Marsh of yore--"the greatest paradise for game and fish in the northwest."

Then he described it in 1925--"Not a drop of water in all this great ditched and drained territory."

"Let us fight for the old heritage, the sights our fathers saw," Curly shouted. "Restore them for the tomorrow of our boys and girls is my plea."

It was not to be until 1946 that the Marsh was completely restored, but restored it was, with state and federal funds. Today the wildlife refuge at Horicon is probably the home of more Canada geese than ever darkened its skies in prehistoric times.

April 24, 1948, was one of the first real spring days in the valley of the Wisconsin. The sun glinted brightly on the swollen river, frogs croaked incessantly in the sloughs. In the air, the piquant smell of grass-smoke as farmers went about their annual burning. Down in Sauk County, one grass fire got out of hand. A neigh-bor ran over to help. He filled a bucket of water and disappeared in the billowing smoke. He never came back.

And yet the man has really never left. Indeed, his presence is a growing force in America. He was Professor Aldo Leopold, father of wilderness areas, framer of Wisconsin's Conservation Commission, founder of the science of game management, and the sparkling essayist whose book, <u>A Sand County Almanac</u>, has played such a mighty role in inspiring America's present demand for environmental husbandry.

You may find the meaning of Wisconsin in her seas of green forests. It wasn't always that way. Wisconsin's worst disaster, and one of the worst in the history of the world, was the great Peshtigo fire in 1871. It burned over a million acres in eight counties. The human toll was more than 1,000 dead, 350 missing, 1,500 seriously injured, and 3,000 made homeless and destitute. Property loss was at least $5 million, not counting two billion trees and thousands of animals. All northeastern Wisconsin was a howling hell of flames. The death toll was five times more than that of the great Chicago fire the same night.

Today's forest fire protection would render a Peshtigo fire impossible.

For a dramatic era they bestrode Wisconsin in the boots of Paul Bunyan. We know them today for the names they left on maps, public buildings, and whole institutions: Washburn, Woodman, Knapp, Stout, Sawyer, Stephenson, Spooner, Weyerhaeuser, Vilas, and others. They were the lumber barons.

With them were the lumberjacks, men like Jim Stewart, who won the first national logrolling championship at Eau Claire in 1901.

Together they cut the forests. In the philosophy of the day, as one of them said: "If God had not meant Wisconsin's pineries to be cut to build Chicago, he would not have caused the rivers of the state to flow southward."

Today Wisconsin is green again, thanks to farsighted reforestation taxes and laws, and to a new breed of lumberman, the professional forester.

The northern third of Wisconsin was in deep trouble in 1925. More than four million acres of cutover, burned-over timberlands and abandoned farms were reverting to the counties as tax-delinquent property.

University economists, practical foresters, and paper company leaders like D.C. Everest came up with a novel idea. They sponsored several forest crop laws that said to those counties, in effect:

"The state will bail you out now if you'll zone those lands, and replant them to trees, and then you can repay us when you have a harvestable crop of timber."

Today, one of the greatest assets owned by the people of Wisconsin is the land nobody wanted yesterday--our state and county forests--a vast source of raw material for building industries, and a big public playground.

You may find the meaning of Wisconsin in her magnificent farmlands and farm folks. Your way may take you past sprawling homestead, rugged red barn, sparkling milkhouse. You watch farmers performing that most ancient and honorable of rituals--cutting hay. You smell the subtle fragrance of alfalfa and timothy.

To a pioneer mother in a frontier cabin goes the credit for starting Wisconsin off to more than a century of dairy leadership. Back in 1840 Armine Pickett arrived from Ohio with a few cows. He had done some dairy farming back home, and saw promise in the wild grasses flourishing in Jefferson County's oak openings. But the problem was how to produce butter and cheese on a profitable scale without a lot of cows.

His wife, Ann, solved the puzzle. According to old county records, she proposed: "We have 10 cows and between our neighbors I can count up 10 more. Let's pool our milk, and I will make it into cheese right here in our kitchen."

The idea worked, and spread, and by 1876 dairy products from Wisconsin crossroads factories won more medals than dairy products from any other state at Philadelphia's Centennial Exposition. We've never been headed since.

You may find the meaning of Wisconsin country in her small towns. Lake Mills is both typical and special.

In the memorable Spring of 1933 there began for me a rather torrid love affair which has not dimmed despite the passage of time. It is a somewhat complicated affair in that there are two "girls" involved. One is a lake and the other is the small town on its shores--Rock Lake at Lake Mills in Jefferson County.

From hindsight I can see that I reserved my initial infatuation for the lake itself. To a boy reared in the driftless area of

southwestern Wisconsin, moving to a lakeshore was a revelation. A lake is a special treasure--sparkling in the Summer sunset, mirroring Fall foliage, daring under sodden Winter skies, surging to life again in Spring thaws. A lake can get under your skin. It can even set the tone for an entire community, almost as if a magic spirit of the waters pervaded Main Street. It may be that there is nothing really special about Rock Lake except that she is "mine." For a suitor, that is enough. I pay her court every June with a spinning rod and every November with a shotgun. She never breaks a date. True, I have to share her with more people today than I did in 1933, but I don't care so long as they are Lake Mills natives.

Like their lake, Lake Mills people seem special to me. They have had the grace to reach out to a prodigal with affection and regard. To the itinerant son of an itinerant preacher, that is everything. Lake Mills is a good town, you know what I mean? Not many very famous people have ever come out of it that I know of. But then there aren't any skeletons in the closet, either. Whisking past Lake Mills on the I-highway between Madison and Milwaukee, it's easy to ignore the town, but if you turn off and drive around the picture-postcard square or stop in at Eddie Detmann's spa, you can get something of the flavor of America's backbone.

The earliest tombstones in the cemetery up on the hill read 1840-1850--Atwoods, Taylors, Joeckels, and Fargos--same names as are around there today, strong-minded people who came a long way to be independent. The Creamery Package manufacturing plant is expanding now and a subdivision is inching its way around the lake, but Lake Mills folk still pay a lot of attention to things like birds, and trees, and plants. Country-style, they watch the change of the seasons with deep interest and awe. I suppose you can find in Lake Mills some characters out of Sinclair Lewis--bumbling George Babbitts and frustrated Carol Kennicotts. If you look hard enough, you probably can even find some Peyton Place types. But by and large Lake Mills people defy the TV stereotype. So if I were ever to write an honest novel about my adopted home town, it probably wouldn't sell.

You may find the meaning of Wisconsin in the vibrant, inventive industry that is hers. There is a sailor on the Wisconsin state flag because great lakes and harbors are the gateway to Wisconsin-- dramatic inland oceans, a sweep of water heaving off its icy shackles to lie steaming in hesitant sunshine, a freighter impatiently tugging at its anchor.

Yet is was not a fortune in furs, fish, or farmland that first lured to Wisconsin a large number of permanent settlers. It was the lead in the hills of southwestern Wisconsin. So there's a miner on Wisconsin's state flag, too.

Some miners came up from Illinois in the spring and retreated in the fall, like fish in a stream. They were called Suckers. Some stuck it out year round, and built, against the cliffs, stone huts that looked like so many dens. Those miners were called Badgers. Then came the expert "powder" miners, the Cornish and Welsh. We can still see their "diggings" today, magnificently preserved along shakerag Street at Mineral Point, where John Sheldon opened the first federal land office in the fall of 1834, and did literally a "land office" business.

Mining as a principal industry has been no more in Wisconsin for many years, yet it may come once again to impact on our economy and politics.

One of the first successful gasoline automobiles, the outboard motor, a pig-iron casting machine--these and others were all important discoveries by Wisconsinites. But the typewriter may be Wisconsin's most significant invention. It revolutionized business practices, and women's proficiency in operating it did much to overcome the notion that woman's place was in the home.

The inventors were Christopher Sholes, Carlos Glidden, and Samuel Soule. The first typewriter was built across the street from the present <u>Milwaukee Journal</u> Building. Sholes patented the device in 1868 and, in 1873, contracted with Remington to manufacture the forerunner of today's efficient typewriters.

You may tour Wisconsin's largest manufacturing firm. Once there was but a little shop bearing a sign reading, "Decker and Seville--Manufacturers of French Burr Millstones, Grist, and Sawmill Supplies." Today Allis-Chalmers is a multimillion dollar worldwide corporation, turning out revolutionary saw mill equipment, roller flour mill machinery, mine pumps, large electrical generators, huge turbines, miles of farm tractors.

Next door you may find Wisconsin in the beer that made Milwaukee famous. We brew enough beer in Wisconsin to float a battleship, or at least to make it stagger. Surprisingly enough, it was three Welshmen who built Wisconsin's first brewery--in Milwaukee naturally--in 1840. They were rapidly overtaken by a quartet of German brewers--Pabst, Blatz, Mueller, and Schlitz.

You may find the meaning of Wisconsin in the classrooms, laboratories, and libraries of a great University, where an agricultural chemist developed a simple, inexpensive, and rapid way to measure the butterfat content of milk; where an historian speculated about the interplay of the frontier with the life, politics, and character of Americans; where a president phrased a ringing defense of academic freedom; where county agents were trained to render the boundaries of the campus the boundaries of the state; where a physics professor fabricated a pioneer educational radio station; where biochemists discovered life-preserving drugs; where generations of Wisconsin youths have shared that spent and sacred moment between halves of a football game to sing together the mighty song, "Varsity".

On February 5, 1849, Professor John Sterling rapped 17 students to order in a preparatory class in a borrowed room in the Madison Female Academy. Thus, without a building, without an operating budget, without qualified freshmen, and without a president, there was opened, under provisions of the infant state constitution, the University of Wisconsin.

Said a University Regent with vision:

"We are about laying the foundations of an institution of learning which we believe is destined to exert a great and salutary influence on the moral, intellectual, and social character of the people of this State, for all time to come."

Today that institution is one of the 10 largest and most distinguished in the cuntry, serving some 38,000 students in Madison, 24,000 in Milwaukee, and 80,000 more at 25 other campuses throughout the state.

As a faculty member I of course may be prejudiced, but I like to think of Wisconsin's great University as somehow being akin to Wisconsin's great river. It is indigenous to this soil and this people. Its headwaters are everywhere throughout the state. It is a thing of beauty, where overhanging trees from opposite shores meet and arbor the way. It is utilitarian. In its quiet reaches it ministers to pastures and fields, at its power dams to municipalities and factories. In its Dells and rapids it is active and turbulent. In its forest oxbows it is the setting for abundant contemplation and irresistible change. Where it spreads itself in shallow sloughs it becomes muddied with the silt of the watershed, but where it flows in ageless channels its waters are a magnificent blue. Wisconsin's University and Wisconsin's river are physically contained within the state. But through other currents they give themselves to the seas of the world. Wisconsin water laps at the base of Gibraltar. Wisconsin sacrifice is entombed on Okinawa. Wisconsin ideas enrich the capitals of the nations. From this spot, where 125 years ago there was but a tricklet, there has

welled forth in the past century-plus a flood of achievement which
has only begun to roll on toward broader lands and fairer days.

You may find the meaning of Wisconsin in the spirit of those youths
who have gone from Camp Randalls to defend their country: the
Black Hats of Wisconsin's Iron Brigade storming the approaches to
Antietam or swinging down a Pennsylvania pike to a rendezvous with
destiny at Gettysburg; lumberjacks turned engineers to build a
river dam that would save a Union fleet; a governor's wife earning
the affectionate nickname "the Wisconsin angel" as a hospital nurse
in the forerunner of the Red Cross; the Red Arrow 32nd sacrificing
itself in Belleau Woods; 332,000 Badgers serving in uniform around
the globe in World War II.
    In the summer of 1925, the U.S. Army courtmartialed a certain
brigadier general from Milwaukee. They busted him to colonel, and
suspended him from active duty.
    Billy Mitchell was no chair-borne officer. He had won the
Croix De Guerre and the Distinguished Service Cross in France. He
was no upstart. The son of a U.S. Senator from Wisconsin, he was a
West Point graduate.
    And his crime was no "cover-up." Quite the contrary. His
crime was to attack publicly what he called "the hidebound bureaucrats
of the Army" for their refusal to face the importance of air power
in any future war.
    Even as a civilian Billy Mitchell kept preaching air power.
In 1935 he warned that the United States might expect a surprise
attack from Japan. He did not live to see his prophecy fulfilled.

You may find the meaning of Wisconsin in her diverse cultural
heritage. They opened the Erie Canal in 1825, and this great
public work of New York helped channel the first flood of immigration to Wisconsin. From New York's Harbor, up the Hudson,
through the Erie Canal, and on to Milwaukee by lake sail or steam--
that was the route. A reporter stood on the Milwaukee docks in
1843 and wrote: "The torrent of immigration swells very strongly...The
refugees arrive daily in their national dresses...Here, on the
pier, I see disembarking the Germans, the Norwegians, the Swedes,
the Swiss, the Irish." Other nationalities would join the flood.
Today their descendants lend a proud richness to the state.
    Another culture was here first.
    Was she Wisconsin's <u>first</u> "first lady"? Perhaps. At any rate
we know she was an Indian maiden buried about 800 years ago in
unusual circumstances. Her body, swathed in many beads, was entombed
in a ceremonial grave in a town square.
    The town was a remarkable walled Indian village on the banks
of what is now the Crawfish River. It contained not wigwams but
houses, and featured earth structures that looked like miniature
Aztec pyramids.
    Exactly where this fascinating culture came from, and where it
went, we're not absolutely sure. But you can see the remains of

this unique Indian city at Aztalan State Park. And the skeleton of the famous "Princess of the Many Beads" is preserved behind glass in the Milwaukee Public Museum.

Named Outstanding Young Woman of America in 1966 was a young Wisconsin woman--Ada Deer. Born and reared on the Menominee Indian Reservation in Wisconsin, Ms. Deer has devoted much of her life to furthering the welfare of native Americans.

From its very beginning she has been active in the Menominee Movement, heading Menominee Enterprises, Inc., and assuming the leadership in persuading Congress to reverse the "termination" policy of the federal government by passing the Menominee Reservation Restoration Act in December, 1973.

A social worker with the Department of the Interior, the Peace Corps, and Upward Bound, and a UW-Madison professor, Ms. Deer has also found time to serve on the boards of key organizations concerned with mental health, planned parenthood, religion, student services, child welfare, and American Indian rights--all with professional skill and compassionate devotion.

You may find Wisconsin in all these things, and see that they are all Wisconsin. But you may most surely find the meaning of Wisconsin in her greatest natural resource--her people.

In 1873 Judge Edward G. Ryan was addressing a University of Wisconsin Law School assembly. He said:

"There is looming up a new and dark power...The enterprises of the country are aggregating vast corporate combinations of unexampled capital...The question will arise, and arise in your day...which shall rule--wealth or man; which shall lead--money or intellect; who shall fill the public stations--educated and patriotic free men, or the feudal serfs of corporate wealth."

In the audience was a young man who later would say the event was the turning point in his remarkable career. The magic name: Robert Marion La Follette. With consistent high ideals and actions, "Old Bob" was to dominate 30 years of Wisconsin history and make his mark as well on national political thought and deeds.

Two days after he landed in Milwaukee in 1836, Increase A. Lapham made the first of the botanical and geological studies that were to lay the basis of Wisconsin's ecological knowledge. Carl Shurz began in his early thirties the political career in Wisconsin that climaxed in Washington in his pioneer defense of American Indians and America's forests. As a young widow Carrie Jacobs Bond began composing the lyrics that made her "the unpretentious wild rose" of songdom. Belle Case LaFollette joined her husband on the stump to inveigh against the special interests that held the Wisconsin legislature hostage.

Dr. William Beaumont's early discoveries about the digestive process--carried on at an Army fort in the Wisconsin wilderness-- brought important advances to medicine. Michael Frank--Kenosha newspaper editor, village president, and territorial legislator-- led the campaign for one of the first free public school sessions outside of New England. Five Ringling brothers put together "the greatest show on earth." Under the leadership of Governor Francis E. McGovern, the 1911 Wisconsin Legislature compiled an astonishing record of progressive legislation. Frank Lloyd Wright created some of the most striking buildings of the modern world. Georgia O'Keeffe pioneered a form of painting that renewed the art in America. Vince Lombardi made Green Bay "Titletown, U.S.A." Lorraine Hansberry wrote the prizewinning play "that tells the truth about people, Negroes, and life"--<u>Raisin in the Sun</u>.

In 1975, Number 44 strode quietly to the plate as cheers pulsed through the stadium like a great wave. His hearty wrists cocked the bat, and the pitchers thought twice before hurling anything good anywhere near the strike zone.

Twenty-one years before, almost to the day, he had broken into the majors here, a slight, unknown Black outfielder.

He wasn't unknown for long. His potent bat helped the Milwaukee Braves win two pennants and a World Series. Then he left to become baseball's new home-run hitting king of all time, surpassing the unsurpassable Babe Ruth. Now he was back in Milwaukee uniform again. And each home run was a new record.

He is "Hammerin' Hank"--Henry Aaron.

"There is a special place in my heart for Milwaukee," he says, "and for the special people of Wisconsin."

It was Wisconsin campus youths who made Earth Day, 1970, the symbol of a new national environmental conscience.

Those youths are still at work in the spirit of Wisconsin country. Examples: one of them, Dick McCabe, almost single-handedly saved a Madison marsh from becoming a parking lot. Cyndy Samson made the Wisconsin Environmental Council a force to be reckoned with. Jeff Smoller is the vibrant chief of public information for the Wisconsin Department of Natural Resources. Dallas Miner holds a similar position in the U.S. Office of Coastal Zone Management. Chris Visser is DNR's sharp legislative representative. Jeff Nedelman helps plot Senator Gaylord Nelson's environmental legislation. Within a year after writing it, Lowell Klessig converted his Ph.D. thesis into the Wisconsin Lake Rehabilitation Program. Keith Stamm trains environmental communicators at the University of Washington, as does Bill Witt at UW-Stevens Point. Bill Vogt edits <u>National Wildlife</u> in Milwaukee. Wisconsin country is in their blood.

What new Muirs will leave the campus to scale new peaks of environmental understanding and action we can only guess. Tomorrow's Wisconsin country will know.

CLAY SCHOENFELD is a hybrid. He is the only university professor in the country with credentials in both journalism and ecology. As such he chairs a teaching and research program with the jaw-breaking title of the University of Wisconsin-Madison Center for Environmental Communications and Education Studies. But at heart this Wisconsin native is really just a rank-and-file fan of the Wisconsin outdoors—a hunter, fisher, hiker, bird-watcher, botanizer, and cabin attendant who spends as much time as he can down the sideroads of his home state. It is from this perspective that he recounts pleasures in outdoor recreation that are everybody's for the finding close at hand.

Schoenfeld photograph by the University of Wisconsin-Madison Department of Photography-Cinema. Metz photograph by Jim Dale Vickery.

DAN METZ is a self-taught artist whose illustrations of wildlife and the out-of-doors have appeared in numerous books and magazines. Though a native Minnesotan, the young artist's search for authenticity in his depictions has taken him as far afield as Alaska. He is an ardent backpacker, canoeist, and photographer not only because these activities are necessary to his work but because he loves the wilderness.

Other fine products from TAMARACK PRESS —

- Wisconsin
- Yarns of Wisconsin
- A Sand County Almanac, Illustrated
- Barns of Wisconsin
- A Season of Birds
- My Life on Earth
- Canoe trails of Southern Wisconsin
- Wisconsin Bike Trips
- Bicycle Escape Routes
- Easy Going-Northwoods
- Easy Going-Door County
- Easy Going-Madison and Dane County
- Easy Going-Sauk and Columbia Counties
- Easy Going-Grant, Iowa, and Lafayette Counties
- Pioneer Photographer: Wisconsin's H.H. Bennett
- Down Wisconsin Sideroads
- Wisconsin Country Cookbook and Journal
- Wild Things
- Wisconsin trails Magazine
- Wisconsin trails 1980 Wall Calendar